An Introduction to Evolutionary Ethics

An Introduction to Evolutionary Ethics

Scott M. James

WILEY-BLACKWELL

A John Wiley & Sons, Ltd., Publication

This edition first published 2011
© 2011 Scott M. James

Blackwell Publishing was acquired by John Wiley & Sons in February 2007. Blackwells publishing program has been merged with Wileys global Scientific, Technical, and Medical business to form Wiley-Blackwell.

Registered Office
John Wiley & Sons Ltd, The Atrium, Southern Gate, Chichester, West Sussex, PO19 8SQ, United Kingdom

Editorial Offices
350 Main Street, Malden, MA 02148-5020, USA
9600 Garsington Road, Oxford, OX4 2DQ, UK
The Atrium, Southern Gate, Chichester, West Sussex, PO19 8SQ, UK

For details of our global editorial offices, for customer services, and for information about how to apply for permission to reuse the copyright material in this book please see our website at www.wiley.com/wiley-blackwell.

The right of Scott M. James to be identified as the author of this work has been asserted in accordance with the UK Copyright, Designs and Patents Act 1988.

Library of Congress Cataloging-in-Publication Data

James, Scott M.
   An introduction to evolutionary ethics / Scott M. James.
       p. cm.
   Includes bibliographical references and index.
   ISBN 978-1-4051-9397-9 (hardcover : alk. paper) – ISBN 978-1-4051-9396-2 (pbk. : alk. paper)
   1. Ethics, Evolutionary–Textbooks. I. Title.
   BJ1311.J36 2011
   171'.7–dc22

A catalogue record for this book is available from the British Library.

Set in 10.5/13 pt, Minion-Regular by Thomson Digital, Noida, India
Printed and bound in Malaysia by Vivar Printing Sdn Bhd

01   2011

To M.B.

Contents

Introduction: A Philosopher and a Biologist Walk into a Bar . . .

> *Any animal whatever, endowed with well-marked social instincts, the parental and filial affections being here included, would inevitably acquire a moral sense or conscience, as soon as its intellectual powers had become as well developed, or nearly as well developed, as in man.*
> *(Charles Darwin, The Descent of Man)*

In 1975 the Harvard entomologist and father of sociobiology E.O. Wilson famously suggested that "scientists and humanists should consider together the possibility that the time has come for ethics to be removed from the hands of philosophers and biologicized" (Wilson 1975: 520). Philosophers, apparently, had had their shot and didn't have much to show for their efforts. Now biologists, armed with a comprehensive understanding of human evolution, were standing by to explain that most human of traits: a sense of right and wrong. But in their enthusiasm, Wilson and his sympathizers had failed to articulate exactly what "biologicization" meant. For despite the impression left by Wilson's suggestion, it was immediately pointed out (by philosophers, alas) that biology could play – and has played – a *variety* of roles in moral theory, ranging from the uncontroversial to the highly contentious.

What this means, first and foremost, is that the real question is *not*: Does biology play some role in the explanation of morality? (Surely it plays *some* role.) The real question is: What *sort of role* does biology play in the explanation of morality? How, in other words, should the story of human evolution influence what we think about our moral lives – our moral judgments, our moral feelings, our moral differences, our tendency to avoid wrongdoing, our admiration of self-sacrifice, our hostility toward

An Introduction to Evolutionary Ethics, by Scott M. James. © 2011 Scott M. James

wrongdoers, and so on? This question, roughly stated, lies at the heart of what we think of as evolutionary ethics.

As a first step toward understanding the many ways in which biology might influence moral theory, consider the following menu of options proposed by Philip Kitcher (1985):

1   *Explaining our moral psychology.* Biology might provide (at least some part of) an evolutionary account of how our species came to acquire moral concepts and make moral judgments. Biology might explain, that is, how recurrent features of our ancestral environment (for example, social or moral features) led some of our ancestors to think in moral terms.

2   *Constraining or expanding our moral principles.* Biology might offer new insights into human nature that may *constrain* or *expand* the moral principles we already accept. We may learn, for example, that humans tend to value some practices that ethicists had not previously recognized; this in turn might expand the practices that ought to be morally protected.

3   *Determining the metaphysical status of moral properties.* Biology might settle, once and for all, questions about morality's objectivity. For example, some have argued that evolution "fooled" us into believing that some acts *really are* wrong (where nothing *in reality* is wrong), since believing as much would have promoted cooperation, which in turn would have advanced our ancestors' biological fitness.

4   *Deriving new moral principles from evolution. Biology* alone might tell us what our moral obligations are. Social Darwinists, for example, argue that since the survival of our ancestors depended critically on promoting "social harmony," we thus have a moral obligation to promote social harmony.

As you can see, "biologicizing" ethics can mean different things to different people. The philosophical significance of this point cannot be overstated: a commitment to one project does *not* necessarily entail a commitment to any other project. For example, one might argue that the story of human evolution explains in part how we came to have the moral psychology that we have (option 1 above), but *deny* that the nature of moral obligation is determined by this (or any other) biological fact (option 3). To see why, consider an analogy. Psychologists attempting to understand the nature of visual perception study how the body's visual system – a system whose structure was refined over thousands of generations – processes an external stimulus, such as a cat. What psychologists expect to learn (and have learned) is something about *visual processing*; what they do *not* expect to learn is something about the nature of cats. Once identified, the lesson is obvious: if you want to know what makes a cat a cat, ask a zoologist, not a psychologist. Similarly, one might argue that moral psychologists expect to learn something about the *processing* of moral and social "information"; they do not expect to learn something about the nature of morality itself. If you want to know what makes wrong acts wrong, ask a moral philosopher, not a psychologist. Or so some have argued.

To take another example, one could argue that biology indeed uncovers facts about human nature that bear on our moral obligations (option 2), but *deny* that our moral obligations are *derived from* these (or any) biological facts (option 4). Consider another analogy. Some evolutionary psychologists reason that since our early ancestors faced the recurrent problem of getting enough calories from what they ate, one adaptive solution would have been to develop an innate craving for fatty foods. (In case, being from another planet, you doubt we have such cravings, anthropologists have indeed observed this tendency across cultures.) The point, however, is this: *even if* it is true that our evolutionary past has disposed us to crave and consume fatty foods whenever available, does it seem correct to conclude that we *ought* to crave and consume fatty foods whenever available? Surely not! If the 2004 film *Super Size Me* (documenting one man's ill-fated attempt to subsist on a McDonald's-only diet) demonstrated anything, it was that we *ought to resist* our craving for and consumption of fatty foods. How is this relevant to biology's role in moral theory?

Suppose it is true (as anthropologists have noted) that humans tend to discriminate against outsiders. We are, it appears, far less likely to assist strangers than those who are near and dear. Does this mean that we *ought* to discriminate against outsiders? Let's test the idea. Suppose you are visiting another country and happen to fall in a shallow pond. Because you can't swim, your life is suddenly threatened. Now, does the native observing all this have any reason to toss you the life preserver at his feet? I have a hunch that you'll say (with confidence) "Yes." Why? Because (you might argue) the fact that you are an outsider is *morally irrelevant* to the native's reason to assist you. Indeed, we might go further and maintain that we *ought to resist* our biologically based disposition to discriminate against outsiders. But if this is right, then we must reject the idea that our moral obligations are *derived from* our biologically given dispositions. Or so some have argued.

The overarching point, however, is worth repeating: offering support to the "biologicization" of ethics settles almost nothing. Our evolutionary past *is* relevant to understanding our present moral experience (at least in the secular moral tradition), but this leaves open the precise nature of that relationship. Hence, our task is to look hard at the details – both biological and philosophical. And that's what we'll do throughout this book.

***

The book is divided into two thematic parts, each of which is relatively freestanding. Part I explores the ways in which evolution may have shaped our *moral psychology*. We will explore some contemporary work in evolutionary psychology, anthropology, primatology, and even neurobiology. We will set to one side – as far as possible – questions about the nature of morality itself and focus instead on how the processes of evolution by natural selection could have produced creatures that not only help others, but often do so because they are, as Darwin noted, "impelled simply by the deep feeling of right or duty."

In part II we will move to the normative or evaluative realm by asking: What actions or practices, if any, does our evolutionary past *justify*? Social Darwinists (and even some contemporary philosophers) argue that our biological past is a source of both psychological descriptions *and* moral norms. That is, evolution tells us not only how things *are* (biologically speaking), but also how things *ought to be* (morally speaking). Such efforts to derive norms from descriptive facts confront some standard objections (one of which we discussed earlier), so we will explore the extent to which these views can survive these objections.

We will also tackle in part II the question of morality's objectivity. Some of the most exciting and provocative arguments in contemporary moral philosophy contend that believing in "moral facts" is unjustified once we have a complete *descriptive* account of the origins of our moral psychology. The reason, according to some, is that evolution explains all that needs explaining. Our feeling – indeed, our thinking – that some acts are *objectively* wrong is explained by the need for cooperation among our ancestors. This, then, is supposed to undercut any *independent* reason to suppose that moral properties, such as wrongness, really exist. We'll look at some objections to these arguments and consider, too, realist (or quasi-realist) alternatives to the anti-realist view just discussed.

It is important to emphasize, however, that although discussions in one part of the book may have implications for other parts, the observations made several paragraphs back should caution us against hasty inferences.

There is an impressive array of combinations in logical space. We would not want to prejudge which combination is most plausible.

***

Let me acknowledge, in closing, several issues that one might have expected to find discussed in a book on evolutionary ethics – but which will not receive attention here. First, there exists a pervasive (some might say, regrettable) temptation to link discussions of evolution with atheism and atheism with immorality. Thus one might regard the very idea of "evolutionary ethics" as contradictory, since (a) evolution eliminates God's role in humanity's affairs, and (b) as a God-less humanity lacks any reason to be moral, the choice is evolution or ethics – but *not both*. As tempting as this bit of reasoning may be, it's deeply problematic. Neither (a) nor (b) is obvious, and efforts to make them obvious would involve considerable argumentation that would lead us into distant philosophical terrains. That, at any rate, would not be a book on evolutionary ethics, but a book on philosophy of religion and secular ethical theory. That said, it should be apparent from our discussion thus far that we *will* be assuming that the human species possesses many of its traits (including some psychological traits) by dint of evolutionary forces. But accepting this assumption does not entail acceptance of atheism or moral nihilism.

A second, perhaps more subtle, discussion one might have expected from a book on evolutionary ethics is a discussion of *biological* or *genetic determinism*. The concern, as I understand it, is as follows. Since (1) our evolutionary past determines our individual genetic makeup, (2) our genetic makeup determines our behavior, in a suitably strong sense, and (3) we cannot be morally responsible for behavior that is determined, our evolutionary past undermines moral responsibility. This argument, like the previous one, may have some initial appeal. But the reason I've decided not to include it here is that, on reflection, it goes wrong at pretty much every turn. Claims (1) and (2), as we'll see in the coming chapters, result from confusion about evolutionary theory. As any biologist will tell you, nature alone determines almost nothing – just as nurture alone determines almost nothing. These two are not competitors, they're counterparts. Even if your genetic makeup were not distinct from any other (as in fact it is), a dizzying variety of environmental differences will distinguish you from others. But setting even that aside, genes are not destiny. While evolution may (*may*) have disposed you to have certain emotions or preferences, you retain the ability to *choose* whether or not to act on those preferences.[1] You can say to yourself: 'As much as I would like to give this job to my son, I have to be fair to all the applicants, so I had better not.' Even (3) is not immune from criticism (though I'll leave that for another time).

Suffice it to say that the issue of genetic determinism has unfortunately become something of a bogeyman haunting discussions of evolution and human nature.[2] And while I could add one more stone to the mountain of criticism, I prefer to let that mountain speak for itself. So for the reader harboring lingering doubts about the issue, I have (alas) nothing to offer.[3] There are enough battles to sort through without revisiting that long-dormant one. As we speak, new insights into the evolutionary under-pinnings of human nature are being uncovered, but the pace of moral theory is struggling to keep up. Part of the problem, as we've just seen, is running together the variety of ways in which biology might influence moral theory. Now that we've sorted that out, we can begin to close the gap that separates our biological understanding of ourselves from our moral understanding of ourselves.

Part I

From "Selfish Genes" to Moral Beings: Moral Psychology after Darwin

You get a lot more with a nice word and a gun than with a nice word.
(Al Capone)

In the opening passages of *The Selfish Gene*, Richard Dawkins has us imagine a gangster (let's call him Sonny) who managed to live a long and prosperous life in the Chicago underworld. Dawkins asks us to consider the kinds of qualities Sonny must have had to survive so long in such an environment. Well, we might reasonably guess that Sonny was *not* uniformly benevolent or generous or tenderhearted. At the very least, Sonny must have been tough. He must have been keenly aware of others' loyalty. He must have been quick to spot deception and merciless with competitors. He must have been, according to Dawkins, "ruthlessly selfish" at the core. (Fans of *The Sopranos* will have no trouble getting the picture.) The point of Dawkins' story, however, is that Sonny is our mirror: insofar as we're prepared to ascribe these qualities to Sonny, we should be prepared to ascribe these same qualities to *ourselves*. We are, after all, survivors of our own rough neighborhood. Here's how Dawkins explains it.

Our genes have survived millions of years in a highly competitive environment. But this was possible only because genes are self-serving. And creative. Along the way genes developed ingenious *vehicles* to ensure their survival and reproduction. Some of those vehicles are quite simple. Others verge on the miraculous. But simple or miraculous, the underlying idea is the same: the living forms we see around us – birds and bees, ferns and foxes – are, in the end, "gene machines." And so it is with us: *Human beings*

An Introduction to Evolutionary Ethics, by Scott M. James. © 2011 Scott M. James

are just another kind of gene-machine. Although we dress better than mollusks and make better sandwiches than baboons, we are in principle no different from them. We're just more sophisticated means of making more genes; after all, we are only here for *their* sake. But, as Dawkins notes, since "gene selfishness will usually give rise to selfishness in individual behavior," we have every reason to believe that, despite appearances to the contrary, each of us is ruthlessly selfish at the core. "Scratch an altruist," writes the biologist Michael Ghiselin, "and watch a hypocrite bleed" (Ghiselen 1974: 274). Each of us harbors our own little inner gangster. Almost apologetically, Dawkins concludes: "Much as we might wish to believe otherwise, universal love and the welfare of the species as a whole are concepts that simply do not make evolutionary sense."

And yet, when we step back and observe ourselves, there is something about Dawkins' story that doesn't make sense. For if he's correct, then people would never have an interest in doing the right thing (never mind *knowing* what the right thing to do is); people would never admire virtue, rise up against injustice, or sacrifice their own welfare to benefit strangers. If human beings are ruthlessly selfish at the core, then we should find *unintelligible* Adam Smith's observation that man possesses capacities "which interest him in the fortunes of others, and render their happiness necessary to him, though he derives nothing from it, except the pleasure of seeing it" (Smith 2010/1759: 9). But we don't find Smith's observation unintelligible. Even the cynic has to admit that people do sometimes have an abiding interest in doing the right thing (even those who don't *know* what the right thing to do is). A surprising number of people work on behalf of the poor and disenfranchised. Consider that in 2004 private American citizens gave more than $24 billion of their own money to aid complete strangers (Hudson Institute 2007: 14). This hardly sounds like the work of a band of "ruthlessly selfish" creatures. At the very least, people seem to care about how their actions will be received by others. More striking still is the fact that people seem to care deeply about acting in accord with their own *conscience.* One of the great themes of literature is the psychic peril of "getting away with the crime": merely knowing that we've acted wrongly can be its own punishment. So perhaps the analogy with the gangster is inapt. Perhaps humans transcend their evolutionary roots in a way that cannot be explained by biology. Indeed, perhaps we've hit upon what separates humans from the rest of the natural world: our ability to grasp a (the?) moral order. This would render biology irrelevant to the study of moral psychology.

So where does this leave us? I began with a biological picture of human beings that appeared to exclude the moral. I then presented a moral picture of human beings that appeared to exclude the biological. We thus have a decision to make. We can: (a) embrace the biological picture and *explain away* the moral part of ourselves; (b) embrace the moral picture and *explain away* the biological part of ourselves; (c) or *reconcile* the biological and moral pictures. As implausible as this last option may sound, a growing number of theorists from across the spectrum are throwing their weight behind it. (Not that the idea doesn't sound odd: "In the same way that birds and airplanes appear to defy the law of gravity yet are fully subjected to it, moral decency may appear to fly in the face of natural selection yet still be one of its many products," writes the renowned primatologist Frans de Waal 1996: 12.) Indeed, one of the aims of this book is to defend the idea that moral decency does have its roots in biology.

In addition to the growing empirical and philosophical body of work outlining various means of reconciling our moral and biological natures, there is the cost of embracing one of the other options. On the one hand, we are moving inexorably towards a picture of human nature that is richly informed by evolutionary theory; robust trends are appearing in anthropology, sociology, psychology, economics, and philosophy. It is difficult to imagine, then, abandoning biology in any serious quest to understand human nature. On the other hand, any picture of human beings that leaves out our moral sensibility is fatally incomplete. This isn't to say that we are uniformly good or even decent. It is to say that our practical lives are indelibly marked by moral thought: we make moral judgments; we deliberate over what the right thing to do is; we experience moral emotions (e.g. guilt and benevolence); we punish wrongdoers and reward the virtuous.

Hence, if we are not yet prepared (as theorists) to overlook our moral natures *or* the power of biological explanations, then we assume the burden of reconciliation: How can we bring these two pictures of ourselves into alignment? Attempting an answer to this question is the task of the first part of this book. I say "attempting an answer" because the state of the field (what might be called *evolutionary moral psychology*) is still quite young – and speculative. Although there appears to be consensus at some very basic levels, as you'll see, there remain deep disputes. Much of our work will consist in surveying these disputes. But I will also attempt to offer what I take to be more promising lines of research. After all, I have my own theories regarding the evolution of morality. At any rate, the next five chapters are united around two general questions: (1) *Why* might natural selection have favored hominids who thought and (sometimes) behaved morally? And (2) *How* did natural selection fashion – out of preexisting materials – hominids who thought and behaved morally?

1

Natural Selection and Human Nature

In a single stroke, the idea of evolution by natural selection unifies the realm of life, meaning and purpose with the realm of space and time, cause and effect, mechanism and physical law. It is not just a wonderful idea. It is a dangerous idea.

(Daniel Dennett, Darwin's Dangerous Idea)

To be human: To be the place where the falling angel meets the rising ape.

(Terry Pratchett, Hogfather)

In order to get some traction on the question of natural selection's role in the development of our moral psychology, we first need to refresh ourselves on the basics of Darwin's theory. In this chapter we review some of the basic features of evolution by natural selection. We will not bother too much with the details. What's important is to highlight the general principles that have led some moral psychologists to claim that evolution played a critical role in shaping our moral mind. I'll start with the general story, which is actually quite easy to tell. Then, with that story firmly in place, I'll dispel some common misconceptions about the view. In the final sections, I'll explore the ways in which this story has been extended to psychology, where it is claimed that, like our bodies, our minds contain specialized adaptations.

1.1 The Basic Story

At the center of what might be called the Darwinian Revolution, amid the myriad details and disputes, refinements and revisions, field tests and

An Introduction to Evolutionary Ethics, by Scott M. James. © 2011 Scott M. James

computer models, is a very simple, very elegant idea. Here's a glimpse of it in Darwin's own words:

> More individuals are born than can possibly survive. A grain in the balance will determine which individual shall live and which shall die, – which variety or species shall increase in number, and which shall decrease, or finally become extinct. (Darwin 2003/1859: 467)

Buried in this passage are three conditions on which the entire edifice of evolution by natural selection stands: *variation, differential reproduction,* and *inheritance.* Let's look closely.

One background assumption, left unstated in the passage, is that the number of reproducers in a given population will eventually outgrow an environment's resources; hence, "more individuals are born than can possibly survive." But, Darwin implies, all individuals are not created equal: speed, strength, coloration – these *vary* within a population. Some (but *only* some) of these variations – in the particular environment individuals inhabit – will over time alter an individual's reproductive success; there will be, that is, *differential reproduction* within a population. For example, the individual moth that happens to be grey tends to be overlooked by predators in her environment, whereas the individual moth that happens to be white makes for an easy meal in that same environment. That tiny difference in color, that "grain in the balance," may well affect not only that individual's chances of survival and reproduction, but the makeup of the species as a whole. Why? Because if we assume that variation in color can be *inherited,* then offspring will tend to exhibit that color variation as well. And since grey moths have a small reproductive advantage over white moths, grey moths (all things being equal) will come to dominate the population. Mother Nature will "select against" white moths in that environment. In sum, some *variations* that occur naturally among reproducing organisms improve an individual's *rate of reproductive success* in relation to its neighbors; when these fitness-enhancing variations are passed on to off-spring, you have evolution by natural selection.[1]

As simple and mindless as this process may sound, its power is hard to overstate. The evolutionary biologist Theodosius Dobzhansky went so far as to claim that "nothing in biology makes sense except in the light of evolution" (1964: 449). First, the theory offers a direct and uncluttered explanation for much of the diversity of organic structures we observe across time and across the biological world, an explanation that does not draw on anything more controversial than, say, the workings of genes. With enough time, the pressures of an unforgiving environment – together perhaps with picky neighbors – will yield any number of exotic forms, from flying squirrels to jellyfish to redwoods.

Second, the theory delivers what was once thought *un*deliverable: an explanation of design that does not depend on a designer. Who could deny that the human eye or the finch's beak is exquisitely suited to its environment? It would seem from any commonsense perspective that that fit *had* to be the result of some kind of engineer, someone who understood both how the design would integrate with the other workings of the organism and how it would mediate the organism's interaction with its environment. But that perspective is distorted by, among other things, our place in time. Were we capable of "rolling back the tape" and observing each generation, with its incremental alterations and minor reproductive successes, we would find the development of the human eye, for example, almost unremarkable. The philosopher Daniel Dennett (1995) compares the process to selecting a tennis champion. How does every tennis tournament always select a champion? Easy, she's the last person standing after all the rounds. Remember: we do not see the 99 percent of genetic mutations that do *not* advance an organism's fitness; we only see the "winners." Success in design is inevitable and ubiquitous for the simple reason that creatures ill suited to their environment have, as the philosopher W.V. Quine put it, "a pathetic but praiseworthy tendency to die before reproducing their kind" (1969: 126).

Finally, the core logic of evolutionary explanations is not limited to the shape of organs or the strength of bones, but extends rather smoothly to observable *behaviors*. Beginning in the 1960s, biologists following the work of Konrad Lorenz and Nikolaas Tinbergen developed methods of analyzing the underlying structure of animal behavior, a field that came to be known as *ethology*. Here, critical focus was directed on the adaptive purpose(s) of certain behaviors, for example, the phenomenon of "imprinting" observed in ducklings.[2] The assumption among ethologists was that there existed a series of evolutionary events – or *adaptive pressures* – that ultimately led to the behavior. This would explain, if anything did, what the behavior was for. And this in turn might aid in understanding the developmental influences that lead to the expression of the behavior in individuals.

From here, it is only a few short steps back to our main subject: the human moral sense. (For the time being, think of a *moral sense* as a tendency to make moral judgments and experience moral sentiments.) *If* – and I stress the *if* – one wanted to argue that our moral sense is the product of evolution by natural selection, the general shape of the argument must look something like the following. Through the process of genetic variation, some individual (presumably some early hominid) developed something approximating a moral sense. While perhaps only slightly distinct from its evolutionary precursor, that sense enabled its possessor to survive and reproduce at a rate that exceeded, if only slightly, the rate of her neighbors. Left unchecked, the process of natural selection yielded a population dominated by individuals who possessed this moral sense.

Let me emphasize, however, two things: first, this argument amounts to little more than a general schema; all of the details needed to make this argument remotely plausible have been left out. In later chapters we will explore these details. Second, one could maintain that evolution by natural selection contributed to the development of our moral sense, but only *indirectly*. Two positions present themselves.

One of the positions that we will discuss later asserts that our moral sense was, if you will, a "by-product" of some other system that was directly selected for. As a point of comparison, consider the color of human blood. No one seriously believes that the redness of human blood was directly selected for. What was directly selected for was the oxygen-carrying properties of blood; the redness "came along for free." That was an accidental property of blood.[3] In the same way, some wish to claim that our moral sense was an accidental property of other cognitive adaptations – for example, our capacity to reason about the consequences of our actions.

A distinct but related position states that our moral sense did evolve according to the laws of natural selection; however, the function that our moral sense originally served has been replaced (due to changes in environmental circumstances) by a more recent function, which in turn can alter its structure. A popular example of this kind of biological sleight of hand is the structure of the human lungs. Some biologists insist that human lungs originally evolved, millennia ago, to aid predatory fish in pursuing prey (Farmer 1997). But once the ancestors of these fish began their forays onto land, those "swim bladders" were well suited to respiration. Thus one might argue that our moral sense may have originally evolved to serve a purpose entirely unrelated to its present purpose.[4] The exact structure of these views will have to wait. In the meantime, let me warn against some common misunderstandings of Darwin's theory.

1.2 Some Common Misunderstandings

The theory of evolution by natural selection does *not* entail the claim that every feature of every organism is an adaptation. It is consistent with the theory that some (some insist on many) of the organic structures we observe are not the result of the pressures of natural selection. Some are the result of random genetic mutation; others are the result of what biologists call *founder effects*, according to which a dominant characteristic (e.g. coloration) of an isolated sub-population is the result of an arbitrary feature possessed by the founders of this sub-population. So, for example, a group of green-winged finches becomes separated from the main colony of finches, only a fraction of the birds in which are green-winged. Assuming "green-wingedness" does not influence reproductive success, we will nevertheless observe "green-wingedness" come to dominate this population even though this form of evolutionary change is not the result of natural selection. Some organic changes are the result of *genetic bottlenecks*. Like founder effects, genetic bottlenecks occur when a population shrinks rather suddenly (e.g., following an earthquake), leaving only a subset of the genes of the original population.

It's worth pausing a moment to point out what these alternative processes of evolution might mean for our main inquiry. One could, for example, claim that our moral sense evolved, but that its evolution was not the result of natural selection. According to a story like this, our moral sense was not an adaptation. Its existence might be the result of a process no fancier than that which produced "green-wingedness." If this were the case, it would be fruitless to search for the (biological) purpose of our moral sense. It has no purpose. As we move forward, it's important to keep these alternatives in sight.

Another common misunderstanding of Darwin's theory is that evolutionary change is, in some sense, *forward-looking*, or deliberate. Part of the problem stems from terminology: to say that over time organisms *adapt* to their environments strongly invites the mistaken idea that Mother Nature – or the organisms themselves – actively solve adaptive problems by altering their structure. In the standard example, the giraffe reasoned that reaching the leaves in the high trees required a long neck, and so – *voilà!* – a long neck. This of course is nowhere near the truth. We have to remember that natural selection can only "act" on those variants that happen to exist, and which variants happen to exist is quite arbitrary, since variation is by and large the result of genetic "errors" during DNA replication. This is not to deny that some organisms are exquisitely suited to their environment. But it is almost always the case that, on much closer inspection, those adaptive "solutions" are surprisingly jerry-rigged: instead of designing the most efficient or reliable or economic solution, Mother Nature appears to have rigged together pieces and parts of other existing designs (a bone here, a ligament there) to enable the organism to get by. Daniel Dennett (1995: 211) refers to them as "perversely intricate solutions." If the raw material on which natural selection acts is genetic variation, then this is precisely what we should expect to see: tinkering. She may be clever, but Mother Nature is nonetheless a tinkerer.

1.3 Mother Nature as Tinkerer

At least part of the resistance to the idea that our moral minds are the product of natural selection comes from a deep suspicion that natural selection, despite its force, could never lead to a mode of thinking as rich and emotional and powerful as moral thinking. Mother Nature is simply not that clever. One way that biologists have tried to ease this suspicion is by having us think about other more familiar processes that, despite their rigidity, produce quite original and unexpected results. Here's a common method biologists and philosophers use to loosen our resistance:

Your assignment is to compose an original Petrarchan sonnet. In case you've forgotten, a Petrarchan sonnet is a poem consisting of fourteen lines; each line should contain, with only one or two exceptions, ten syllables, where every other syllable is accented. The proper rhyme scheme is: *a-b-b-a/ a-b-b-a/c-d-e-c-d-e*. Although I leave the theme up to you, it is expected that the first eight lines should introduce a problem or dilemma; the remaining six lines should seek to resolve the problem.

I'm going to bet that you would not relish the thought of completing such an assignment. It's just too constricting. Even if you manage to hit upon an agreeable theme rather quickly, what promises to take up all your time is fitting that theme into the poem's rigid confines. Obviously, you can't designate in advance your rhyming words ("bird," "heart," "start," "blurred") without making your task nearly impossible. Instead, you just have to strike out in a general direction. Put some words on paper and be prepared to make lots of adjustments. You should expect of course that most of your early efforts will have to be trashed. It's not enough to find a word that rhymes with "deranged"; the word has to fit both *locally* (that is, grammatically) and *globally* (that is, thematically). In some cases, a particularly effective turn of phrase may necessitate restructuring the entire stanza. As unpalatable as this assignment may seem, I would wager that if you were to stick with it, if you were to wrestle your poetic imagination into the poem's form, you would surprise yourself. You wouldn't necessarily proclaim, "I'm a poet after all!" You would, however, produce some quite original and unpredictable lines, and apart from the music of the poem, they would express some quite original thoughts. (The price of doubting me on this, of course, is writing your own sonnet.) But the reason such an exercise is likely to yield unexpected results lies precisely in the *restrictions of the form.* Poetic "energy" has to be channeled, often in unnatural directions. The mathematician Stanislaw Ulam observed that poetic form "forces novel associations and almost guarantees deviations from routine chains or trains of thought. It becomes paradoxically a sort of automatic mechanism of originality" (1975: 180). In the process of wearing out the delete key on your computer eliminating all the obvious expressions (simply because they don't fit), eventually something clicks. It fits the meter, it sets up the rhyme, and it advances the larger theme. Ingenious! Moreover, what are the chances you would have come up with that expression in the absence of such restrictions?

The point of this little example is to emphasize the unlikely power of *form* or *law* in the creation of solutions. To be sure, writing a sonnet and designing species are dis-analogous in a variety of ways. Most notably, there is no analogy to the role of poet in the case of evolution; the metaphor of "tinkerer" is just that, a metaphor. There is selection going on in both instances, but the most that can be said in the case of evolution is that species are being selected for by the processes outlined above. Still, the metaphor is instructive: Mother Nature "tinkers" with the different designs that genetic mutations make available, just as we would tinker with words in composing a sonnet. Of course, like the vast majority of words you can think of, most organic alterations won't fit within the imposing confines already set up. Such alterations either don't fit locally (they're incompatible with the organism's internal structure) or globally (they decrease an organism's reproductive success relative to its neighbors). But every now and then, a slight modification of existing structure fits. Mother Nature's tinkering pays off. And, as in the case of writing the sonnet, the originality can be breathtaking: webbed feet, echolocation, poisonous venom, photosynthesis. Perhaps even thought.

So maybe we should take Richard Dawkins' advice: "Never say, and never take seriously anyone who says, 'I cannot believe that so-and-so could have evolved by gradual selection.' I have dubbed this kind of fallacy 'the Argument from Personal Incredulity.' Time and again, it has proven the prelude to an intellectual banana-skin experience" (1995: 70).

In the next section we build on these earlier scientific developments and explore the exciting (and controversial) new field of evolutionary psychology. As the name suggests, evolutionary psychology proposes to study the human mind in the same way that evolutionary biologists study organic form: by applying the principles of Darwinian selection. In this case, the objects of study are patterns of human behavior, patterns of human thought and desire. The study is directly relevant to our main focus, for it is often within the field of evolutionary psychology that some theorists locate the evidence for an evolved moral sense.[5]

1.4 Evolutionary Psychology and Human Nature

You may have no problem accepting a Darwinian explanation for the structure of the human eye. Ditto for the human lungs, liver, colon, and circulation system. But what about jealousy? What about friendship? What about men's proneness to violence, or women's interest in looking young? What about language? *These* things, you say, are another matter. Perhaps not, say evolutionary psychologists.

Today, Darwin's ideas about evolution occupy an interesting place. On the one hand, when it comes to explaining the *bodily* features of human beings (the human heart or the human hip joint), most people have no problem appealing to evolution by natural selection. On the other hand, when it comes to explaining the *psychological* features of human beings, people resist appealing to evolution by natural selection – if it occurs to them at all. Apparently, there is an explanatory divide between the human body and the human mind. That divide is perpetuated (I suspect) by the weatherbeaten distinction between nature and nurture.

The prevailing assumption is that the human body is as it is *by nature* (for example, you didn't learn to grow legs instead of fins), whereas the human mind is as it is *by nurture.* Your attitudes about what makes a desirable mate, for example, were primarily shaped by your environment. That divide between body and mind, however, is eroding. In this section, we explore what some are calling the new science of the mind, evolutionary psychology, which actively seeks to integrate psychology and evolutionary biology.

Contrary to the prevailing assumption, evolutionary psychology maintains that there is a common explanatory framework underlying both human physiology and human psychology: evolution by natural selection. A complete understanding of the human mind, according to evolutionary psychologists, requires understanding the evolutionary pressures that shaped it so many millions of years ago. We do not come into the world as blank slates, as many commonly assume. Instead, they argue, our heads are full of psychological *adaptations*.

Of course, when asked to think of evolutionary adaptations most of us think of *anatomical* features like a duck's webbed feet or a lizard's camouflaged skin. According to the standard account, webbed feet initially arose as a result of a genetic mutation; because webbed feet enabled their possessor to out-reproduce its neighbors (all things considered), over time webbed feet spread to the entire population. Evolutionary psychologists are proposing a similar account for *mental* features. At some point in the distant past, a certain mental system arose in an individual as a result of a genetic mutation; this system altered her psychology – the way she thought or felt or reasoned or desired. And because this system enabled her to out-reproduce her neighbors (all things considered), over time that mental system spread to the entire population. Speaking grandly, we might say that just as webbed feet are part of a duck's nature, so, too, certain ways of thinking or reasoning or desiring are part of human nature.

Returning for a moment to our main theme (i.e. the human moral sense), we can put our question this way: Is having a moral sense part of human nature, where that nature is best explained by evolution by natural selection? As we'll see below, in order to answer that question we will need to look carefully at the kind of adaptive problem (if any) that our moral sense was designed to solve. Webbed feet, for instance, helped solve the problem of efficient movement through water. If our moral sense is indeed an adaptation, then there should be good evidence that possession of such a sense helped to solve (or to solve more successfully than one's neighbors) a particular adaptive problem. But we're getting ahead of ourselves. Let's look more closely at the details of evolutionary psychology.

1.5 An Evolved Mental Tool-Box

Evolutionary psychologists hypothesize that the human mind is equipped with many (some say very many) different evolved psychological mechanisms. Instead of viewing the mind as containing a single all-purpose "problem-solver," evolutionary psychologists view the mind in roughly the way we view the body. We know the body does not contain a *single* anatomical mechanism to deal with the body's journey through the world. Rather, it contains *different* mechanisms to confront *different* problems: a liver to filter out toxins, lungs to take in oxygen, antibodies to fight off bacteria and viruses, and so on. It's true that each mechanism is profoundly limited in what it can do (your digestive system is a pretty bad listener), but this cost is more than offset by the benefits. With only one task to complete, each system should be able to do it efficiently, economically, and quite reliably.[6] And even if other systems break down (you lose your eyesight, for example), most other systems should remain operational.

Evolutionary psychologists contend that this is the way we should understand the human mind.[7] Like the body, the mind requires different mechanisms to deal with different tasks. After all, the alternative to this picture – a single, all-purpose psychological mechanism – is, say evolutionary psychologists, hard to accept:

> The idea that a single generic substance can see in depth, control the hands, attract a mate, bring up children, elude predators, outsmart prey, and so on, without *some* degree of specialization, is not credible. Saying that the brain solves these problems because of its "plasticity" is not much better than saying it solves them by magic. (Pinker 1997: 75)

What we're left with, then, is what some psychologists call a "modular" account of the mind: many distinct modules designed to solve many distinct problems. That is, many distinct "tools" to take on many distinct problems. It's an *evolutionary* account because natural selection is responsible for the design. But what are these modules?

According to David Buss, a leading evolutionary psychologist, an evolved psychological module or mechanism is "a set of procedures within the organism that is designed to take in a particular slice of information and transform that information via decision rules into output that historically has helped with the solution to an adaptive problem" (2007: 52). What does this mean? Well, first, by "a set of procedures," Buss is acknowledging that there may be many subsystems involved in delivering information from the environment to the mechanism. Visual systems, auditory systems, chains of logical inference, all of these may deliver information to the mechanism. Nevertheless, the mechanism is designed to take in *only* "a particular slice of information." The mechanism for choosing mates, for example, will not process information regarding the color of the grass or the taste of the berries or the speed of passing clouds. Instead, that mechanism (it is alleged) is designed to take in and process only that information that is relevant to choosing a mate, and which information is relevant will depend on the operative "decision rules." Such rules (we can imagine) amount to "If . . . then" clauses: *if* the mechanism registers so-and-so, *then* do thus-and-so and/or think so-and-so.[8] Because these rules do not process information about innumerable other things (just as your house-key does not open innumerable locks), that mechanism is described as *dedicated* or *domain-specific*.

Finally, the presence of *this* mechanism – as opposed to some other mechanism – is explained by the fact that, given the preexisting materials of the hominid brain, *this* mechanism helped to solve an adaptive problem that confronted our hominid ancestors. This last part is extremely important. The psychological mechanisms that evolutionary psychologists claim fill the mind did not evolve to in response to problems we confront today. They *may* help in solving similar problems today, but that's not why we possess them. We possess them because they solved recurrent problems confronting our distant ancestors. And since they haven't been "selected out" of the population, current populations still posses them. As evolutionary psychologists like to say, our modern skulls house stone-age minds.

1.6 Some (More) Common Misunderstandings

As you might imagine, when the topic turns to human nature (and the alleged evolutionary roots of that nature), the landscape is suddenly awash in landmines. From the rather straightforward biological story above, it is easy to find oneself concluding all sorts of dubious things. I want to spend a few moments warning against several dangerous missteps: (1) conflating adaptation and adaptiveness; (2) conflating explanation and justification; (3) misunderstanding the scope of an evolutionary explanation; and (4) succumbing to the temptation of genetic determinism.

Conflating adaptation and adaptiveness

One of the most seductive confusions in this area concerns the distinction (and there *is* one) between adaptations and adaptiveness. Simply put, what is adaptive is not necessarily an adaptation, and adaptations are not necessarily adaptive. Some examples will help. Going to your doctor for an annual physical is adaptive insofar as it increases your chances of survival and reproduction; however, no one is going to conclude that the mind possesses a "going to the doctor" mechanism, dedicated to identifying doctors and motivating the organism to seek out their counsel. Going to the doctor is, if you will, a *learned* behavior – at least for those who learned it. The point is that we should be careful not to conclude that a piece of behavior is (or, more carefully put, is produced by) a psychological adaptation *just because it happens to be biologically adaptive.*

What is perhaps less obvious is the claim that adaptations are not necessarily adaptive. When an evolutionary psychologist claims that a piece of behavior is produced by a psychological adaptation (let's call it *A*), she is *not* claiming that *A* produces adaptive behavior. She is claiming, instead, that *A, on average*, tended to produce behavior that was more adaptive than competing designs *in the environment in which A evolved.* But the environment in which *A* evolved may not resemble our current environment; hence, there is no guarantee that *A* will be adaptive in this current environment. Think of it this way. By most estimates, 99 percent of our species' history consisted of hunting and gathering under the harsh conditions of the African savannah. So the psychological mechanisms that evolved evolved in response to *those* conditions. But now imagine transplanting that "stone-age mind" into the skull of a citizen of the modern world, with its maze of office cubicles and public transportation, its online dating and jury duty, its Google and Facebook, its GPSs and ATMs. Is it any wonder that some of our stone-age solutions (to adaptive problems) are not up to the task of the problems of the modern world?

Return to an example discussed in the Introduction: our preference for fatty foods. It should be immediately obvious that early humans regularly confronted the problem of getting enough to eat. One solution to this problem would have been a greater discrimination in respect of what one ate: preferring fatty foods increased one's chances of increasing caloric intake thereby increasing one's store of energy and so on. But that same solution – a strong preference for fatty foods – that was so adaptive during the period of hominid development is decidedly *non*-adaptive in environments rich in cheeseburgers and chocolate doughnuts. Again, the point to bear in mind is that when it is claimed that such-and-such is a psychological adaptation, the claim should be understood, first and foremost, as a claim about our *evolutionary past*, about a particular psychological solution to an adaptive problem that repeatedly confronted our distant ancestors. Whether or not that solution is well suited to our current environments is a separate matter.

Conflating explanation and justification

One might reasonably suspect that some of the popular resistance to contemporary evolutionary psychological accounts stems from a confusion over what these accounts are aiming at. Some critics of evolutionary psychology mistakenly suppose that such accounts amount to an endorsement or justification of the relevant behavior. So when, for example, they hear that the male tendency to prefer multiple sexual partners (assuming such a tendency exists) is accounted for by the forces of sex selection, it is all too tempting to think that such an account is meant to excuse males ("How can you blame him? It's in his genes!"). But this temptation must be resolutely fought. As the old saying goes, "To understand is not to forgive."

Simply put, evolutionary psychologists seek to *explain*, not to *excuse*. They are attempting to describe the causal processes that lead to observed human behavior; they are *not* attaching value either to the processes or to the behavior. They are *not* claiming, for example, that male promiscuity is good or bad, virtuous or vicious. Such claims are – or, at least should be – left up to those who seek to understand the nature of goodness and badness, virtue and vice. So while you may hear evolutionary psychologists describe a psychological mechanism as "fitness-enhancing" or "effective" or "reliable" or "detrimental," none of these adjectives should be thought of as ascribing value (or disvalue) to the mechanism *beyond the merely biological context.* If we seek to know whether a mechanism is good *all things considered*, presumably we must look beyond biology. As this discussion makes clear, the distinction between explanation and justification carries particular significance in the moral realm. As such, we will be revisiting this subject in part II.

Misunderstanding the scope of evolutionary explanations

If you want to understand why you do the things that you do, it would be a mistake to turn to evolutionary psychology for anything but the most indirect and abstract explanation. To see why, consider an analogy. If I want to figure out what kind of music you like (without your assistance, that is), I might choose to conduct a poll to find out what *most* people in your demographic like in the way of music. Suppose I find out that, based on a representative sample, 73 percent of those in your demographic prefer hip-hop. How confident should I be that *you* like hip-hop? Well, sort of confident; it's better than flipping a coin, I guess. But a better approach would be to investigate the kinds of music you were exposed to growing up, especially through your teenage years – what your parents listened to, what your siblings listened to. Most of all, I would want to know what your friends listen to. These lines of detail are going to be essential in forming predictions about the kinds of music *you* like. Polls might help narrow down the field, but only crudely.

Similarly, evolutionary psychological accounts of human behavior are like polls in this sense: they measure large-scale trends. They predict what *most* humans will be like. Actually, such accounts are more general than even this. Evolutionary psychological accounts predict what most humans will be like *under specified circumstances*. Even the most ardent defender of evolutionary psychology will recognize the tremendous adaptability of the human mind. We are fabulous learners (even if we are notorious forgetters). What this means is that psychological adaptations rely critically on environmental input, a point that can't be over-emphasized. That's why knowing why you do the things you do will require knowing a lot about your environment. At best, the psychological adaptations posited by evolutionary psychologists might provide the framework for some probability claims about you: you will *probably* prefer this over that or think this rather than that, *in the presence (or absence) of these specific environmental inputs*. But this is a very "low-resolution" picture. This is like a charcoal outline of who you are. For a "photo-realism" picture, you need to supply all the rich details of your environment. Thus, the *scope* of evolutionary explanations about human psychology is notably limited. They explain, at best, patterns at the level of populations; they won't tell you much about what makes you, in all your rich detail, you.

Succumbing to the temptation of genetic determinism

I warned against this temptation in the Introduction, but it bears repeating. Although the structure of your mind is partly the result of your genes (at least according to evolutionary psychology), and although you have the genes you do in part because of your evolutionary history, none of this *determines* how you will behave, in the sense that there is only one course of action open to you. (So you're not likely to get much mileage out of the excuse: "Darwin made me do it!") The reason is, there is simply no causal chain linking gene sequence ABC to behavior XYZ. Gene sequence ABC will tend toward a *range* of behaviors depending on, among other things, other genetic structures, learned behaviors, and ongoing environmental input. You are not, as the biologist Paul Ehrlich emphasizes, "captives of tiny self-replicating ... genes" (2002: preface). Genes do not, he says, shout commands at you; "at the very most, they whisper suggestions." Remember: your genes represent but the barest outline of the kind of person you are. Your environment (your parents, your friends, your culture) plays a critical role in shaping how you will respond to various situations.

Indeed, when we note the tremendous impact your upbringing has on your behavior, one has to wonder whether genetic determinism should worry us less than *environmental* determinism, according to which your behavior is determined by (or, let's say, strongly influenced by) the environment in which you were brought up. Just think of the variety of excuses that have made their way into courtrooms: "the abuse excuse, the Twinkie defense, black rage, pornography poisoning, societal sickness, media violence, rock lyrics, and different cultural mores" (Pinker 2002: 178). The truth is, the worry over genetic (or biological) determinism is actually a symptom of a deeper philosophical mystery, one that philosophers are still actively wrestling with: the problem of moral responsibility. It is not that behavior-caused-by-genes is any more (or less) morally problematic than behavior-caused-by-environment; the morally problematic notion, in the eyes of philosophers at least, is the mere notion of behavior-that-is-caused. After all, can we not *ultimately* link the causes of one's behavior to some force(s) outside one's skull? "If we *ever* hold people responsible for their behavior," Pinker maintains, "it will have to be in spite of any causal explanation we feel is warranted, whether it involves genes, brains, evolution, media images, self-doubt, bringing up-ke, or being raised by bickering women" (2002: 180). In conclusion, whatever the prospects of evolutionary psychology, they do not rise or fall with the set of philosophical problems raised by the specter of determinism. Even if your genes shouted commands at you (which they do not), this wouldn't show that evolutionary psychology was a defective scientific hypothesis. Unsettling, yes. Untrue, no.

So, let's review the missteps to avoid. First, the search for psychological adaptations is *not* the search for adaptive behavior, but rather the search for those psychological traits that were adaptive during the long period of our species' evolution. Second, to explain a piece of human behavior in terms of evolution is *not* to justify (or endorse or recommend or applaud) that same piece of behavior. Third, to explain on evolutionary grounds why humans, as a group, tend to behave in the ways they do does *not* explain – in any interesting detail, that is – why you or I performed *that* action at *that* moment. Finally, you are not condemned to act in the ways that are (at most) "outlined" in your genes; at most, your genes, mediated by your brain, *suggest* lines of action.

So how do these missteps bear on our main inquiry, the evolution of the human moral sense? First, it would be a mistake to conclude that our moral sense is *not* a psychological adaptation on the grounds that it does not produce biologically adaptive behavior in *this* environment. Second, if our moral sense is indeed an adaptation and if a given piece of behavior (call it *B*) is indeed produced in part by that sense, we cannot automatically conclude that *B* is good or virtuous or whatever. (Conversely, if *B* is not produced by that sense, we cannot conclude that *B* is bad or vicious or whatever.) And finally, in case it was not already obvious, having a moral sense does not guarantee moral behavior. More importantly, it would be a mistake to conclude that our moral sense is not a psychological adaptation on the grounds that *not everyone* behaves morally or makes correct moral judgments. After all, we don't conclude that our visual system is not an adaptation on the grounds that our eyes sometimes fool us. The existence of an evolved moral sense is compatible not only with different moral judgments (concerning the same event, say), but also with wide-ranging differences in moral behavior. This is an under-appreciated point. Psychological adaptations, if there are any, do not entail universal – or even near-universal – similarities in thought or behavior. This might be the case if the environment did not have a role in shaping our psychology. But we know that just the opposite is true.

1.7 Conclusion

In this chapter I've tried to present the building blocks for understanding evolutionary adaptations – in particular, psychological adaptations. All adaptations have this in common: they started out as genetic mutations; because those mutations tended to give their possessors a reproductive advantage, however slight, they eventually spread to the entire population. The central tenet of evolutionary psychology is that, like the body, the mind contains an array of adaptations, each designed to assist an individual in managing a particular kind of recurrent adaptive problem. Narrowing our focus even further, we can see how proponents of an evolved moral sense are going to go about making their case: such a sense tended to give our ancestors a reproductive advantage (however slight) over other members of the species. The moral sense is presumably specialized, in the sense that its function is distinct from other functions of the mind, and this is so even if it draws on the operations of other subsystems.

There are, however, other building blocks that need to be laid in place before approaching our main subject. For, as it turns out, natural selection has apparently "primed the pump" for moral thought.

Biologists going back to Darwin have observed in non-human animals behavior that might be described, loosely at least, as *moral* behavior: sharing, self-sacrifice, cooperation, and the like. But such observations seem plainly at odds with natural selection's competitive nature. Indeed, the sight of worker bees sacrificing themselves to protect their hive deeply unsettled Darwin, for his theory had no way to explain this "special difficulty." Such behavior, feared Darwin, was not just "insuperable," but "actually fatal to the whole theory" of natural selection (2003/1859: 236). But through a series of recent breakthroughs, modern biology has erased the unease. Natural selection can actually explain these behaviors. What this means for our purposes is that when early humans came onto the scene they already possessed, by way of inheritance, the mental mechanisms responsible for moral-like behavior, however distant these behaviors are from *genuine* moral behavior. In the next chapter we will explore these recent breakthroughs and consider what natural selection may have added to those early minds to give us the moral minds so special to our species.

Further Reading

Barkow, Jerome, Leda Cosmides, and John Tooby (1995) *The Adapted Mind: Evolutionary Psychology and Generation of Culture* (Oxford University Press).

Buller, David (2006) *Adapting Minds: Evolutionary Psychology and the Persistent Quest for Human Nature* (Bradford Books, MIT).

Carruthers, Peter, Stephen Laurence, and Stephen Stich (eds.) (2005/6) *The Innate Mind*, vols. 1 and 2 (Oxford University Press).

Darwin, Charles (2003/1859) *On the Origin of Species* (Signet Classics).

Darwin, Charles (2009/1871) *The Descent of Man* (Dover Publications).

Dawkins, Richard (1995) *The Selfish Gene* (Oxford University Press).

Dennett, Daniel C. (1995) *Darwin's Dangerous Idea: Evolution and the Meanings of Life* (Simon & Schuster).

Ehrlich, Paul R. (2002) *Human Natures: Genes, Cultures, and the Human Prospect* (Penguin).

Lorenz, Konrad, and Robert D. Martin (1997) *The Natural Science of the Human Species: An Introduction to Comparative Behavioral Research* (MIT Press).

Mayr, Ernst (2002) *What Evolution Is* (Basic Books).

Pinker, Steven (1997) *How the Mind Works* (Norton).

Pinker, Steven (2002) *The Blank Slate: The Modern Denial of Human Nature* (Viking).

2

The (Earliest) Roots of Right

Call it a clan, call it a network, call it a tribe, call it a family:
Whatever you call it, whoever you are, you need one.
                                        (*Jane Howard, Families*)

Commitment is healthiest when it is not without doubt but in spite of
doubt.
                            (*Rollo May, The Courage to Create*)

Defenders of Darwin have some explaining to do. The theory described in
the previous chapter asserted that genetic mutations that tended to increase
an individual's ability to survive and reproduce would, all things being
equal, eventually spread to the entire population. This seems to imply that
genetic mutations that tended to *decrease* an individual's ability to survive
and reproduce would eventually be eliminated from the population. So
when we look out into the world, we should not observe individuals
regularly sacrificing their own reproductive advantages for the reproductive
advantages of others. For how on earth could such individuals ever get a
foothold in the population, let alone come to dominate it? After all, didn't
Darwin himself insist that "any variation in the least degree injurious would
be rigidly destroyed"? What we should observe, then, is a world of *pure
egoists*. Clear enough. But there's only one problem. That's not the world
we observe!

Set aside human behavior — which contains too many acts of cooperation,
sharing, and self-sacrifice to name – and focus simply on non-human
animals. Every school-age child knows that puppies and ducklings, kittens
and cubs, foals and piglets, all have mommies and daddies, and mommies
and daddies care for their babies. But school-age children will also tell you
that birds (and baboons and bears and even beetles) care for their brothers

An Introduction to Evolutionary Ethics, by Scott M. James. © 2011 Scott M. James

and sisters. And those children would be right. But where's the self-interest in all this? Doesn't Darwin's theory imply that individuals should only behave in ways that benefit *themselves*?

It gets worse. Vampire bats regularly donate foodstuff (i.e. blood) to other bats (some related, some not) who have failed to feed on a given night (Wilkinson 1984). Ground squirrels and vervet monkeys regularly risk their own lives by alerting others to terrestrial predators (Seyfarth and Cheney 1984). When a ground squirrel sees a coyote, it will often emit a high-pitched call that allows other squirrels to escape to safety; the danger of course is drawing the coyote's attention to the alarm-caller (Dunford 1977). The famed primatologist Frans de Waal has documented thousands of cases of compassion, nurturing, and sympathy among primates (e.g., de Waal 1989, 1996, 2006).[1] Among birds, white-fronted African bee-eaters, like bluebirds and scrub jays, will delay and sometimes forgo reproduction in order to help raise a neighbor's clutch of baby birds (Emlem and Wrege 1988). Social insect colonies (ants, bees, termites, and wasps) represent perhaps the most pronounced obstacle to Darwinian theory: instead of reproducing, these individuals devote their lives to sustaining the hive and the queen.

Evidently, the world contains not just occasional altruists, but *pure* altruists as well! So should we conclude (as one website promoting creationism does) that Darwin's theory is "badly flawed"? If so, should we abandon evolution as a source of explanation for our moral impulses? The answer to both of these questions is *No*. In this chapter, we will consider how some breakthroughs in evolutionary biology (namely, inclusive fitness and reciprocal altruism) account for the sorts of helping behavior noted above. More importantly, we will explore how these breakthroughs can account for at least some of the human behavior we think of as *moral behavior*. In chapter 3, I will try to point out what these breakthroughs do not explain as far as our moral lives are concerned. For although most theorists agree that inclusive fitness and reciprocal altruism can go some way toward explaining our moral lives, disputes remain as to whether these forces can go all the way.

2.1 Together We Stand?

Perhaps there's an easy way out of the puzzle for Darwinians. They might argue that helping behavior in the natural world evolved to benefit *groups* –

not individuals. Surely a group of individuals working toward the greater good will have a reproductive advantage over a group of egoists. A group of ground squirrels, say, containing individuals disposed to alarm-calling will, over time, survive more coyote encounters than another group of squirrels, none of whom tends to alert others of nearby coyotes. (When it's "every man for himself," every man tends to suffer.) The natural result, then, would be selection for groups of (moderately) self-sacrificing individuals. The logic was good enough for Darwin: "a tribe including many members who ... were always ready to give aid to each other and sacrifice themselves for the common good, would be victorious over most other tribes; and this would be natural selection" (2003/1859: 537).

Unfortunately, modern evolutionary biology has all but shut down this escape route. In the mid-1960s the idea of group selection suffered a pretty serious setback: several prominent biologists – most notably, G.C. Williams (1966) and J. Maynard Smith (1974) – showed (to the satisfaction of most) that group selection is, at best, an extremely weak evolutionary force. True, under unusual experimental conditions, where parameters are carefully calibrated, group selection might yield some significant evolutionary results; however, those conditions only very rarely could be expected to obtain in the natural world. (That's why they're "unusual.") Without getting too bogged down in the details, the problem of group selection as an explanation for helping behavior is this: a group of helpers is almost always vulnerable from *mutant egoists* within. Dawkins called it "subversion from within." Egoists, by definition, act in ways that ultimately promote their own good, so when an egoist pops up in a population of helpers (presumably by mutation), he will exploit the generosity of his neighbors for his own good. Assuming that "his own good" translates into *reproductive advantage*, it will only be a matter of time before the egoism mutation drives helpers into extinction. On this model, nice guys do not finish first; they become extinct.

Reports of the "total demise" of group selection are, however, premature. Some biologists and philosophers continue to maintain that group selection plays a more notable role in evolutionary explanations than the canonical view allows (e.g., Sober and Wilson 1998). Some argue, for example, that inclusive fitness and reciprocal altruism are in fact special cases of group selection. This is not – thankfully for us – a debate we need to take up, for whether or not such forces count as instances of group selection, there can be little doubt that they are potent biological forces. It's time now to reveal how these forces work.

2.2 Inclusive Fitness and the "Gene's-Eye" Point of View

Richard Dawkins famously described genes as "selfish." Taken literally, this is of course nonsense: genes are no more selfish than toenails. To be selfish requires self-interested *motives*, and genes, as sophisticated they may be, have no motives – selfish or otherwise. But Dawkins was making a different point. Viewing genes as selfish – as "interested" in their own good – serves to locate the *level* at which natural selection works. And this in turn locates where most of the (biological) explanatory work is done. When you want to understand the workings of a big scandal, journalists will tell you: follow the money. In this case, when you want to understand the workings of evolution, biologists will tell you: follow the genes. Here's why.

The theory of natural selection, as it was presented in the previous chapter, encouraged the idea that (as Dennett puts it) "what's good for the body was good for the genes and vice versa . . . The fate of the body and the fate of the genes are tightly linked" (1995: 325). After all, a genetic mutation that allows a gazelle to run faster will eventually lead to more gazelles with copies of those genes. But what happens when what's good for the genes is not good for the individual, or vice versa? What happens when an individual gazelle forgoes feeding in order to protect her brothers from a predator? Because her brothers share 50 percent of her genes, such an act promotes the survival of her genes, but it surely threatens her own survival. Good for her genes, not good for her. You might think that such an individual, with her particular genome, is headed for extinction. Not so.

In 1966 William Hamilton demonstrated that when the interests of an individual conflict with the interests of its genes, natural selection will tend to reward the genes. Since the gazelle's brothers share 50 percent of her genes and since the gene(s) responsible for helping kin is likely to be *among* those genes, promoting her brothers' survival is another way of replicating (copies of) her own genes, including the gene(s) responsible for helping kin. Thus, what may not be good for the body may still be good for the genes – and that's what drives the evolutionary engine. Dawkins offered a vivid way of appreciating the point: our genes are not here to make more bodies like these; instead, our bodies are here to make more genes like these. A body is simply a gene's way of making more genes.

The most immediate consequence of adopting this "gene's-eye" point of view is that it illuminates the *biological value of relatives*. To repeat, our relatives share – to differing degrees – our genes. And since natural selection, strictly speaking, is driven by the replication of genes and not the replication of individuals, it does not matter if copies of a gene are replicated through me or through a relative – *so long as they're replicated*. For this reason, biologists speak of *inclusive fitness*, a concept Dawkins describes this way:

> The inclusive fitness of an organism is not a property of himself, but a property of its actions or effects. Inclusive fitness is calculated from an individual's own reproductive success plus his effects on the reproductive success of his relatives, each one weighted by the appropriate coefficient of relatedness. (Dawkins 1982: 186)

To get a grip on this concept, let's consider again alarm-calling in ground squirrels.

If an individual squirrel was disposed, by some slight genetic mutation, to emit an alarm call to *anyone* in the vicinity of a predator, that genetic mutation faces a bleak future. The reason? If we can assume that the majority of the individuals who benefit from that alarm call do *not* have that mutation, then the costs of making alarm calls are not offset by the benefits to individuals with that mutation. Ground squirrels without the mutation – and, hence without the disposition to alert others – enjoy the benefits of being alerted, but without running the risks that come with doing the alerting. Hence, *indiscriminate alarm-callers* will quickly be driven to extinction. But change the scenario slightly. Imagine a genetic mutation that disposes an individual ground squirrel to emit alarm calls in the presence of predators *but only when it senses the presence of kin*. Although that individual now runs a greater risk of attack, if that individual can manage to survive and pass on that mutation to offspring, over time, the costs of alarm-calling to any individual squirrel will be offset by the benefits to the gene for that mutation – which happen to be located in genetic relatives. While non-alarm-callers may reap the occasional benefit of an alarm (by being in the right place at the right time), they will eventually be driven, if not to extinction, at least to a minority position in a population. The genes for discriminate alarm-callers have an inclusive fitness advantage over both *indiscriminate* alarm-callers and *non*-alarm-callers.[2]

This is just one example of a phenomenon that, according to Hamilton, should cut across the biological realm. According to inclusive fitness theory, natural selection will favor helping behavior in almost every instance in which (what we now think of as) Hamilton's Rule is met:

$$c < rb$$

The rule states, roughly, that for any act of assistance, the benefits (**b**) to a given relative, multiplied by the genetic relatedness (**r**) of actor and recipient (.5 for parents, children, and siblings; .25 for grandparents, grandchildren, half-siblings, uncles, aunts, and so on), are *greater than* the cost (**c**) of performing that act. (Benefits and costs are measured in terms of reproductive successes.) In concrete terms, this means that if a kind of behavior typically produces a benefit to one's full sibling that is more than twice the cost of producing it, we can expect natural selection to favor that kind of behavior. This rule makes it clear why indiscriminate alarm-callers, for example, will eventually be driven to extinction: the cost of the behavior is greater than the benefit to recipients, since the coefficient of relatedness among the recipients is quite small.

On the other hand, the rule should smoothly explain the instances of helping behavior with which we began the chapter. For example, white-fronted African bee-eaters, bluebirds, and scrub jays, it turns out, *selectively* assist others in rearing their young: the recipients almost always bear a genetic relation to the donors (Emlem and Wrege 1988). Among Japanese macaques, defending others from attack and food-sharing occur almost exclusively among kin (Chapais et al. 2001). The inclusive fitness theory also dissolves the mystery of sterility among social insect colonies: in a unusual twist of the genetic lottery, females within the *hymenoptera* order (ants, bees, wasps, sawflies) can share up to 75 percent of their genetic material with sisters, but only 50 percent with offspring. According to Hamilton's rule, with a coefficient of relatedness this high, natural selection will strongly favor behavior that benefits sisters, even at the cost of not reproducing themselves. Adopting the gene's-eye point of view, then, should bring into focus the root of many kinds of helping behavior among non-human animals.

Before concluding this section, let me address a question that may have arisen in the course of this discussion: Do we need to suppose that animals who assist kin take an active interest in promoting their genes? Of course not. Non-human animals – not to mention a sizable portion of humans – are entirely unaware of their genetic legacy precisely because they have none of the relevant concepts. (And even those who *do* grasp the relevant concepts may be entirely uninterested in their genetic legacy.)

It might be said that natural selection operates on a *need-to-know* basis: to solve a given adaptive problem (such as giving preferential treatment to kin), natural selection has to work with what it has been given, and this is usually not much. In most cases, substantive deliberation on, say, who to help in a fight is out of the question: we're talking about bird brains here! Instead, solutions are likely to be crude, allowing for only a limited amount of flexibility. But this is as it should be. From the gene's-eye point of view, there's no need to turn over any more executive control to the organism than is necessary; the point is to maximize genetic replication, not score high on IQ tests. As far as inclusive fitness goes, all that's really required is a special motivational system that's triggered by recognition of kin – an instinct, if you will. From the point of view of the organism, there need be no question of *why* or *how*. In most mammals, it is enough that their behavior is internally constrained by the recognition of kin.

2.3 Love Thy Neighbor – But Love Thy Family First

When we turn to our own case, do we observe the kinds of preferential treatment to family that inclusive fitness theory predicts? We do. Indeed, the point hardly seems worth arguing for: it's almost a truism that, in times of need, family comes first.[3] Still, it's worth mentioning a few large-scale trends observed by researchers. After all, large-scale trends are what give support to the idea that evolution has played a role in explaining our moral lives, where this would include helping behavior toward family. If the theory of inclusive fitness is correct, then we should observe in humans not merely a tendency to favor family members over strangers, but a tendency to *calibrate* one's assistance according to genetic relatedness. In other words, the more closely (genetically) related you are to someone the more likely you are to offer assistance. To test this idea, researchers have subjected the inclusive fitness theory to a range of tests.

In one study (Essock-Vitale and McGuire 1985), researchers interviewed 300 adult women in Los Angeles who described some 5,000 instances of receiving help and giving help. As predicted, the women were more likely to receive and give help to close kin than to distant kin, and this trend remained even when corrected for differences in residential proximity. In another study (Burnstein et al. 1994), researchers asked subjects to consider hypothetical scenarios in which subjects had to decide who (and who not) to help. Some of the scenarios involved life-or-death decisions; others involved more minor decisions, like picking up a few items at the store. Again, researchers found that who a subject chose to help almost always corresponded to genetic relatedness: brothers were chosen over cousins; mothers over grandmothers; nephews over second cousins.

Help of course can come in different forms. Consider financial help. According to the inclusive fitness theory, when people draw up their wills and decide who should receive their wealth, we should see the same pattern as above: all things being equal, the more closely related you are (genetically) to a benefactor, the greater the share of their estate you receive. When, in 1987, psychologists examined the bequests of 1,000 randomly selected decedents in British Columbia, Canada, this is just what they saw (M.S. Smith et al. 1987). Of a given decedent's estate, 55 percent was bequeathed to genetically related kin. Significantly, a full 84 percent of what was bequeathed to kin went to immediate offspring and siblings. Nieces, nephews, and grandchildren received only 15 percent of what was bequeathed to kin. Cousins received less than 1 percent. Spouses received about 37 percent of a decedent's estate; this can be explained by the fact that spouses should be expected to distribute wealth to their mutually related offspring. All told, kin and those expected to care for kin (i.e., spouses) received more than 92 percent of a decedent's estate; non-relatives received less than 8 percent.

These studies indicate that humans strongly resemble other species in the favoritism they show toward relatives. According to evolutionary psychology, this resemblance at the surface level is best explained by a force acting at the gene's-eye level: namely, inclusive fitness. Early members of the human family who either never helped anyone apart from themselves or helped anyone and everyone eventually found themselves at an evolutionary dead end. We, on the other hand, are descended from those early humans who possessed that genetic mutation that disposed them to treat relatives differently. Since those individuals fared best, they passed that behavioral tendency on to their offspring, who passed it on to their offspring, who passed it on to their offspring, who . . . in the end, passed it on to us. If this account is on the right track, then there is a perfectly straightforward Darwinian explanation for behavior that bears at least some of the hallmarks of *moral* behavior: caring for and assisting relatives. In case you don't see the *moral* component here, put yourself in the following situation.

You're a lifeguard at a local public pool. Staff shortages require that you watch over two pools, one next to the other (your lifeguard stand is situated between them). On this particular day, your little brother is at the pool. Suddenly, the air is full of screaming: you quickly discern a small boy drowning in the east pool and a small girl drowning in the west pool. The small boy, you realize, is your little brother. You do not know the little girl. Now, setting aside for a moment what you *would* do, consider: what *should* you do? What would be the morally right thing to do?

Here's what I think you'll say: "I should attempt to save my brother first." Or, "saving my brother first is morally justified." Indeed, you might insist that saving the little girl first would in fact be morally *wrong*. Either way, I don't believe that we're stretching the notion of morality when we say that morality allows for, indeed requires, giving special treatment to family.[4] But this is precisely what the theory of inclusive fitness predicts. Giving preferential treatment to relatives makes good evolutionary sense. That we're unable to say why – to produce some cogent ethical argument in defense of that treatment – is also unsurprising. From a gene's-eye perspective, the point is to get us, occasionally, to *act* in ways that benefit relatives – not *think about why we should act* in ways that benefit relatives. (If we needed an opinion, evolution would probably have given us one.) A more direct solution to the problem is to bypass the operation of rational thought and outfit organisms with powerful *emotions*, since these are more reliably connected to motivation. After all, simply telling Jones that there's a snake in the other room won't move Jones to flee unless Jones happens to fear snakes. The subject of emotions and their role in human morality will occupy us in the next chapter, so I'll hold off on further discussion until then.

2.4 False Positives and Core Systems

I've just argued that natural selection – by way of the processes of inclusive fitness – can account for one part of our moral lives, namely, our tendency to assist and care deeply about family members. It's natural to suppose, therefore, that any assistance to *non*-relatives must be explained by some other process. Actually, it's more complicated than this. There are two reasons to think that the processes of inclusive fitness may well explain some helping behavior to some non-relatives. First, we have to focus on a subproblem that inclusive fitness raises: in order to give special treatment to relatives, organisms have to know who their relatives are. In most species, relatives are identified by scent. Humans' sense of smell is far less developed.

So how did our earliest ancestors overcome this obstacle? So far as we know DNA tests were unavailable. Language, presumably, was also unavailable – at least to our earliest ancestors. But the problem was nevertheless solved. How? The philosopher Richard Joyce proposes the following.

Suppose some early hominid developed, as a result of some slight genetic mutation, a special concern for those around whom she lived. For example, when her closest neighbors were in trouble, she instinctively desired to help them; when she had food to share, she instinctively desired to share it with them. How would this genetic mutation have solved the sub-problem described above? The thought is this: such an individual, despite having made no judgment about her neighbors' genetic relation to her (after all, what does she know about genes?), would likely be helping her relatives because *her close neighbors would likely be her relatives*. If the people our ancestor spent most of her time with happened to be her relatives, then a disposition to care for those people is a cheap but fairly reliable means of improving one's inclusive fitness. Remember: Mother Nature is a frugal tinkerer. If a solution to an adaptive problem can be had on the cheap, chances are, natural selection will take it. But what does this have to do with *non*-relatives?

If in fact we did inherit a psychological tendency to care for and assist those around whom we live, then we should expect occasional *false positives* – especially now that we have exchanged life on the African savannah for life in densely packed cities. In densely packed cities, you are in close contact with the same people over the course of many years, many of whom are not your relatives (for example, close neighbors, shopkeepers, fellow congregants). But since the psychological mechanism we're hypothesizing does not itself discriminate between relatives and non-relatives, it's expected that you would care for these individuals *as if* they were your relatives. True, knowing these individuals are not family may temper your affection, but your affection is nevertheless real. This would also explain why the emotional bond between adopted children and their parents is typically as strong as the bond between children and their biological parents.

A second reason the processes of inclusive fitness may well explain some helping behavior to some non-relatives is that those processes may be responsible for the very structures that natural selection later bent into other tasks – such as helping non-relatives. When we recall that natural selection is an inherently conservative process, jerry-rigging new solutions out of old structures, we may well have inclusive fitness to thank for putting core psychological systems in place that made later moral (or quasi-moral) behavior possible. That is, since early humans were *already* disposed to care about those closest to them (thanks to inclusive fitness), it's not too difficult to imagine a few more mutations, aided by regular environmental pressures, delivering a disposition to care about a much wider range of folk (and fauna and flora).

What sorts of "regular environmental pressures" do I have in mind? First and foremost, the pressure to cooperate. The selection pressure on early hominids to cooperate led to what some theorists regard as the critical turning point on the road to morality: *reciprocal altruism*.

2.5 A Quick Note on "Altruism"

Up to this point I have been reluctant to make use of the term "altruism," despite the fact that theorists routinely use it in biological discussions. My reluctance stems from what I (and other philosophers) regard as a certain terminological carelessness. In less formal settings, we can get away with describing the vampire bat or the ground squirrel as *altruistic*. But to seriously suppose that the vampire bat is altruistic implies that (a) it possesses certain motives and (b) some of those motives are other-regarding. Neither (a) nor (b) is easy to defend. I take it that, according to the standard sense, to be altruistic requires a certain *motive* – namely, a reason or desire to help someone *for her own sake*. Thus I'm supposing that someone is made altruistic not by her actions, but by her motives. After all, I can be altruistic but fail to help someone (because of some unforeseen accident), and I can help someone but fail to be altruistic (again, by some unforeseen accident). If you conflate helpfulness and altruism, this will be hard to see.

Whether I'm right about this, for the purposes of the discussion here I plan to go on the assumption that altruism is a function of an organism's motives. If an organism has no "other-regarding" motives, then (strictly speaking) it's not altruistic – even if it regularly helps others. And if an organism lacks any motives at all (because it's a cockroach, say), then obviously it's not altruistic.[5] I am also going to assume that typical humans are – sometimes, at least – altruistic. (I won't take a stand on whether non-human animals are sometimes altruistic.) The role that altruism plays in our own moral lives will be addressed in the next chapter. The important thing now is to see that, although biologists frequently invoke the concept of altruism (e.g., reciprocal altruism), we should be careful not to assume they mean altruism in the standard sense.

Unfortunately, it's too late in the game to be changing names, so I'll continue to follow tradition and refer to the next biological process as reciprocal altruism. Perhaps the best thing to do is this: when you see the term "reciprocal altruism," read it as *reciprocity*.

2.6 Reciprocal Altruism

We all know the expression "You scratch my back, and I'll scratch yours." But you may not realize the power of this idea. It would not be an exaggeration to say that exercising this idea has settled labor disputes, passed legislation, put government factions in power, put government factions *out* of power; it has rearranged corporate hierarchies, saved marriages, even averted wars. The idea gets traction in those moments when we cannot get what we need or want, since what we need or want cannot, under the circumstances, be gotten alone. But even without the help of friends or family, our situation is not hopeless. Remember: others have needs of their own.

Consider: Farmer A needs to harvest his field in order to have enough food for winter, but Farmer A cannot do it alone. Farmer A's neighbor Farmer B (no relation) has an interest in Farmer A's crops, but being a rather disagreeable fellow, Farmer B has no interest in helping Farmer A. Farmer B, however, has problems of his own. Farmer B needs to harvest *his* field in order to have enough food for winter, but can't do it alone. Farmer A has an interest in Farmer B's crops, but Farmer A, being a disagreeable fellow himself, has no interest in helping Farmer B.

Now it should be glaringly obvious what Farmer A and Farmer B ought to do: *agree to help each other out!* If Farmer B agrees to help Farmer A harvest his crops this week, then Farmer A should agree to help Farmer B harvest *his* crops next week. Thus, at the end of two weeks, both have enough food for winter. It's not as if they have to be friends or even like each other. As they say, it's just business. But a business that delivers real payoffs. For together, Farmer A and Farmer B do substantially better than, for example, Farmer C and Farmer D who *cannot* agree to help each other out. (In fact, in this case the failure to agree might cost Farmer C and Farmer D their lives!) The biologist Robert Trivers (1971) described this phenomenon as *reciprocal altruism*. Paralleling what Hamilton had done for inclusive fitness, Trivers argued that reciprocal altruism would evolve across the biological realm provided that certain conditions were met.

First and foremost, the cost of providing a benefit to a non-relative *now* must be reliably outweighed by the reciprocation of some *future* benefit. (The other conditions largely concern an organism's ability to keep track of the relevant facts, for example who gave what to whom and when. Alas, this is going to exclude a rather wide swath of the biological population.) According to field biologists, where these conditions have been met, we observe instances of reciprocal altruism.

For example, the pattern of food-sharing in vampire bats indicates that while the majority of food-sharing occurs between mother and pup (roughly 70 percent), a substantial percentage of food-sharing (some 30 percent) occurs between non-relatives. Evidently, inclusive fitness is not the only force at work here. Closer study reveals that food-sharing among non-relatives is a direct function of past associations (Wilkinson 1990). The more likely it is that a given vampire bat (let's call her X) has shared food with another bat (let's call her Y) in the past, the more likely Y will be to assist X in the future. The vampire bats have, in effect, a buddy system. And preserving this buddy system is a matter of life or death: two nights without food is pretty much fatal for vampire bats.

Perhaps the most vivid example of reciprocal altruism in non-human animals is the grooming behavior observed in primates and monkeys. For us, the maxim "You scratch my back, and I'll scratch yours" is a figure of speech; for some primates and monkeys it's a serious request. A vervet monkey, for example, has to deal constantly with external parasites, some of which can cost him his life. But he can't reach all the parts of his body that might be vulnerable (ever tried putting sunscreen on the middle of your back?). So he needs a *groomer*, another monkey who will spend thirty minutes or so carefully picking out parasites from his head and back. Thirty minutes might not seem like a lot of time, but it's time that could be spent hunting or foraging, attracting potential mates or caring for young – in other words, advancing his *own* reproductive fitness. If grooming behavior occurred strictly within the family, then one need only appeal to the processes of inclusive fitness. But biologists routinely observe monkeys grooming *non-relatives*. Why? As in the case of vampire bats, something else is going on here. What's going on, according to biologists, is reciprocal altruism. In study after study (most recently, Schino 2007), primatologists observe that whether one monkey (P) grooms another monkey (Q) *now* is directly related to whether Q has groomed P in the past. Moreover, the length of time spent grooming is proportional to the time spent in past exchanges.

In another study, anthropologist Craig Packer (1977) showed that whether or not a vervet monkey (R) was disposed to assist an unrelated monkey (S) calling out for help is directly related to whether S had groomed R in the recent past. If S *had* recently groomed R, R was far more likely to look around and move in the direction of S's calls of distress. By contrast, if S had *not* recently groomed R, R simply ignored the calls. (Interestingly, this discrepancy does not appear among kin; there, calls for help are responded to whether or not grooming has taken place.) So it appears that vervet monkeys are "keeping score." And for good reason: doing favors for one's neighbors pays. Equally important are the *costs*. With the exception of a few dominant individuals at the top of the social hierarchy, vervet monkeys that do not return the "grooming favor" significantly increase their chances of contracting a disease.

As a general rule, then, *mutual cooperation* is better for everyone involved than *mutual defection*. Mutual cooperation, we'll say, consists of individuals benefiting others in return for some future benefit. Mutual defection consists of individuals refusing to benefit others in return for some future benefit. If Farmer A and Farmer B aren't willing to assist each other, then Farmer A and Farmer B face desperate futures. Clearly, mutual cooperation is a far better alternative. But this is not the end of the matter.

Although mutual cooperation yields higher returns for everyone than mutual defection, *any individual* stands to gain even more under a different arrangement: she defects while others cooperate. This is the fabled *free-rider*. If Farmer B helps Farmer A harvest the latter's crops but Farmer A does not return the favor, then Farmer A has received a sizable benefit without having to pay the cost (of returning the favor). If, that is, this were a one-time affair (because, let's say, Farmer A immediately packed up his harvest and moved to the other side of the continent), then we'd have to say that Farmer A did better under this arrangement than under mutual cooperation. As far as Farmer B is concerned, this arrangement is *even worse* than mutual defection since he made a sizable sacrifice on Farmer A's behalf but received nothing in return. We can thus add two more general rules to our list. First, the best arrangement for *any individual* is one in which she defects (i.e., receives help, but doesn't help others) while others cooperate. Second, the worst arrangement for any individual is one in which she cooperates while others defect.

Perhaps the best way to appreciate the intricacies of reciprocal exchanges is by considering the game "Prisoner's Dilemma," first developed in the

1950s by Merrill Flood and Melvin Dresher of the Rand Corporation. The game itself can be played with money, M&Ms, mating partners, whatever – so long as there is some benefit each participant desires. In the original example, Jack and Jill are arrested (for looting a store, let's say) and placed in separate holding cells. Although Jack and Jill were jointly participating in the looting, Jack and Jill do not know each other. The police make the following offer to Jack:

> If you identify Jill as the perpetrator of the crime and Jill refuses to talk, I will release you right now and, with your eye-witness testimony, charge Jill with the maximum penalty (ten years behind bars). If you refuse to talk and Jill identifies *you* as the perpetrator, I will charge you with the maximum penalty and I'll release Jill right now. If you identify Jill as the perpetrator and Jill identifies you as the perpetrator, I'll see to it that each of you receives five years behind bars. If both of you refuse to talk, I can only charge each of you with the minimum penalty (two years behind bars). You think about what you want to do while I go down the hall and make the same offer to Jill.

Figure 2.1 illustrates the various "payoffs" for Jack and Jill.

If we assume that Jack wants to avoid as much jail time as possible and Jill wants to avoid as much jail time as possible, what should Jack do? Well, let's think about this. If (unbeknownst to Jack) Jill decides to STAY

JILL

		Stay Silent (*Cooperate*)	Identify Jack (*Defect*)
JACK	Stay Silent (*Cooperate*)	Jack: 2 years Jill: 2 years	Jack: 10 years Jill: 0 years
	Identify Jill (*Defect*)	Jack: 0 years Jill: 10 years	Jack: 5 years Jill: 5 years

Figure 2.1 A Prisoner's Dilemma payoff schedule for Jack and Jill

SILENT, then Jack would do better to IDENTIFY JILL, since going free beats two years in jail. If Jill IDENTIFIES JACK, then – again – Jack would do better to IDENTIFY JILL, since five years in jail beats ten years in jail. In other words, *whatever Jill decides to do, Jack does better DEFECTING.* According to game theorists, DEFECTING is said to "strictly dominate" under these conditions; that is, under all conditions, DEFECTING maximizes an individual's interests. So what makes the Prisoner's Dilemma a *dilemma*? This comes into focus when we turn our attention to Jill.

We're assuming that Jill is just like Jack in that she wants to avoid as much jail time as possible. And, by hypothesis, Jill is offered the same deal as Jack. If Jill goes through the same deliberative processes as Jack, then she, too, will recognize that DEFECTING strictly dominates as a strategy: whatever Jack does, she does better DEFECTING. But if Jill acts on this strategy and Jack acts on this strategy, then both end up worse than if they had both STAYED SILENT. For surely Jack and Jill would each rank two years in jail ahead of five years in jail. The dilemma that the Prisoner's Dilemma so elegantly raises is this: rational calculation recommends DEFECTING, but when everyone calculates in this way, when everyone DEFECTS, *everyone does worse than he or she could have done.* When everyone goes for the top, everyone ends up near the bottom.

Putting the point more generally, we can see that from the perspective of any thoughtful individual, defection will always be the most tempting option. By defecting, you at least have the chance of exploiting your neighbors' help; by cooperating, you give up that chance. Moreover, by defecting, you protect yourself from being exploited by others (I mean, who can you trust?). Cooperation, by contrast, almost always comes with the risk of giving without getting in return. And in an unforgiving environment, where resources are scarce and time is limited, giving without getting in return can exact a heavy price. But this way of thinking, when adopted by all, drives everyone down: a group of strictly rational individuals who all appreciate the payoffs of defecting and act accordingly are going to be considerably worse off than a group of individuals who are, by some means, committed to cooperating. In other words, such social environments appear open to invasion by individuals capable of engaging in ongoing cooperative exchanges.

Trivers' hypothesis was that natural selection seized on mutations disposing individuals to cooperate, if only occasionally. If we assume that, in a particular environment, the cost–benefit ratios are relatively stable and opportunities for cooperation are recurrent, the adaptive pressure is there for a kind of reciprocal altruism to evolve. A genetic mutation that disposes an organism to enter into cooperative exchanges with others will evolve if such exchanges can regularly be preserved. But this is much easier said than (biologically) done. As biologists are quick to point out, the Prisoner's Dilemma (despite its elegance – or perhaps because of it) can distract us from all the intricacies and complexities of real-world exchanges, in both the human and the non-human realms. Perhaps the most apparent point is the fact that *single* exchanges between strangers with little chance of future interaction are surely the exception and not the rule. Even among nomadic animals, in-group interactions will be frequent and participants familiar. This puts new constraints on how a Prisoner's Dilemma-type game is played. Furthermore, it potentially changes the payoffs for each player. For example, in *iterated* games there may be future costs associated with defecting when another cooperates that do not arise in single exchanges. (Think of the difference between a situation in which Farmer A "flees the scene" of defection, as in our original example, and a situation in which Farmer A defects but remains in proximity to Farmer B. The latter situation is, you might say, combustible.) In the next chapter we'll explore these details more fully. More specifically, we'll look at the engineering ways in which evolution may have solved the problem of preserving cooperative exchanges – at least in humans. This will move us decidedly into the terrain of the moral.

2.7 Conclusion

My aim in this chapter has been to clarify and support the following idea: the theory of natural selection has the potential to explain at least some of the helping behavior we observe in the world. To the extent that human instances of such behavior amount to *moral* behavior, then evolution can (to that extent) explain a piece of human morality. For example, you might insist that we have strict moral obligations to our family members; this may be evidenced by our strong emotional bond to their well-being. The theory of inclusive fitness, by redirecting our focus to the gene's-eye level, may provide an explanation for *why* we tend to think that we have these strong moral obligations to our family members: such thoughts, ignited by strong emotions, reliably disposed our ancestors to care for and protect relatives. And by caring for and protecting our relatives we were, in a sense, caring for and protecting copies of our genes. A strong moral commitment to one's family, after all, has high biological payoff.

Even in the case of self-sacrificing behavior toward *non-relatives*, evolution may offer some explanation. It may be, on the one hand, that the psychological system put in place by the processes of inclusive fitness is not "fine-grained" enough to distinguish relatives from non-relatives. From the point of view of natural selection, it was good enough that we were attuned to those around whom we live. So in environments where many of the people in your close proximity are *not* biologically related to you, you may nevertheless see yourself as having a moral duty to protect *their* well-being, too. On the other hand, self-sacrificing behavior toward non-relatives may be a function of the high value we place on preserving cooperative relationships. We may regard it as a moral imperative to "follow through on our commitments" or to "keep our promises" or to "repay our debts." But insofar as these attitudes dispose one to preserve cooperative relationships, they serve ultimately to advance one's biological fitness. Mutual cooperation pays. You get by with a little help from your friends – and they get by with a little help from you.

Important pieces of the puzzle, however, remain to be filled in. I have said very little about morality itself. I have only hinted at the role of emotions. And I have only gestured at the intricacies of real-world cooperative exchanges. In the next chapter we'll fill in these details, and by doing so we'll begin constructing the bridge from these earliest roots of morality to morality as we know it and experience it.

Further Reading

De Waal, Frans (1996) *Good Natured: The Origins of Right and Wrong in Humans and Other Animals* (Harvard University Press).

Dugatkin, Lee Alan (2006) *The Altruism Equation: Seven Scientists Search for the Origins of Goodness* (Princeton University Press).

Hamilton, W.D. (1998) *The Narrow Roads of Gene Land: The Collected Papers of W. D. Hamilton. Evolution of Social Behavior* (Oxford University Press).

Joyce, Richard (2006) *The Evolution of Morality* (MIT Press).

Maynard Smith, J. (1982) *Evolution and the Theory of Games* (Cambridge University Press).

Skyrms, Brian (1996) *Evolution of the Social Contract.* (Cambridge University Press).

Sober, Elliott and David Sloan Wilson (1998) *Unto Others: The Evolution and Psychology of Unselfish Behavior* (Harvard University Press).

Trivers, R.L. (1985) *Social Evolution* (Benjamin/Cummings).

Trivers, R.L. (2002) *Natural Selection and Social Theory: Selected Papers of Robert L. Trivers. Evolution and Cognition Series* (Oxford University Press)

Williams, G.C. (1966) *Adaptation and Natural Selection* (Princeton University Press).

3

The Caveman's Conscience: The Evolution of Human Morality

Zigong asked: "Is there any single word that can guide one's entire life?"
The master said: "Should it not be reciprocity? What you do not wish for
yourself, do not do to others."

(*Confucius*)

Good and evil, reward and punishment, are the only motives to a rational
creature: these are the spur and reins whereby all mankind are set on
work, and guided.

(*John Locke, Some Thoughts Concerning Education*)

We have reached the point in our discussion where we are ready to take on the evolution of morality itself. The stage for this discussion has, I hope, been set. We've discussed the fundamentals of Darwin's theory; we've seen how natural selection can generate surprising solutions to adaptive problems; we've explored the "gene's-eye" point of view and seen how aiding relatives is a standard biological imperative; and we've seen the advantages and risks of reciprocal exchanges. It is time now to connect these early stages with morality itself. In this chapter, I want to present a sketch of how natural selection may have produced our moral minds. I call the forthcoming a "sketch," but it may as well be called a *distillation* because it attempts to distill a single story from a family of different of views. As we proceed, I'll make a point of noting the differences that separate these views; however, the larger aim is to present the core idea that runs through these views.

That idea, put simply, is this: moral thought, together with our moral feelings, was natural selection's way of ensuring social harmony. And this, by extension, fostered reliable reciprocal exchanges. So, for example, feeling

An Introduction to Evolutionary Ethics, by Scott M. James. © 2011 Scott M. James

bad about a certain action or believing that an action is *bad* or *morally wrong* serves a purpose: it "keeps us in line," which (it is thought) yields long-term biological advantages. Those individuals *not* disposed to think morally or who did not experience moral emotions were at a distinct disadvantage, for (as we'll see) they jeopardized important reciprocal relations. The goal of this chapter is to present this idea, taking note of differences among authors. I will conclude the chapter by laying out some of the questions and concerns raised by critics of the idea.

But first things first. Any hope of sketching out a plausible evolutionary account of human morality requires getting clear on what morality is – or, better yet, what we take ourselves to be doing when we are "morally aroused." The point is not to settle basic philosophical questions about the nature of justice or wrongness or rights. Rather, the point is to identify as clearly as possible what it is that makes moral creatures like us *moral*. That is, if we want to assert that evolution is responsible for the human moral capacity, we had better have a very clear picture in mind of what that capacity looks like – without any specific regard for evolution. Here, moral philosophy comes in handy, for moral philosophers have long been involved in the quest to understand what we are doing when we engage in moral thought. So we'll begin by forming a picture of the human moral capacity.

3.1 What Makes Moral Creatures *Moral*

It might be thought that what it is to be moral is to *behave morally*. As tempting as this thought is, it is almost surely mistaken. If we define behaving morally as simply behaving in ways that accord with accepted moral standards (e.g., not harming others needlessly, helping our neighbors), then we'll be forced to count many creatures as moral that, on reflection, probably aren't. For example, just because a rat doesn't murder his neighbor, it would be stretching things to say that, for *that* reason, the rat is moral. (By the same token, it seems strange to call a rat a murderer if it *did* kill its neighbor.) Likewise, calling a vampire bat moral because it shares blood with a hungry neighbor seems inappropriate. Suppose I design a robot that assists me with yard-work, does it follow that the robot is moral? It seems not. The lesson is that, for a given creature, simply behaving morally (a welcome trait, perhaps) is not *sufficient* for calling that creature moral. Indeed, it may not even be *necessary*. If you tell a lie for personal gain, it seems a bit excessive to conclude that you are therefore not a moral person.

True, what you *did* was immoral, but you still count as moral. What this should reveal is that being moral – while surely connected behavior in some way – is not the same thing as simply behaving morally.

This parallels our discussion of altruism in the previous chapter. There, I insisted that altruism was not determined by a creature's behavior, but by a creature's *motives*. Something similar is being proposed here. Being moral has to do with, first and foremost, what's going on *inside* a creature. The standard philosophical approach is to describe our moral capacity as the capacity to make *moral judgments*. Now, I will be understating things when I say that philosophers are deeply divided over the nature of moral judgment. About the most one can say – without getting into too much philosophical hot water – is that moral judgments consist of certain *attitudes* individuals have toward actions, persons, institutions, and the like. This, however, is not saying much. For on some views these attitudes are essentially *beliefs*, as in *Jones believes that capital punishment is wrong*. On other views, these attitudes are nothing more than (non-belief-like) *expressions* of one's emotional attitude, as in *Capital punishment, yuck!* And these views just scratch the surface. Suffice it to say that whatever a moral judgment is, there is at least this much that (most?) philosophers will agree on: it's distinct from mere behavior. To avoid diverting our attention too much, I will return to moral judgment later on.

What we're trying to characterize here are the surface-level features of our moral experience – in particular, the experience of judging that something is wrong.[1] For these are the features an evolutionary account is supposed to capture. To move things along, let's focus on an example that you'll probably recognize. Walking across campus one day, you pass by a group of students chanting "Abortion is murder!" They display photos of aborted fetuses and graphs depicting global abortion rates. Occasionally, they manage to engage passers-by in discussion. What's going on here? What is it these students think they are doing when they insist that abortion is murder?

Set aside the question, *Is* abortion murder? That's a question about the moral status of abortion. Focus instead on what's going on inside the minds of these students: what do they take themselves to be doing? Now the question might seem a bit thick-skulled. (*Isn't it obvious? They're expressing their moral views!*) In fact, what's going on here requires careful analysis.

First, you might infer from the students' statements that they themselves would not want to have an abortion, that they themselves possess a strong aversion to having an abortion. While that's probably a safe inference, it misses the point. By asserting that abortion is murder, the students (at least think they) are *doing more* than expressing a strong desire not to have an abortion. After all, if, by their assertion, they mean nothing more than that, why are they bothering to advertise it to the campus community? It would be like me "protesting" the campus community with: *I don't desire the taste of lobster! I don't desire the taste of lobster!* This is why, incidentally, defenders of abortion miss the point by insisting (as some bumper stickers do) that "If you don't like abortion, don't have one." In asserting that abortion is murder, our student activists are not *just* expressing an aversion to an abortion. So, then, what else is going on?

One reasonable suggestion is that by asserting that abortion is murder, the students are asserting that abortion is *prohibited*, that it's something that should not be done by anyone. Presumably, if you ask the students whether you yourself should have an abortion, the answer is going to be *No*. But if moral assertions were nothing more than expressions of one's inhibitions, then the answer would be *It depends*. It depends on your inhibitions. But it would be very surprising indeed if our student activists had this in mind in asserting that abortion is murder.

According to the philosopher Richard Joyce (2006), one of the essential ingredients of any moral capacity is understanding *prohibitions*, that is, understanding that some things shouldn't be done because they're wrong. The distinction that Joyce is highlighting is the distinction between *judging* that some act is prohibited and *being disinclined* to perform that act. They often go together, but not always. Joyce (2006: 50) offers this example. A friend prepares you a rather large helping of your favorite meal. After working your way through most of it, your friend says: "Don't feel obliged to finish it." You say (because it's your favorite meal and you're particularly hungry): "I don't. I really *want* to finish it." Joyce's point is that *wanting* to do something is different in an important way from judging that you *ought* to do something. After all, you could have been full. You could have thought that not finishing would have hurt your friend's feelings. Since you think you ought to avoid hurting your friend's feeling, you could have thought: "I *ought* to finish the meal." In the former case, there is no reason at all to suppose that your action is motivated by anything like morality. You simply want to continue enjoying the meal. In the latter case, your motivation is clearly moral.

The larger lesson here is that creatures that fail to understand prohibitions fail to possess a moral sense. This means that even if members of a species sometimes benefit their neighbors (e.g., vampire bats) or show sympathy toward the suffering of others (e.g., chimpanzees), this is not enough to deem them *moral* creatures. A race of creatures with a strong desire to treat others kindly and no desire to harm others, who genuinely love each and every neighbor, will not, on Joyce's view, count as *moral* creatures. We can perfectly well describe this race of creatures as nice and friendly and loving and so on. But we cannot describe them as moral *unless* they regard some acts as prohibited.[2] For our purposes, this means that any attempt to explain our moral sense must account for this distinct appreciation of prohibitions. Explaining human sympathy or empathy or compassion, while part of the package, is not sufficient.

Talk of desires prompts a second observation. Suppose you respond to the abortion protesters by saying, "But I actually *desire* to have an abortion. Indeed, it's been one of my lifelong pursuits. So is it wrong for me?" Undoubtedly, the students will insist: "Yes!" The wrongness of abortion (if it is wrong) does not disappear for those individuals who actually desire to have an abortion. Abortion, the students will insist, is murder *whatever your desires are*; that is, what makes abortion wrong does not depend on what you or I or (perhaps) anyone desires. Telling someone that they shouldn't have an abortion because it's wrong is not a piece of advice – as in, "You shouldn't eat so many French fries." The judgment that someone shouldn't eat so many fries rests on the reasonable assumption that the listener *desires* to live a long and healthy life. Asserting that abortion is murder rests on no such assumption. And so it goes for other acts: when we assert that something shouldn't be done because it's morally wrong, we seem to mean that it shouldn't be done – period – whatever your desires or interests happen to be. If moral judgments weren't like this, then our student activists would happily revise their judgment that abortion is murder when confronted with someone who positively desires to have an abortion or genuinely does not care about being punished. So an explanation for our moral sense must explain the sense in which moral judgments appeal to prohibitions, where these prohibitions are distinct from our desires.

Granted, the students may use the threat of punishment (e.g., eternal damnation) as a means of getting their listeners to comply, but this is very different than saying that the threat of punishment is what makes abortion wrong. That would be getting things backwards. It would be strange if expressing our moral views were not like this. Imagine being the brutal and powerful dictator of some reclusive nation, and imagine that you desire to have some nondescript peasant killed – because, let's say, he insulted you (remember: you're brutal). Since you face no threat of punishment, does this mean that killing the peasant is therefore not wrong? That seems absurd.

If you cheat on an exam and get away with it, does this mean that your cheating was, for that reason, morally permissible? No. The correct thing to say in both cases is that *you got away with your crime.* It was still a crime; you just went unpunished. By invoking crimes and criminal behavior, I do not mean to suggest that morality and legality are the same, that what makes something wrong is that it's illegal. To see why, return your attention to our abortion protesters.

Suppose our protesters are protesting in the United States. Surely they know that first- and second-term abortions are protected under the United States criminal code? If the law was the sole determinant of an act's morality, then it would be hard to make sense of the protesters' actions. Why would they be seeking to change the law, unless they thought that the law was, in some way, mistaken? If legality made morality (so to speak), then we would regard the protesters the way we would regard someone staging a moral protest (in the US) against the practice of driving on the right-hand side of the road. Such a person would be utterly confused. The law requiring that US motorists drive on the right-hand side of the road does not derive from some deep metaphysical truth about how people should drive. It's merely a convention, inherited from tradition. But we do not regard the abortion protesters that way. We may disagree with their moral (or perhaps theological) views, but we don't believe that they're utterly confused. The upshot—and this is my third observation about morality—is that it seems the moral prohibitions at the heart of our moral judgments are distinct from human convention. Human legal conventions – we might say – should reflect the underlying moral order.

A fourth observation we might make from our abortion example is that we expect a tight link between the students' moral views and their *motivation.* Consider, for example, how mystifying it would be to see one of the student activists, later that same day, on her way into the abortion clinic.

"What – did you change your moral view?" you ask.
"No," she says. "Abortion is still murder."
"But you're having an abortion anyway?"
"Sure," she says.
"Because . . . it's an absolute necessity?" you ask.
"Nope. Just 'cause."

Three things seem possible here. Either she's *lying* about her moral view of abortion, or she's a shameless hypocrite (with, perhaps, sociopathic tendencies), or she simply fails to grasp the concept of murder. What does not seem possible here, given our implicit understanding of morality, is the combination of the following three things: (a) she sincerely believes that abortion is murder; (b) she understands that murder means wrongful killing; and she is not motivated in the least bit to refrain from having an abortion. This combination seems impossible because sincerely believing that abortion is murder entails the belief that one should not have one, and believing that one should not have one implies – if not entails – that one is *motivated*, however slightly, not to have one. This is not the same thing as saying that one will not, as a matter of fact, have an abortion. After all, people regularly act in ways that they regard as immoral. But someone who acts immorally, without the least bit of reluctance and without a hint of regret or shame or guilt, should make us seriously doubt that she sincerely believes that that act is immoral. What this suggests is that a sincere moral judgment is somehow connected to motivation. We have a hard time making sense of someone who repeatedly insists that abortion is murder but could not care less whether she has one.

A fifth feature of morality that emerges from our abortion example is this: someone who knowingly violates a moral prohibition – in this case, a prohibition on abortion – *deserves* (at least in the minds of our protesters) *punishment*. Whether or not she is actually punished is a different matter. The point is that in judging that abortion is prohibited, the students are implying that punishment would be justified. To sharpen the point, Joyce has us imagine creatures who regularly assert that some acts must be done and other things must not be done, but when someone refuses to act as she must, there is no sense among the creatures that she should "pay" for what she has done. No one thinks that the violation *demands* retribution. Joyce suspects, therefore, that "these creatures must … lack a central element of the notion of *justice:* the element pertaining to getting what one deserves" (2006: 67). Part of what makes moral creatures moral, then, has to do with thinking that acting in ways that are forbidden *deserves* punishment while acting in ways that are (for example) selfless *deserves* praise.

This is not the case with a wide range of other acts we think should or should not be done. Suppose I tell you that you shouldn't go see the movie you're contemplating seeing because (let's say) the acting is terrible. Suppose you see the movie anyway. I might regard your decision as imprudent or dumb, but I wouldn't think that you deserve to be punished for going. When you tell me that I ought not to build my house so close to the ocean shore because it will be threatened by a storm surge, you might think me unwise for going forward with my plans, but you wouldn't think me sinful. Moral "oughts," however, are different. When we assert that you morally ought not do something, this implies that we (or at least someone) would be warranted in punishing you for your deed. If wrongdoing was not tightly connected to punishment in this way, then we should have no trouble at all imagining our abortion protesters feeling entirely neutral about someone who willfully decides to have an abortion. But this would be quite surprising indeed.

In the background of this observation is a distinction that needs underlining. Believing that an action will *provoke* hostility is distinct from believing that an action *merits* hostility. This distinction may not be obvious, so let me spell it out. Believing that an action will provoke hostility requires only that one should believe that a given type of action is normally followed by another type of response – in this case, hostility. It is merely the recognition of a *regularity*, not unlike the recognition of other regularities: for example, thunder regularly follows lightning. It would be silly to think that lightning *justifies* or *warrants* thunder; the two are merely "regularly conjoined." The point is that we can easily imagine creatures that can recognize social regularities (actions of type T are normally followed by hostility), but fail to recognize that hostility is justified or warranted. In short, the recognition of social regularities, by itself, does not presuppose morality.

Someone could believe that abortion is regularly followed by hostility *without* believing that abortion is morally prohibited. How? Well, maybe she does not believe abortion is murder! Or maybe she's an expert on human behavior but simply lacks a moral sense (maybe she's a psychologist from another galaxy). The upshot, however, is that among the distinctive features of our moral sense is the recognition that some responses are merited or deserved. Joyce (2006: ch. 2) sees the distinction this way: it is one thing to understand that an action is *accepted*, another thing to understand that it is *acceptable*. (Give that distinction a minute to play out in your mind.) An important implication of this distinction is that even if creatures display the recognition of social regularities (and we see this in lots of higher mammals), it does not automatically follow that they are moral creatures. For that, they would need to recognize more than behavioral regularities; they would need to recognize that some behaviors are "called for."

Finally, in connection with the previous point, creatures like us appear to internalize the attitudes of others. This internalization is part of what we think of when we think about the feeling of *guilt*: we feel that our wrongdoing *deserves* punishment. Indeed, the feeling itself can be its own punishment. This is what we mean we say that someone must suffer the pangs of his own conscience. "How can you live with yourself?" we ask of someone unrepentant in his wrongdoing. "You should be ashamed of yourself!" Part of being a moral creature, then, appears to involve norms of feeling: guilt or shame are appropriate feelings in response to one's own (acknowledged) wrongdoing. To say the least, we regard with suspicion those who feel no guilt or remorse for their crimes. It is perhaps not surprising that such individuals are commonly classified as *antisocial* or *sociopathic*, for at least one of the checks on immoral behavior is missing: the pangs of one's own conscience. (More on this in the next chapter.)

It is important to note as well the behavioral element associated with guilt. When we feel guilty about something we've done, we desire, if only slightly, to *make amends*. We feel the need to apologize, to repair whatever damage we've caused. Our pride may stand in the way so that we do not carry through with the reparation, but the feeling is undeniable. And it is often the case that the feeling does not dissipate *until* we've made amends. Criminals who for years have gone unidentified commonly express a sort of relief upon being caught; part of the relief, evidently, consists of no longer having to live under the weight of the guilt. Thus an explanation for our moral sense, within the context of evolution, should also illuminate the fact that guilt compels us to make things right.

A quick review. What makes moral creatures moral apparently involves a number of things. The following seem to represent some conceptual truths about the making of moral judgments. (1) Moral creatures understand prohibitions. (2) Moral prohibitions do not appear to depend on our desires, nor (3) do they appear to depend on human conventions, like the law. Instead, they appear to be objective, not subjective.[3] (4) Moral judgments are tightly linked to motivation: sincerely judging that some act is wrong appears to entail at least some desire to *refrain from* performing that act. (5) Moral judgments imply notions of desert: doing what you know to be morally prohibited implies that punishment would be justified. (6) Moral creatures, such as ourselves, experience a distinctive *affective* response to our own wrongdoing, and this response often prompts us to make amends for the wrongdoing.

3.2 The Evolution of Morality

For those theorists who believe that evolution played a central role in the development of our moral sense, a general storyline has developed. The aim of this section is to trace that storyline. However, instead of approaching our subject directly, I'm going to ask you to consider an analogy, a case that, though drawn from evolutionary psychology, is entirely unrelated to morality. The point of the analogy of course is to get you primed for the evolution of morality. More specifically, I want to rehearse a common evolutionary lesson: sometimes what we – as biological organisms – regard as intrinsically good (call it A) is not what natural selection "regards" as intrinsically good (call it B). However, given the contingencies of our environment, the pursuit of A has the reliable effect of securing B. This can explain why our attitudes toward A evolved. This phenomenon is probably more common than we think. So here's the analogy.

For sexually reproducing creatures such as ourselves, it is important that individuals do not waste time mating (or attempting to mate) with non-fertile members of the opposite sex. Considering the substantial efforts one might expend attracting and securing potential mates, we can thus expect that organisms developed means of *discriminating* between worthwhile mates and, well, less-than-worthwhile mates. It would only be a matter of time before those individuals who couldn't make those discriminations lost out to those individuals who could. So how might this general constraint have affected early humans? Let's take early males. If it is fair to assume that the peak fertility of ancestral females resembles the peak fertility of contemporary females (i.e., ages 19–25), then males who selectively pursued females *outside* the years of peak fertility would fare worse than males who selectively pursued females *within* the years of peak fertility, since mating with females outside those years would (all things being equal) result in fewer viable offspring. Hence, there would have been adaptive pressure on early males to attract and pursue only the most fertile females.

But this raises a new problem. How would early males know when females in their vicinity were most fertile? After all, early females did not wear labels announcing their relative fertility. They did not advertise their ages for the simple reason that they wouldn't have had any concept of calendar years. It's not impossible that early women released sex pheromones (an odor males might detect), but this would have required intimate contact, precisely the kind of contact early males were deciding whether or not to make. So how did early males in fact solve this problem?

Once you think about it, the answer is obvious. The most fertile females simply *look* different from most other females (that is, from pre-pubescent and post-menopausal females). Evolutionary psychologists have proposed and provided empirical support for the idea that early males distinguished between fertile and non-fertile females on the basis of specific *visual cues*. Suppose that an early (post-pubescent) male, as a result of some mutation, possessed strong preferences for females with many of the following physical traits: symmetrical face, clear complexion, full lips, small nose, big eyes, lustrous hair, full breasts, and a waist-to-hip ratio of approximately 0.7. Why these traits? Simple: women with these traits are the most likely to be healthy and fertile. The male who possessed desires for those traits (as opposed to others) and could attract females with those traits would over time out-reproduce other males precisely because those females were more likely to reproduce than females without those traits.[4]

But let me underline the important point here: there would be *no need whatsoever* for that male with those desires to have any knowledge of – let alone, concern for – the correlation between those traits and fertility. As we've seen again and again, natural selection operates on a "need to know" basis. And, here, there's no need for males to know about that correlation. Design males to be attracted to females with those traits and reproductive success will take care of itself.

So here is an example of natural selection settling on a psychological mechanism that does not attach importance to what is, biologically speaking, good in itself, but to some other *intermediate* good instead. In other words, what males regard as intrinsically valuable (e.g., clear complexion, lustrous hair, full breasts) is not the same as what natural selection "regards" as intrinsically valuable (e.g., female fertility). Of course, if natural selection *did* equip males with a concern for female fertility *itself*, then we should expect to see males exhibiting a strong *aversion* to the use of contraception. For the point of contraception is to positively frustrate a woman's fertility by preventing her from becoming pregnant. But this is not at all what we observe. The desire for females with those traits remains (very much) in effect with or without the use of contraception. But this mismatch is tolerable since, for creatures like us, with all of our biological idiosyncrasies, pursuing females with those traits has the reliable effect of achieving reproductive success, all things being equal.

With this story firmly in mind, let's turn to morality. As we saw in the previous chapter, the biological value of establishing and preserving cooperative alliances among one's neighbors would have been critical for the survival (and reproductive success) of early humans. While the processes of inclusive fitness would have ensured at least some resources coming one's way, this would be far from optimal. Anthropologists and ethnographers hypothesize that early humans existed in small bands of about thirty-five individuals. And these bands may have coexisted with other bands totaling some 150 people. One might have treated some of these individuals as relatives, but a sizable number would be mere neighbors. An individual who could routinely count on these non-relatives for assistance – in return for giving assistance – would have possessed a pronounced advantage over an individual unable or unwilling to forge such relationships.

As in the case of our discriminating males, however, it's one thing to identify what is biologically advantageous, another thing to design individuals capable of regularly reaching it. We cannot expect that our earliest ancestors calculated the long-term value of establishing cooperative alliances. This is no more plausible than the idea that early males calculated female fertility rates. But the adaptive sub-problem here is even more pronounced than in the case of mate selection. For we have to remember that there would have been persistent pressure to *resist* cooperating. Recall our discussion of the Prisoner's Dilemma in the previous chapter. Cooperating in Prisoner's Dilemma games is hardly the most attractive option: first, it means forgoing the highest payoff (i.e., exploiting the cooperation of another) and, second, it opens one up to being exploited. If early humans had enough sense to know how to reason about what was good for them, then they would have been leery of setting themselves up for a fall. But as Prisoner's Dilemma games so elegantly make clear, when everyone takes that attitude, everyone suffers. So the adaptive problem in need of solution was this: design individuals to establish and preserve cooperative alliances *despite* the temptation not to cooperate.

The solution (you guessed it) was to design individuals to *think morally*. One of the earliest philosophers to push this specific view was Michael Ruse: "To make us cooperate for our biological ends, evolution has filled us full of thoughts about right and wrong, the need to help our fellows and so on" (1995: 230–1). Cooperating is not merely something to be desired (at least when it is); it's something we regard as *required*. "Morality," says Ruse, "is that which our biology uses to promote 'altruism.'" A recent proponent of this view, Richard Joyce, provides the most explicit account of the steps leading up to our moral sense. It's worth pausing over a longer passage:

> Suppose there was a realm of action of such recurrent importance that nature did not want practical success to depend on the frail caprice of ordinary human practical intelligence. That realm might, for example, pertain to certain forms of cooperative behavior toward one's fellows. The benefits that may come from cooperation – enhanced reputation, for example – are typically long-term values, and merely to be aware of and desire these long-term advantages does not guarantee that the goal will be effectively pursued, any more than the firm desire to live a long life guarantees that a person will give up fatty foods. The hypothesis, then, is that natural selection opted for a special motivational mechanism for this realm: moral conscience. (Joyce 2006: 111)

If an early human (let's call him Ogg) believed that not performing certain actions (e.g., killing, stealing, breaking promises) was good for him, then although he would routinely avoid these actions, nothing prevents Ogg from occasionally *changing course* in the face of an even more attractive good, for example, his neighbor's unattended stash of fruit. "Not stealing is good, sure, but just look at those ripe papayas – they're *great!*" So Ogg could be counted on as a reliable neighbor – except, well, when he couldn't be.

But in order for cooperative alliances to work, in order for each to truly benefit, there must be a guarantee that each sticks to his commitment, that neither is tempted to back out when more attractive options arise. Recall Farmer A and Farmer B from the last chapter: each needs the other's help, but helping puts each at risk of exploitation. What each needs is the assurance that the other is *committed* to this cooperative arrangement. And what is true at the level of two individuals is true at the level of groups: each person needs assurances that the sacrifices she makes for the group (e.g., defending against invaders; participating in hunts) are not in vain. This is where morality steps in.

The introduction of moral thinking, characterized along the lines discussed in the previous section, provides the missing guarantee. If Ogg believes that stealing his neighbor's (unattended) fruit is not merely undesirable but *prohibited*, and if this belief is strongly tied to Ogg's motivation, then this would be the best guarantee that Ogg will not commit those actions.[5] And by not committing those actions, Ogg would avoid the very kinds of behavior that would threaten cooperative alliances. We have to remember that, in small groups, it's not just what Ogg's actual partners think of Ogg; it's also what potential partners think of Ogg. We call it *reputation*.[6] After all, would *you* trust someone who wouldn't hesitate to deceive or kill another human being?

But here's where the lesson we began with matters: there would be *no need whatsoever* for Ogg to have any knowledge of – let alone concern for – the correlation between what's right and wrong, on the one hand, and cooperative alliances on the other. It is enough that Ogg is convinced that some things *just shouldn't be done* – no matter what. He need not also recognize that attitudes like that have a biological payoff. (In fact, we might insist that success actually depends on the absence of any such recognition, for again the point is to block deliberation and lock in cooperation.) Design humans to think (and feel) that some actions are prohibited, and cooperative success will take care of itself.

Well, almost. There are several wrinkles to iron out here. Perhaps the most pressing concern is this: What prevents clever amoral individuals from invading and taking over a population of moral creatures? Won't the strong disposition to refrain from immoral acts dangerously handcuff such individuals? These and other concerns will be addressed in the next chapter. In the remaining part of this chapter, I want to show two things. First, this evolutionary account of morality parallels in interesting ways hypotheses about the evolution of religious belief and ritual. Second, and more important, this initial sketch of morality's evolution nicely explains the surface features of moral thinking outlined in the previous section. As I'll try to show, those features are precisely what we would expect to see if the sketch just rendered is correct.

Recall the lesson of the Prisoner's Dilemma: cooperating with others can deliver real benefits, *so long as* you have some guarantee that others are likely to play along. You need a reason, that is, to trust others. The behavioral ecologist William Irons (2001) has argued that religious rituals, backed by deep religious beliefs, can provide just such a reason. The key, says Irons, is *signaling*. Someone who regularly engages in religious ritual, making repeated costly sacrifices, signals to others her commitment to her faith. Someone who goes to the trouble of wearing heavy garments, or praying, or eating only certain types of food, and so on, demonstrates the kind of fidelity to a group that can provide others with the assurance that this person can be trusted. The anthropologist Richard Sosis summarizes the idea this way: "As a result of increased levels of trust and commitment among group members, religious groups minimize costly monitoring mechanisms that are otherwise necessary to overcome free-rider problems that typically plague communal pursuits" (2005: 168). In other words, members spend less (valuable) time worrying who among them can be trusted. This hypothesis yields a number of testable predictions. To name just one, the more costly constraints a religious group puts on a member's behavior the more cohesive the group should be. And one indication of cohesiveness should be the *duration* of the group's existence. Sosis (2005) compared the demands various nineteenth-century American communes placed on their members and how long such communes survived. Indeed, Sosis found that the more demands a commune placed on its members, the longer such a commune remained in existence.

We can't say exactly how these results (if they stand up) bear on the question of the evolution of morality. It may be that they are unrelated. But if they are connected, it would help explain the powerful connection people very commonly draw between religion and morality. How, these people ask, can you have one without the other? As Donald Wuerl, the archbishop of the Roman Catholic diocese of Washington, DC, recently put it in a homily, "ethical considerations cannot be divorced from their religious antecedents."[7] Perhaps the disposition to feel a connection to a religious group is part of the same disposition to regard actions as right or wrong. Perhaps one triggers the other. At any rate, what we can say is that this area remains almost entirely unexplored. Let me move on to my other closing point.

3.3 Explaining the Nature of Moral Judgments

In the previous section we identified six features of moral thinking in need of explaining. The first thing we noted was that moral thinking requires an understanding of prohibitions. To judge that abortion is wrong is not merely (if at all) to express a desire not to have an abortion; it's to assert that abortion is *prohibited*, that it should not be done. This distinction makes a practical difference. For regarding some acts as prohibited, as *wrong*, has a way of putting an end to the discussion; it's a "conversation-stopper." If I believe that the act is wrong, then that's it. It shouldn't be done. Moral thinking has a way of overriding my other modes of practical deliberation. It's worth contrasting this with our desires.

We're pretty good at getting ourselves to do things we don't desire, even things we passionately hate (for example, getting ourselves to the dentist or cleaning the bathroom). But getting ourselves to do things we think are *immoral* is a different matter. I would bet that no amount of persuasion will get you to steal your neighbor's car or beat up the elderly couple down the street – even if I could guarantee that you wouldn't get caught. This is not to say we're incapable of such things; tragically, we are. The point is that there appears to be a substantial difference between doing something you (strongly) desire not to do and doing something you sincerely believe is (seriously) immoral. Most would agree that it takes considerably more psychological effort to do what we think is seriously wrong than to do what we strongly desire not to do. Part of it has to do with the psychic "cost" of living with ourselves after committing an immoral act.

Now this difference, according to the evolutionary account, has critical biological consequences. For if we assume that reproductive success in creatures like us depended so critically on forging and preserving our social bonds, then this deep reluctance to do what we regard as prohibited is precisely what we should expect to see. Designing creatures with a psychological mechanism that *overrides* practical deliberation when moral matters arise ensures that an individual will not act in ways that might jeopardize future cooperative exchanges. As Joyce noted above, merely desiring not to perform certain actions allows for too much wriggle room: after all, keeping promises may not seem very desirable once we've already benefited from the initial arrangement (as with Farmer A).

This should also explain the sense that prohibited acts remain prohibited *even if one desires to perform them*. We noted earlier that if you judge that no one should have an abortion because abortions are wrong, this judgment remains firm even when applied to someone who positively desires to have an abortion. What this seems to imply is that the truth of a moral judgment does not depend on people's desires, their interests, their moods, and so on. The wrongness of an action is apparently grounded on something more, something transcendent. This fits perfectly with the suggestion above that the recognition of moral wrongness halts further deliberation; it overrides our decision-making. Someone whose moral judgments *did* depend on his desires in this way would run a serious risk of undermining his reputation by acting in antisocial ways whenever his desires overwhelmed him. In general, individuals who could so easily back out of their commitments or steal from their neighbors or murder their enemies – simply because their desires shifted – would have a substantially more difficult time making and keeping cooperative arrangements.[8] (Test yourself: what kind of person would you trust in a Prisoner's Dilemma-style game?)

Built into these observations is the assumption that moral judgments are tightly linked to *motivation*, another feature of morality we discussed. Again, if we assume that evolutionary success (for creatures like us) really depended on preserving social arrangements, then for moral thinking to play its biologically significant role it has to *move* us – even in the face of "internal resistance." Moral thinking should not be idle. It's not like thinking that the sky is blue or that Ogg is a sloppy eater or even that the red berries are tasty. Moral thinking should very reliably "engage the will." And this is just what we see. For example, you can pretty much guarantee that if someone sincerely believes that abortion is murder, you won't see her having an (elective) abortion later that day. Whatever else moral thinking is, it's practical. It moves us. And it can move us to retaliate. We noted in the previous section that moral thinking implies notions of desert. The next chapter is devoted to exploring how this idea relates to punishment, reputation, and feelings of guilt. Some of the more interesting work coming out of behavioral economics and psychology highlights the strategic importance of punishment and reputation. Indeed, my own view has developed partly in response to these findings.

3.4 Conclusion

My aim in this chapter has been to describe, first, the important features of moral judgment and, second, an evolutionary explanation for those features. Making a moral judgment involves, first and foremost, an appeal to *prohibitions*. And these prohibitions seem to transcend merely legal or cultural norms. Moreover, our recognition of these norms involves being moved to act in accordance with them. The evolutionary account purports to explain these (and other) features by highlighting the advantages of cooperating in social interactions. But the value of cooperating, so the story goes, cannot be secured by merely having creatures like us *desire* cooperation. Instead, a system of moral judgment, with all of the its attendant features, evolved as powerful mechanism to keep us in line. This explanation receives further support from analyses of the structure of punishment. In the next chapter, we look at how punishment may have figured in moral thought and biological evolution.

Further Reading

Frank, Robert (1988) *Passions within Reason: The Strategic Role of the Emotions* (Norton).
Joyce, Richard (2006) *The Evolution of Morality* (MIT Press).

Ruse, Michael (1995) Evolutionary Ethics: A Phoenix Arisen. In P. Thomson (ed.), *Issues in Evolutionary Ethics* (SUNY Press).

Wilson, E.O. (1978) *On Human Nature* (Harvard University Press).

Wright, Robert (1995) *The Moral Animal: Why We Are the Way We Are. The New Science of Evolutionary Psychology* (Vintage).

4

Just Deserts

One sole desire, one passion now remains
To keep life's fever still within his veins,
Vengeance!
(*Thomas Moore, Poetical Works*)

As we noted in the previous chapter, one of the defining features of moral thought is its connection to punishment: judging that someone has acted wrongly involves judging that he deserves to be punished. Any account of the development of moral thought must make sense of this feature. In this chapter we take up the issue of punishment, as well as some associated issues: reputation and moral emotion. This chapter, like the next, draws on a range of empirical work in economics and psychology. Among the questions researchers are focusing on are the following: *When* do people punish? *Why* do they punish? *How* might punishment benefit an individual or a group? And how is punishment related to one's reputation and feelings of guilt?

The evolutionary account of morality outlined in the previous chapter provides a rough explanation for this phenomenon. First, if individuals regarded the violation of prohibitions as punishable offenses, then this would keep both oneself and others in line. If I know that my community is likely to deprive me of something I value if I act in ways that are prohibited, then this just reinforces my commitment to do the right thing. And likewise for every other member of the community. In this way, a common framework is established – or, if you like, a *balance*. The threat of punishment acts as a leverage against the temptation to defect.

But this exposes a limitation in pure Prisoner's Dilemma games: in the single-play version, defecting delivers either a big pay-off to you or a paltry pay-off to everybody. But social exchanges in real life, if they resemble

---

the Prisoner's Dilemma at all, resemble a game played over and over. To see how this alters the outcomes, put yourself in the following kind of situation.

Suppose you and I are among a group of individuals playing Prisoner's Dilemma games over the course of a year, where pay-offs are made in cash (and if you like, to up the stakes, imagine that this is your only source of income). Assume there are no restrictions on who plays whom or how many times a game is played. Before play begins, however, we have a week to interact with our fellow participants. What would you look for? What kind of person would strike you as an attractive counterpart? What kind of person would you avoid? Would you try to make explicit arrangements? Suppose that you and I decided to play our first round together. We both promise to cooperate. But when play begins, I break my promise: you cooperate, but I defect. I receive a nice chunk of change and you receive nothing. How would you feel? What would be your first response? Well, you might begin by slinging a few choice words my way. But how would you play the *next* round? One option would be to play me again. But why? Surely you would be doing it out of spite; you'd be looking to give me some of my own medicine. And since you know that I'm not stupid, you know that I would *expect* you to defect. So you could expect *me* to defect in anticipation. This is beginning to look like a loser's bargain.

Instead of throwing good money after bad, the smartest thing to do after I go back on my promise is to dump me, move on, find someone new. But why stop there? Since it costs you next to nothing, you probably shouldn't hesitate to point out – to anyone who'll listen – that I'm not to be trusted. "He double-crossed me," you would say with a sneer. And it wouldn't be long before this information got around. Now this might sound like idle gossip, but remember: with so little information to go on, participants have every reason to use that gossip in deciding how to act. What people say matters because it affects what people do.[1] It's difficult to overstate the critical role that punishment plays in a social group. It doesn't take much to trigger the drive to punish. The following experiments highlight when people punish, and some surprising benefits of doing so.

4.1 The Ultimatum Game

Recent psychological studies reveal how powerful the retributive urge is. Imagine being invited to play what psychologists call the Ultimatum Game.

You are given twenty one-dollar bills. You are told that you may divide those twenty dollars any way you like with a stranger in another room, someone you'll never meet – but who *is* aware of the amount of money you have to divide. You can offer him whatever you like – $1, $5, $7, $13, whatever. But once you make your offer, the stranger has this choice: he can accept the offer or he can refuse it. If he refuses the offer, *no one gets any money*. The game is over and you go home. So what would you offer? Think for a moment before reading on.

Here's what I bet (and the data suggest) you'll do. If you believe that the stranger in the other room is purely rational – that is, seeks his own economic advantage above all else – you will offer him only $1. Why? Because a purely rational actor, driven solely by his desire to maximize profits, will prefer $1 over nothing, since nothing is what he'll receive if he rejects the offer. But this is *not* the offer I bet you would make. If you're like most people, your offer would come in at around $7. But isn't this irrational on your part? Why are you offering a perfect stranger money that could be yours? The answer is simple: you believe (correctly) that others are driven by more than immediate economic gain: people are also driven by *a sense of fairness*. And this sense of fairness can drive people to *punish* others – even if it costs them personally. The reason you probably would not make a $3 offer is that you would expect the stranger to reject this offer. You know implicitly that he would rather give up $3 to show his disapproval, his righteous indignation, than take the money and be treated unfairly. Study after study has shown just this. People reject most offers under $7. This sense of fairness is so powerful that people are willing to pay to punish people who treat *other strangers* unfairly.

In a variation on the Ultimatum Game, a third-party "observer" is given $50. The observer is told that she will be observing a game between two strangers. In this game, one player, "the allocator," has $100 that he can divide with another player, "the recipient," any way he chooses. Unlike in the Ultimatum Game, however, the recipient has *no choice* but to accept what the allocator offers (economists call this the Dictator Game, for obvious reasons). So if the allocator gives the recipient one dollar, that's what the recipient receives. Here's the wrinkle, though. The observer has the option of stepping in *before* any money is allocated to the recipient. If the observer chooses, she can give up some of her own money to reduce the allocator's take-home pay: for every dollar the observer gives up, the allocator has to give up three. In effect, the observer has the option of *fining* the allocator – except the fine comes from her own pocket.

The results of the game are striking: the number of dollars the observer gives up (i.e. the fine) is directly proportional to the inequity. In other words, the more unequal the split, the higher the fine imposed on the allocator. In fact, observers give up money for just about any offer *lower* than $50. Against the assumption that people always seek their own best interests, these results are remarkable: here is someone giving up her own money to punish a complete stranger who has treated another complete stranger unfairly. All the observer has to do to walk away with $50 is to sit idly by while two strangers interact. But people can't sit idly by.

4.2 The Public Goods Game

Behavioral economists have derived similar results from what are called "public goods" experiments. For example, Ernest Fehr and Simon Gachter (2002) recently performed a set of "public goods" experiments that allowed for punishment. Here's how the experiment works: each member of a group of four receives 20 monetary units (let's just say, dollars) and is given the opportunity to "invest" all or some or none of that money in a group project. Students are allowed to keep any money that is not invested. Notably, however, students are guaranteed a 40 percent return on their investment. So if every student invested $10, they would, as a group, earn $16 to add to the $40 they invested – a total of $56. And since group earnings are always divided evenly among members (regardless of investment, if any), each person would walk away with $24, since each person's $4 earnings plus their $10 investment are added to the $10 they did not invest. If every student invested *every* dollar, each member would walk away with $32.

Here's the thing, however: investments are anonymous. Thus I don't know what (if anything) you're investing and you don't know what (if anything) I'm investing. If I invest $5 but *everyone else* invests $20 each, then I walk away with $22.75. That's a 55 percent return on my investment! Hence, there's an incentive for each person to invest less than his neighbor (indeed, I can *lose* money when I invest much more than others). Of course, when *no one* invests his money, there's no chance to increase one's earnings.

Now, Fehr and Gachter (2002) ran two series of experiments. In one series, subjects played six rounds of the game just as it is described above, where the group makeup changes after each round. Thus, no one ever interacts with the same person twice. In the second series, the game remains the same as above except subjects have an additional option: to *punish* other specific members after each round (though punishers remain anonymous). And punishment works like this: if you decide to punish player A – because, for example, you learn that A only invested $1 whereas everyone else invested $10 – you assign points to A. For every point assigned to A, $3 is deducted from A's earnings. At the same time, $1 is deducted from *your* earnings. Economists refer to this kind of punishment as *altruistic punishment* since punishment in this case not only reduces your earnings, but also means that you cannot ever recoup anything from A since you never interact with A again. So what did the experimenters observe?

Bluntly put, punishment pays – at least in this setting. In the final round of the *no*-punishment series, three-fourths of the subjects invested $5 or less. In the final round of the punishment series, more than three-fourths of the subjects invested $15 or more. Moreover, punishment and the threat of punishment promoted a trend: investments increased from round to round. In the *no*-punishment series, investments decreased from round to round.

To be sure, the threat of punishment was not empty. More than eight out of ten subjects punished at least once; 35 percent of subjects punished in at least five out of the six rounds of the game. The punishment also followed a pattern, a pattern that parallels the Ultimatum Game findings. Fehr and Gachter found that the further a player's investments fell below the average investment of other members the more she was punished. So, for example, when a player's investment fell between $8 and $14 *below* the mean cooperation level of other group members, these members paid on average $4 to punish her. When her investment fell $14 to $20 below the mean, these members paid on average $9 to punish her.

Fehr and Gachter also hypothesized that the decision to punish was mediated, at least in part, by subjects' emotions. Punishment, they suspected, resulted not so much from calculation but from contempt. Subjects were asked to imagine a situation in which they, along with two other members, invested around $16 while a fourth subject invested only $2. How would they feel about this free-rider? Half the subjects reported feeling an anger intensity of 6 or 7 (out of 7); nearly 40 percent of subjects reported an anger intensity of 5. And, not surprisingly, the intensity of anger was directly correlated with the deviation from others' average investment: the more an individual's investments fell below the average investment, the more intense the anger directed at her.

Of equal significance were the *expectations* of anger. Subjects were asked to imagine that *they* were the free-rider; how would others feel if they accidentally met them? Three-fourths of the subjects predicted that others would feel an anger intensity of 6 or 7, and a fifth of the subjects expected an anger intensity of 5. As it turns out, these expectations exceeded reality. People did not report anger intensity levels at the levels people would expect. This is significant since it suggests that we err on the side of caution when it comes to others' anger. We are keenly aware, that is, of how others may perceive our behavior.[2]

4.3 Winners Don't Punish

The experimental results on punishment, however, are more nuanced than my discussion has so far suggested. For example, a leading group of economists and biologists has shown that, as the title of their paper indicates, "winners don't punish" (Dreber et al. 2008). In a variation on the Prisoner's Dilemma, subjects had three choices instead of two: cooperate, defect, or punish. Whereas defection meant gaining $1 (say) at a cost of $1 for the other person, punishment meant paying $1 for the other person to *lose* $4. Subjects played repeated games with the same person, though they were unaware of how long games would continue. What Dreber et al. discovered was that "the five top-ranked players, who earned the highest total payoff, have never used costly punishment" (2008: 349). Winners, it turned out, tended to play a "tit-for-tat" strategy, like the one we discussed in the previous chapter. Their response to defection was defection; losers, on the other hand, responded to defection with costly punishment. To be clear, both winners and losers expressed their disapproval of defection. It's just that the winning strategy consisted of moderate punishment (i.e., defection) instead of costly punishment.

Are these results inconsistent with the Fehr and Gachter's results? Not necessarily. Dreber et al. found that, in environments where punishment is an option, cooperators do better than their counterparts in environments where punishment is not an option. But taking the punishment option is almost always a bad idea. So we have something of a paradox here. Your best hope (in these artificial settings) would be to play nice in an environment where punishment is occasionally meted out. But this requires, quite obviously, punishers. And punishers do really badly. In fact, although cooperation increases in the punishment option setting, the added benefit to cooperators is offset by added losses to punishers, such that the *aggregated payoff of all participants* was pretty much the same whether or not punishment was an option. How do these results make contact with our more general concern with morality?

It's important to remember that the leading idea under consideration here is *not* that judging that an individual has violated a moral norm involves judging that he *should* be punished. The leading idea is that judging that an individual has violated a moral norm involves judging that he *deserves* to be punished. This difference may sound meager, but it's not. For if it's true that natural selection favored a moral sense like ours, then we should *not* observe individuals reflexively punishing others, for, as Dreber et al. seem to show, this strategy founders. Instead, we should observe something less, something more restrained. And that is indeed what we see. People are quick to identify wrongs, but they do not blindly retaliate. When someone cuts us off on the highway, we do not automatically speed up and do the same in retaliation. While we don't hesitate to think that the jerk *deserves* to be cut off, we do hesitate to do so. Our disapproval is handled differently (with unmentionable expressions, say, or a choice hand gesture). It would appear that, in many instances, retaliation is substituted by feelings or affective judgments. What does seem consistent is the tendency to *avoid* the wrongdoer. If we've been egregiously wronged, the need for retaliation can indeed carry us away (see, for example, Hamlet). But when the wrong is less than capital, we simply "write the person off." Or, just as Dreber et al. found, we respond to defection by defecting ourselves – not costly punishing.

All of this research on punishment, however, fails to answer a deeper question: *why punish?* When we punish others, what's driving us? How do we justify (to ourselves, if you like) making wrongdoers pay? These questions encourage us to think harder about punishment's role in our moral sense and may offer us an independent line of support for the idea that our moral sense was indeed an adaptation. The psychology of punishment is quite a new area of research, but some of the findings are suggestive.

Psychologists Kevin Carlsmith, John Darley, and Paul Robinson (2002) tried to get to the bottom of our "naïve psychology of punishment" by testing to see which features of moral norm violations influence us the most in punishment decisions. More specifically, the tests were designed to uncover which of two competing philosophies of punishment people generally adhered to. One philosophy of punishment – the *deterrence* model – is "forward-looking": we punish for the good consequences that follow. It deters not only *this* perpetrator, but potential perpetrators from committing similar violations in the future. The other philosophy of punishment – the *retributive* or *just deserts* model – is "backward-looking": we punish because a wrong was committed and the perpetrator deserves to punished. The punishment is proportionate to the crime, for the aim is to "right a wrong." Interestingly, when subjects were presented with these two models of punishment, subjects generally had "a positive attitude toward both" and "did not display much of a tendency to favor one at the expense of the other" (Carlsmith et al. 2002: 294). However, when the subjects were given the opportunity to actually mete out punishment (either in terms of "not at all severe" to "extremely severe" or in terms of "not guilty" to "life sentence") in response to a specific act of wrongdoing, subjects operated "primarily from a just deserts motivation" (2002: 289). That is, subjects seemed to be responding almost exclusively to the features picked out by the just deserts model (for example, the seriousness of the offense and the absence of mitigating circumstances) while ignoring the features picked out by the deterrence model (for example, the probability of detection and the amount of publicity). The upshot is that, while people may express general support for differing justifications of punishment, when it comes to dealing with a specific case, people are almost always driven by "a strictly deservingness-based stance" (2002: 295).

The results of Carlsmith et al.'s study are consistent with the philosophical picture of moral judgment sketched in the previous chapter. According to that picture, part of the process of making a moral judgment involves judging that someone who violates a moral norm deserves to be punished. What the present research indicates is that moral outrage drives the desire to punish. We do not punish because it deters. We punish because the punished deserve it.

The categorical nature of punishment (i.e., that deservingness is not contingent on the consequences of punishment) does, however, suggest something deeper about punishment and the evolution of morality: if people cannot be reasoned out of the desire to punish, then getting caught for wrongdoing just about guarantees punishment (be it moderate or costly). If you get caught violating a social or moral norm, don't expect your neighbors to be open to discussion – about, say, the disvalue of punishing you. The sense that you deserve punishment is virtually automatic. After all, as Fehr and Gachter (2002) found, the drive to punish is largely a product of anger – not reason. And anger comes unbidden. What this means, I would argue, is that in social settings of this sort there would have been considerable pressure on individuals to avoid getting caught in an act of wrongdoing. And how does one do that? Avoid wrongdoing in the first place! This is effectively the strategy that subjects in Fehr and Gachter's study eventually adopted. When punishment was an option, subjects began to "straighten up and fly right." Instead of investing a little of their money and hoping others invested heavily, they put their trust in the group. They had learned that pretty much anything else guaranteed a punitive response. True, punitive responses could be costly (as Dreber et al. demonstrated),[3] but they could also drive up and secure cooperative arrangements. In the next section, I want to connect this discussion of punishment with the experience of guilt.

4.4 The Benefits of Guilt

Return to our year-long Prisoner's Dilemma game example. The preceding discussion of punishment should make it patently obvious – if it wasn't already – how important it would be for me to pay attention to what others are doing and saying (and you bet I am: after all, I have a year of this game). Others will be quick to pick up on accusations. In the event that I am called out for breaking my promise to cooperate with you, it would be wise to do damage control. I might accuse you of lying. I might claim my defection was an accident ("You mean, D is for *defection*?!"). Probably the most effective response would be contrition: I was foolish, I did wrong, I'm sorry. And most importantly: *It. Won't. Happen. Again.*

Better yet, if I could *actually feel* contrite or guilty, this would do more to repair my image than anything I might say. Socrates had it right: "The way to gain a good reputation is to endeavor to *be* what you desire to *appear*" (see Plato's *Phaedo*). To really feel guilty signals to others, first and foremost, that

I'm actually *experiencing my punishment*, the punishment of my own conscience. And this is just what you and the community seek. After all, if I break my promise to you, retaliation is going to be one of the central things that crosses your mind. One reason has to do with what punishment can do *for you*. Retaliation is the urge to "get back" at someone for something he's done wrong. In our case, it might involve refusing to play me again, telling others about my double-crossing, punching me out. But the urge to punish protects your own interests. This won't likely cross your mind, but punishment serves the purpose of either banishing the wrongdoer from the group ("Whatever you do, don't play *him*"), eliminating the possibility of getting double-crossed by me again, or spurring me to feel bad about my action. In the latter case, a connection between defection and psychic harm is created.

This can be good for you in several ways. In the short run, my feelings of remorse might prod me to make amends, to correct the harm. This can benefit you directly. In the long run, my feelings of being *chastised* function as a sort of internal check on future promise-breaking. Here you might benefit either directly – when, for example, I cooperate with you in a future game – or indirectly – when I do not undermine the general level of trust in a group. Either way, punishment pays.

The general lesson, though, is worth repeating. Through the mechanism of punishment and the corresponding feelings of guilt, a group can effectively insulate itself from cheaters, and this benefits everyone.[4] Gossip helps to inform us of who to keep close and who to watch out for. (Does this explain the strange attraction of reality television? We can't get enough of the backbiting and double-crossing and scheming. There's a reason we call gossip "juicy," for it is to the social mind what fatty foods are to the taste buds.)

Does all this mean that guilt serves only the interests of others? No. My feelings of guilt can serve my *own* interests as well. In most cases, they drive me to repair the damage I've done to my own reputation. I take steps to re-enter the group of participants, to present myself as trustworthy after all, and my emotions can mediate this process. He who feels no remorse might calculate ways of re-entering the group, but people are surprisingly good at smelling out a fraud. People can usually distinguish between he who merely "goes through the motions" and he who goes through remorse. The best way to signal to others that you feel bad about your behavior is to *really feel bad about your behavior*. Remember, we need not assume that you are aware of any of this. Your feeling the need to retaliate, my feelings of remorse, these are quite automatic. And that's a good thing if their behavioral consequents are to do their job: your desire for retaliation must be genuine, not calculated, if I am to believe that my act of promise-breaking has consequences. By the same token, my feelings of remorse cannot be staged, if I am really to convince you that I can be trusted in the future.

The economist Robert Frank (1988) has suggested that emotions like guilt are hard to fake precisely for this reason: they signal to others that one's remorse is genuine. The cost of sacrificing the ability to control some of our emotions is more than made up for by the trust others put in us.

What I've tried to show in this section is that the evolutionary account of morality provides a plausible explanation of why moral thinking is connected to punishment and guilt. An individual who, when wronged, did *not* threaten retaliation or regard punishment as justified was more or less inviting others to exploit him. In the absence of a protective social structure, like a family, such an individual would have been at a distinct disadvantage among his peers. Likewise, an individual who was incapable of experiencing guilt and who could not put on an adequate show of remorse (in most cases, by actually *experiencing* remorse) was similarly at a disadvantage, since he would over time repel potential partners.

The story just told enjoys growing support. Versions of it appear on websites and in popular scientific magazines. The online journal *Evolutionary Psychology* regularly features scholarly articles exploring different facets of the story. Even the *New York Times* recounted it in a feature article in the Sunday magazine. But is the popularity premature? Are we celebrating merely a good story – or a true story? Since its introduction, some theorists have questioned the story's legitimacy. In this section I want to discuss several objections to the account just offered. One objection, despite its initial appeal, is unlikely to unseat the story. That objection runs like this: even if moral thinking happened to evolve in a particular group according to the preceding story, it would ultimately be overrun by mutant immoralists or amoralists. Two objections that cannot be so easily dismissed are: first, while the story does an adequate job of explaining our moral attitudes toward cooperation, promise-breaking, and the like, it does not so easily explain our moral attitudes toward, for example, ourselves, the unborn, or the terminally ill. It's hard to see how these subjects could be captured by an account modeled on Prisoner's Dilemma-style games. Second, when we turn our attention to moral attitudes across different cultures, there appears to be substantial variation; on its face, this is not what the evolutionary account predicts. Some have thus speculated that the evolutionary story only goes so far: it may explain certain other-regarding feelings (e.g., altruism), but what we regard as distinctly *moral thought* is the result of local training. In short, evolution endowed us with powerful learning mechanisms, not an innate moral sense. Let's consider these objections in turn.

4.5 A Lamb among Lions?

Some have expressed doubts that moral thinking could hold its own among individuals who have no concern for morality. Since an individual who possessed a moral conscience would be reluctant to capitalize on golden opportunities (that is, opportunities to advance one's own interests at someone else's cost but without being detected), and since he could be counted on to cooperate regularly, he would seem to do worse than an individual who had no moral conscience, but who could feign moral feelings. Even if the advantage were slight, over many generations this kind of individual would come to dominate a population. Moreover, it's hard to see how a population of non-moral individuals could ever be overrun by moral individuals. So, the objection concludes, the presence of moral thinking exists *in spite of* – not *because of* – evolution by natural selection.

As persuasive as this objection may initially seem, its force is largely the result of underestimating the sophistication of our moral sense. First, it has already been shown that natural selection would have favored, in creatures like us, other-regarding feelings toward those we assume to be relatives. Because uncertainty would have inevitably surrounded the question of who in fact counts as a relative, our ancestors would have developed a general, though limited, disposition to feel empathy toward those around them. Thus the population of individuals out of which morality allegedly evolved was not one of cold, calculating individualists, as the objection seems to assume.

Second, any realistic modeling of social interactions among our early ancestors must assume *iterated plays* – that is, multiple chances to interact with the same core group of people. As I tried to demonstrate above, a year-long series of Prisoner's Dilemma games would quickly reveal the reputation of its participants. And reputation is everything. So add to the adaptive pressures on our early ancestors the pressure of maintaining the appearance of, for example, benevolence and trustworthiness. But what is the cheapest, most reliable means of appearing benevolent and trustworthy? *Actually being* benevolent or trustworthy! Never forget that evolution will favor the quick and dirty solution if the benefits outweigh the costs. Since the flexibility of practical deliberation will occasionally divert us from the kinds of behavior that are in our *long-term interests*, natural selection needed a means of selectively overriding this system: a moral conscience. Written into our genes, therefore, is the imperative to act in ways that others would find acceptable. From our perspective, this is a categorical rule; it has no exceptions. This is a pretty cheap means of achieving important results. From nature's perspective, however, the rule was actually contingent on the ways in which creatures like us interacted over time.

But won't a general disposition to act in socially appropriate ways also attract those who seek to exploit me? Perhaps. But we must remember several things. First, generally speaking, I retain the power to *choose* with whom I interact, and I can retaliate against those who abuse my trust. Second, presenting myself as trustworthy will also serve to attract other *cooperative* individuals who seek mutual advantage. So if I seek out "like-minded" individuals and also advertise a disposition to retaliate (e.g., refusing to cooperate after another's defection), I can decrease the chances of being exploited and capitalize on long-term cooperative relationships.

Game theorists have identified a strategy that embodies this approach. They call it "tit-for-tat." In a Prisoner's Dilemma game, the tit-for-tat strategy is simple: cooperate on the first round, and then, on future rounds, mirror what your partner did on the previous round. Let's assume you and I agree to play. I begin by cooperating. If you cooperate as well, then on the next round, I cooperate again. So long as you play me straight, we reap the benefits of mutual cooperation and, over time, establish an enduring, mutually beneficial arrangement. But the moment you defect, I defect on the next round. In other words, the moment my trust is abused, our relationship is broken. I'll either return the "favor," or leave the relationship. True, you'll benefit on that particular round, but the costs of losing that relationship will very likely exceed that momentary benefit. So the individual with a moral conscience is not a lamb among lions, as the objection seems to assume. A moral conscience does not preclude avoiding or even punishing cheaters ("Vengeance is Mine," says the Lord, "I will repay"). Nor does it mean taking all comers: no one has a moral duty to sacrifice herself to those who wish to do her harm.

4.6 An Explanation for *All* of Morality?

The evolutionary sketch just offered does a fair job of explaining why humans are disposed to regard some acts as morally wrong. The sorts of acts that immediately come to mind are: breaking a promise for no reason, killing a neighbor for no reason, lying to advance one's self-interest. According to the evolutionary account, these acts have the potential to undermine social harmony and trust; they threaten the kind of atmosphere necessary for mutual cooperation. By thinking of them as *wrong*, and hence prohibited, each person is strongly motivated to refrain from doing them. As a result, everyone benefits more than they would if no one thought of them as wrong or if people thought of them as merely unattractive.

But there are some attitudes, some feelings, that seem to deserve to be called *moral* but are not apparently linked to the preservation of social harmony. For example, one might plausibly maintain that we have moral duties to *ourselves*. For example, you have a duty to develop your talents, to care for your health, to take an interest in your future, and so on. Failing to carry out these duties without justification can expose you to moral condemnation. But it's far from clear why these self-directed moral attitudes would do anything to preserve social harmony. Feeling bound to develop one's talents, say, might plausibly be regarded as something good, but why should it be regarded as a *moral* good? The evolutionary story doesn't say.

Alternatively, consider our moral attitudes toward the unborn or the terminally ill. If the evolutionary story is correct, we should not view harming the unborn or hastening the death of a terminally ill patient as a moral matter, since the unborn and the terminally ill cannot exactly participate in the sorts of reciprocal relations at the heart of the evolutionary story. This is important. The evolutionary account was premised on how our actions might influence those with whom we interact or will interact in the near future. This means that the *content* of our moral thinking should be restricted to potential partners in reciprocal relations. But if this is right, then we should be morally neutral about such things as physician-assisted suicide and even abortion, since how the terminally ill and embryos are treated doesn't seem to bear on our cooperative relations. But it's pretty obvious that people *aren't* morally neutral about such issues. Indeed, if one pressed on in this way, it may possible to uncover a range of moral issues that are not easily captured by the evolutionary account. As a sampling, consider: famine relief, child prostitution, civil rights, disability rights, animal cruelty, pollution and environmental degradation, and genetic enhancement. There appears to be quite a distance, for example, between feeling bad about defecting in a Prisoner's Dilemma-style game and feeling bad about favoring a white person over a black person for a job or feeling bad about genetically altering your child. The worry, then, is that the evolutionary story is notably *incomplete.*

Of course, there are worse fates than being incomplete. After all, defenders of the view might begin working to fill in the details, assuming such details are there to be filled in. And work has already begun. The standard approach is to show that, for each of the problematic cases above, our moral attitudes somehow *derive* from the basic evolutionary story. It might be shown, for example, that blatant disregard for the environment is linked to a general disregard for public goods, but someone who exhibited no concern for public goods would run the risk of diminishing her reputation as a "socially conscious" person. Prohibitions on animal cruelty might be explained by the connection people tend to draw between the disposition to harm an animal for fun and the disposition to harm a person for fun. Wanton cruelty to animals has a way of repelling people. But this can be explained, at least in part, by what such cruelty elicits in onlookers: *What kind of person would do that?* This is important because when we consider the kind of person with whom we would want to enter into a cooperative relationship, we'll generally avoid individuals disposed to wanton cruelty. Thus, cruelty to animals (like wanton cruelty in general) will come to be regarded as morally wrong. Now this is little more than an outline. What remains to be seen is whether evidence can be mounted in its defense.

An even more tantalizing proposal stems from recent work in evolutionary psychology. To put it crudely, generosity pays. In one study (Iredale et al. 2008), the focus was on female mate preference. According to the study, females exhibit a preference for generous males. Females, write the authors, "seem to like heroic types for short term relationships, but *altruists* for long term relationships."[5] The authors speculate that "generosity could be a way for men to show their suitability to invest in a relationship and help in rearing offspring." If this is right, then it might be possible to explain the fact that, for example, donating to famine relief, assisting the homeless, and donating blood are generally regarded as admirable. If ancestral females exhibited a preference for males who displayed a tendency toward generosity, then, all things being equal, males who developed that trait would come to dominate the population. This might also explain why such *acts* of generosity are thought of a morally good – at least among female onlookers.

But this is not all. Martin A. Nowak, the director of the Evolutionary Dynamics program at Harvard, recently produced mathematical models of Prisoner's Dilemma-style games that indicated that (again) generosity pays. He writes:

> Mathematical analysis shows that winning strategies tend to be generous, hopeful, and forgiving. Generous here means not seeking to get more than one's opponent; hopeful means cooperating in the first move or in the absence of information; and forgiving means attempting to re-establish cooperation after an accidental defection. (Nowak 2008: 579)

So, contrary to the old adage that goodness is its own reward, goodness may in fact deliver other, biologically critical, rewards. Nowak's research indicates that "if I am willing to let others have a slightly bigger share of the pie, then people will want to share pies with me. Generosity bakes successful deals" (2008: 579).

It's of course far too early to say whether or not this hypothesis succeeds; still, the direction of research indicates that the evolutionary approach potentially has the resources to meet the incompleteness objection. There remains, however, a more serious problem confronting the evolutionary approach.

4.7 Universal Morality or Universal Reason?

There is a concern among some theorists that the evolutionary account does not explain what it seeks to explain. One way to spell out this concern is as follows. If, through the processes of natural selection, our early ancestors evolved the capacity to think morally, and if all extant people have the same ancestors, then we should expect all people to display similar moral beliefs. We should observe, that is, a kind of *universal morality*, according to which people generally make the same moral judgments about the same things wherever they happen to live. We should observe not only a moral consensus across our own country, but across all countries. So whether you're Aborigine or American, Brazilian or Balinese, you should think that killing is generally wrong, charity is good, and so on.

But even someone with a passing familiarity with other cultures knows that this claim is in trouble. There is, it turns out, a breathtaking diversity in moral attitudes across the globe. Even apart from differences in moral attitudes toward such things as food and dress and religious rites, very basic moral differences remain. Take killing for example. While in many parts of the world women are ascribed the same moral rights as men, in some Arab cultures killing a woman who has had sex outside of marriage is not only morally permissible, but morally *obligatory* (Hauser 2006). Among the Ilongot of Luzon, initiation rites require that boys decapitate an innocent person from the nearby village (Rosaldo 1980). Indeed, cannibalism has been a regular part of some cultural traditions for centuries. Name a practice that you're positive is prohibited around the world (infanticide, patricide, brother–sister incest), and the ethnographic record will very likely prove you wrong. When it comes to morality, the world is a mixed bag. One man's vice is another man's virtue.

This diversity is a critical reason why some theorists think our moral minds have a different origin. Evolution, as the philosopher Neil Levy maintains, only "gave us the *preconditions* of morality." But evolution itself is insufficient. "It is only as a result of the *cultural elaboration* of this raw material that we come to be moral beings" (Levy 2004: 205). Thus the real force behind human morality (to the extent that there is a universal human morality) is *human learning*. We learn from those around us which acts are right and which acts are wrong, just as we learn which numbers are odd and which numbers are even. The philosopher William Rottschaefer and his biologist colleague David Martinsen elaborate on this idea, citing "imitation or symbolic learning and reasoning, [and] the inductive moral training" discussed by the psychologist Martin Hoffman. "In inductive techniques, parents point out to their children the beneficial and harmful effects of their action on others in a manner appropriate to their ages" (Rottschaefer and Martinsen 1995: 167). On these proposals, natural selection's role is demoted to that of provider of raw materials.

A position that occupies a sort of middle ground between the evolutionary account and (what I'll call, somewhat misleadingly) the *learning* account is one recently proposed by the philosophers Chandra Sripada and Stephen Stich. Unlike the evolutionary account, the Sripada and Stich (S&S) model denies that humans are innately disposed to think morally, and unlike the learning account, the S&S model denies that humans develop their moral minds from "all-purpose" reasoning mechanisms. What Sripada and Stich propose is that humans are innately endowed with a sort of "rule-detection" system, what they call a *norm-acquisition system*. For the purposes of our discussion, we can think of norms as social rules dictating what can and cannot be done. Stich describes the system in starkly mechanical terms:

> The job of the Acquisition Mechanism is to identify the norms in the surrounding culture whose violation is typically met with punishment, to infer the content of those norms, and to pass that information to the Execution Mechanism, where it is stored in the Norm Data Base. The Execution Mechanism has the job of inferring that some actual or contemplated behavior violates (or is required by) a norm, and generating intrinsic (i.e. non-instrumental) motivation to comply and to punish those who do not comply. (Sripada and Stich 2008: 228)

So a mind equipped with this system will generate a set of moral beliefs that are uniquely keyed to its environment. At the same time, such a mind will generate a set of rules that may (or may not) be classified as moral, but which nevertheless play a constraining role in one's local community (for example, bow to your elders in passing). The reason is that, on the S&S model, evolution has not selected us to be sensitive to *moral* rules; it has selected us to be sensitive to a more general class of rules, call them *social* rules. If the adaptive value of rule-following is great enough, then it's less important that one should discriminate between moral rules and other rules of the community.

The obvious advantage of Sripada and Stich's account – relative to the evolutionary account – is that it will readily explain the world's moral diversity. The moral beliefs that you come to have will be a direct function of the rules you are exposed to in your local community. This will be true of the learning account as well. If my caregivers routinely reward one kind of behavior and punish another, then it's no surprise that as an adult I'm likely to think and behave in ways that reflect those moral attitudes, rather than the moral attitudes of geographically remote communities. A second advantage of these alternatives to the evolutionary account is simplicity: these accounts are simpler than the evolutionary account. As we've seen in various places, natural selection is a highly conservative process. Evolutionary biology reveals time and again that natural selection will "favor" simpler, cheaper solutions to adaptive problems even if they're less effective than more sophisticated alternatives we could dream up.

To be sure, evolution has a role to play in these other accounts; it's just that its role is significantly diminished. Evolution might explain the selection of general reasoning and learning mechanisms or, as in the S&S model, sophisticated norm-acquisition systems. It might also explain general motivational dispositions – for example, caring about the suffering of others. But this picture of morality relies less critically on evolution (after all, on this picture, aliens could be just as successful at developing into moral creatures). On this picture, the principal reason humans are *moral* creatures is that humans are *reasoning* creatures.

In the next chapter we'll explore these accounts in a bit more detail as we turn to the empirical side of the story. What I've tried to do in this chapter is to sketch the processes that may (I stress, *may*) have led to our moral sense. I've said very little, however, about the *structure* of our moral minds. This is what we'll pursue in the next chapter. We'll consider research from across the scientific spectrum, research that helps sharpen our understanding of the structure of the moral mind. For example, we'll look carefully at primatological data suggesting moral-like behavior in primates; we'll investigate the behavior of infants and toddlers for clues on how children develop morally; and, finally, we'll look to neuroscientific data revealing how the brain represents and processes morality, and how it initiates moral responses. I'll also argue that, despite all the information flooding in, we're not in a position yet to articulate the structure of the moral mind. At best, we'll put ourselves in a position to craft the outlines of a plausible theory.

4.8 Conclusion

The aim of this chapter has been to offer a popular historical account of why humans developed the disposition to think and behave morally, a disposition that needs to be sharply distinguished from other sorts of thinking and behaving. That account relies essentially on the biological advantages of cooperation in social interactions.

If we can suppose that moral thinking (or some early prototype) managed to get a foothold in a population of early humans, as some philosophers and psychologists believe, then we can trace out a story explaining why it spread to the population as a whole. For when we contrast a group of individuals that regards certain actions as *morally wrong* – thus making their performance quite rare – with a group of individuals that does not regard those actions as wrong, but perhaps only unattractive, we see that members of the former group, unlike members of the latter group, enjoy biological benefits that favor their selection. As a model of such interactions, Prisoner's Dilemma-style games bear this out – but only if we allow participants the ability to choose whom they interact with and the tendency to punish defectors. How this is achieved may depend on certain emotional dispositions (something we'll explore in the next chapter). What makes this account attractive to its proponents is its ability to capture the distinctive characteristics of morality: for example, the sense that immoral acts are acts that are *prohibited* (and not merely unattractive), do not depend on the interests or desires of any particular person, should elicit guilt in those who commit them, and prompt others to feel justified in punishing wrongdoers.

Critics of the evolutionary account emphasize the diversity in moral attitudes across the globe. If the evolutionary account is correct, they ask, shouldn't we observe more consistency than we do? As an alternative, they suggest that the mind is innately equipped with more general learning mechanisms, and it's these mechanisms that enable humans to develop into moral creatures. Debates over *how* we came to have the moral minds we have will not be settled until we begin to understand *what* the moral mind looks like – that is, its structure. To this we now turn.

Further Reading

Frank, Robert (1988) *Passions within Reason: The Strategic Role of the Emotions* (Norton).

Iredale, W., M. Vugt, and R. Dunbar (2008) Showing Off in Humans: Male Generosity as Mating Signal. *Evolutionary Psychology*, 6/3: 386–92.

Joyce, Richard (2006) *The Evolution of Morality* (MIT Press).

Levy, N. (2004) *What Makes Us Moral? Crossing the Boundaries of Biology* (Oneworld).

Nowak, M.A. (2008) Generosity: A Winner's Advice. *Nature*, 456: 579.

Rottschaefer, William A. and David Martinsen (1995) Really Taking Darwin Seriously: An Alternative to Michael Ruse's Darwinian Metaethics. In P. Thomson (ed.), *Issues in Evolutionary Ethics* (SUNY Press).

Ruse, Michael (1995) Evolutionary Ethics: A Phoenix Arisen. In P. Thomson (ed.), *Issues in Evolutionary Ethics* (SUNY Press).

Stich, S. (2008) Some Questions about The Evolution of Morality. *Philosophy and Phenomenological Research*, 77 (1): 228–36.

Wilson, E.O. (1978) *On Human Nature* (Harvard University Press).

Wright, Robert (1995) The Moral Animal: Why We Are the Way We Are. The New Science of Evolutionary Psychology (Vintage).

5

The Science of Virtue and Vice

To pity distress is but human; to relieve it is Godlike.
(Horace Mann, Lectures on Education)

Why does everyone take for granted that we don't learn to grow arms, but rather, are designed to grow arms? Similarly, we should conclude that in the case of the development of moral systems, there's a biological endowment which in effect requires us to develop a system of moral judgment and a theory of justice, if you like, that in fact has detailed applicability over an enormous range.
(Noam Chomsky, Language and Politics)

Children can be cruel. Insects do not stand a chance around a group of boys with access to fire. Little girls can steal with impunity. Children do nothing to hide their displeasure at having to kiss old Aunt Bettie or getting socks for Christmas. They tease, bully, and harass. They're the inspiration for characters like Dennis the Menace, Bart Simpson, and Lucy from *Peanuts*. So it might come as a surprise to learn that children are a favorite source of evidence about the historical roots of our moral minds. Why? Because their grasp of morality is – in all honesty – impressive. Whether or not they regularly *do* the right thing, they invariably *know* what the right thing is. And this has led psychologists to speculate that maybe morality is not taught. Maybe morality is innate.

Here's the thinking. Suppose children can demonstrate a certain sort of competence from a very young age. And suppose that it is unlikely that they could have learned all the skills associated with that competence from their surroundings. Well, if that competence didn't come from the *outside*, then it must have from the *inside*. That is, the competence must be innate.

An Introduction to Evolutionary Ethics, by Scott M. James. © 2011 Scott M. James

It must be part of a child's "design specification." But this raises a new question: how did this competence come to be innate? Someone or something must have "put" it there. Defenders of the evolutionary approach argue that natural selection put it there – in the form of genes that shape the how the mind works.

Notwithstanding the anecdotal evidence cited by parents and school-teachers, careful studies indicate that children follow a morally rich developmental path beginning from a very early age. Dennis the Menace knows much more about morality than you might think. Now this doesn't mean that children won't be cruel, any more than it means that adults – who are indisputably moral creatures – won't be cruel. What it means is that, absent other powerful outside influences, most children will develop the range o. moral capacities typical of adults *whether or not their caregivers provided them with so-called "moral training."* They may sometimes act like moral monsters, but on closer inspection they're far more attuned to their moral environment than we give them credit for. By studying the moral minds of children we get some insight into our evolutionary inheritance.

But if we're trying to understand where our morality came from we should not stop at young children. We should go even further back. According to the preeminent primatologist Frans de Waal, "the building blocks of morality clearly predate humanity" (2005: 225). De Waal has spent a lifetime observing and writing about his experiences with primates: apes, capuchins, bonobos, and chimps. These observations are significant because primates are our cousins; we share a common ancestor. Hence, what we observe in them provides indirect evidence of what this distant ancestor was like. Characteristics humans have in common with primates tell us some-thing about our distant past and the kinds of adaptations that directed the path of evolution.

Moreover, we can corroborate this story by investigating the structure of the organ responsible for behavior, i.e., the brain. So a third line of investigation concerns how the brain operates when trying to navigate the moral world. It's pretty much agreed that there is no dedicated moral organ or system in the brain in the way that there is a dedicated visual or auditory system in the brain. Instead, it appears as if multiple systems contribute to our moral minds, and through the work of neurologists and neuroscientists we're beginning to understand how these systems contribute to the whole. For when a particular system fails to function properly or is absent entirely, distinct moral deficits result. And this gives us some insight into the function of that particular system. From here, we can perform comparative studies with primates to determine, for example, how old certain systems are and what kinds of adaptive pressures may have contributed to their selection.

So the aim of this chapter is to review some of the fascinating new research on the biology and psychology of morality, from the perspective of developmental psychologists, primatologists, and neuroscientists. With this picture in hand, we can return to the speculative story sketched in the previous chapter to see how well the two cohere.

5.1 Distress Test

The path to the moral mind begins, we might say, with distress. Infants appear to experience a range of emotions even within the first few hours of life, but one emotion in particular stands out: distress. Infants exhibit signs of distress not only in response to their own discomfort but in response to the discomfort of others. Infants appear to be wired to mirror the distress of those around them: cry and the whole world (of neonates nearby) cries with you. The psychologist Nancy Eisenberg interprets this sensitivity to a "rudimentary form of empathy" (Eisenberg and Mussen 1989: 789). When you and I empathize with others, we do not merely come to have beliefs about their states of distress (what we might call sympathy), we actually experience "faint copies" of those states. We *feel* the pain of others. Infants, while they probably do not have any beliefs about their neighbors' emotions, appear to *resonate* to what others are feeling. This distress test is what gets the moral ball rolling. For feeling the pain of others very soon prompts us to act: we want the distress to stop. (It's perhaps too soon to call this a moral emotion since one could have selfish reasons for wanting the distress to stop.)

In a fascinating set of studies, the psychologist Carolyn Zahn-Waxler (Zahn-Waxler et al. 1991) demonstrated that this response begins at a remarkably early age. What Zahn-Waxler et al. found was that 14-month-olds not only experience distress in response to the distress of another person, they move – without prompting – to comfort the distressed person. Zahn-Waxler had family members of the child pretend to cry or to wince in pain. In response the child, as by some instinct, patted the family member or rubbed her injury. Such findings would be less striking if they could be explained by the fact that a child had been *told* how to respond or had observed others responding in the appropriate ways. But the fact is, 14-month-olds are far from mastering a language. And children whose primary caregivers have never displayed signs of distress nonetheless respond empathically.

In fact, children appear to be sensitive to more than just distress. They seem to be natural helpers. Drop a clothespin, say, in the vicinity of a child as young as 14 months and you may be surprised by his reaction. According to Felix Warneken, a Harvard psychologist, he "will toddle over, pick it up and return it to you" even in the "total absence of encouragement or praise" (Warneken and Tomasello 2009: 397). If, instead of dropping the clothespin, the experimenter throws it down, infants do not regularly make an effort to retrieve it. In another set of experiments, Warneken and his colleagues (Warneken and Tomasello 2007) tested what infants would do when an object was placed out of reach of an experimenter, but within reach of the child. When experimenters attempted (but failed) to reach the object, infants routinely helped the experimenter by retrieving the object. Interestingly, the help infants provided was not influenced by a reward. Instead, their tendency to help depended only on whether or not the experimenter made an attempt to reach for the object: when the experimenter did not reach for the object, infants did not help. This suggests, at a minimum, that infants were able to recognize not only that others had goals, but that they needed help in achieving those goals.

All this raises a question. If children display rudimentary forms of empathy and if these forms of empathy do not require language, then perhaps we should look for empathy outside the human species. Perhaps distress-sensitivity is an ancient system. Several lines of evidence support this idea.

The primatologist Frans de Waal contends that responses to distress are commonplace among apes. Like toddlers learning to walk, young apes learning to climb trees occasionally fall. When this happens, according to de Waal, the wailing youngster "will immediately be surrounded by others who hold and cradle it. . . . If an adult loses a fight with a rival and sits screaming in a tree, others will climb toward him to touch and calm him" (2005: 183). And this response is not limited to family members. This response to others can be taken to remarkable extremes. Monkeys and rats will literally starve themselves instead of causing others distress. In one set of experiments (Masserman et al. 1964; Wechkin et al. 1964), the only way for a monkey to receive food was by pressing a bar that would – at the very same time –

deliver an electric shock to another monkey in an adjoining cage. (Monkeys quickly grasped the association.) The acting monkey was thus forced to make a difficult decision: starve or cause distress in a neighbor. Monkeys would routinely go *five days* without eating. One monkey went *twelve days* without eating.

Now to explain what's going on here, we don't have to attribute empathy to these monkeys. The simpler, more direct explanation is that monkeys don't like distress, whether in themselves or in others. In short, distress begets distress. This is of course distinct from being directly concerned about the welfare of others.[1] Still, the findings are provocative because they indicate that *social emotions* (as we might call them) are produced by very ancient systems, systems that proved and continue to prove their biological value. De Waal speculates that such emotions serve to alert us to distress-causing elements in our environment: "if others show fear and distress, there may be good reasons for you to be worried, too. If one bird in a flock on the ground suddenly takes off, all other birds will take off as well ... the one who stays behind may be prey" (2005: 187).

In general, the idea that the capacity for empathy is part of our inherited biology is consistent with the evolutionary sketch offered in the previous chapter, according to which morality serves to promote and protect cooperative arrangements among individuals. If humans are naturally disposed to be distressed at the distress of others, then they will, as far as possible, take steps to avoid actions that cause distress in others. This will require, among other things, a bit of cultural training. Infants have not been around long enough to learn which acts cause others distress. (As we'll see shortly, it may require, for example, the ability to take on the perspective of others.) But once this ability is in place, and once others begin to put their trust in a person, she will be *emotionally* disposed (according to this account) to avoid acts of "defection," since such acts are expected to cause others distress. None of these associations needs to be conscious. This is, if you will, the emotional precursor to the sophisticated moral sense adults possess.

Further support for the idea that humans are wired to mirror the distress of others comes from the work of cognitive psychologists and neuroscientists. What, they ask, is the *brain's* role in empathy? What brain system or systems are involved in taking in the relevant information from the environment, processing that information, and initiating a response? Arriving at this understanding is, to say the least, formidable. Almost nothing in the universe (natural or unnatural) rivals the complexity of the human brain, with its 100 trillion to 1,000 trillion connections (or neural synapses) between more than a trillion nerve cells. All packed into something smaller than a bowling ball. Despite this complexity, researchers looking for the neural bases of morality have managed to produce some intriguing results – largely by way of an unorthodox source: psychopaths. One of the more effective means of learning about the brain is to compare individuals with a very specific cognitive or behavioral deficit, one that does not affect other mental capacities, with individuals *without* that deficit. How, if at all, are their brains different? And what do these differences tell us about the function of different brain systems? In some cases, there are no remarkable differences. In other cases, however, the differences are unmistakable.

Take face-blindness (or *prosopagnosia*), a neurological condition marked by an inability to recognize faces. Prosopagnosiacs have no difficulty passing a wide array of vision tests, and their memories are not noticeably impaired. But faces are entirely forgettable; they do not recognize friends, relatives, even themselves.[2] They can perfectly well describe the person they're seeing. It's just that they don't know *who* that person is. When neuroscientists began subjecting prosopagnosiacs to brain scans, it became apparent that something was indeed amiss with their brains. Specifically, what neuroscientists did *not* see in prosopagnosiacs that regularly appeared in non-prosopagnosiacs was activity in the *occipital* and *temporal lobes* of the cerebral cortex (a portion of the brain involved in memory, attention, and perceptual awareness) along with processing in the *fusiform gyrus*. (Don't worry, this won't be on the test.) The point is that, on the basis of these experiments, it is now believed that these different areas of the brain are critically important in the recognition of faces. Similar results have now been shown in chimpanzees, one of our closest relatives. So what do psychopaths teach us about the brain's role in our moral lives?

Surprising as it may sound, psychopaths possess a rather specific deficit. Despite their larger-than-life personas, psychopaths are remarkably normal when it comes to most cognitive tasks. They can pass almost every psychological skills test you can pass, even tests designed to evaluate moral knowledge. Psychopaths have no more trouble identifying what's right (or wrong) than you do. What separates psychopaths from people like you and me is, at bottom, an *emotional* deficit. It's not so much what they don't *know* that make psychopaths psychopaths; it's what they don't *feel*. (Consider the title of a recent article in the journal *Social, Cognitive, and Affective Neuroscience*: "Psychopaths Know Right from Wrong But Don't Care.") Psychopaths lack empathy. Unlike you and me, they are not disturbed by the distress that others feel, even though they correctly *believe* that their acts cause others distress. More specifically, psychopaths fail to recognize submissive cues, according to the cognitive neuroscientist James Blair (2005). When you (a non-psychopath, I'll assume) observe a grimace, a wince, or a look of sadness in another, it sets in motion a series of involuntary emotional events that serve to inhibit you (if only weakly) from harming him or her. Psycho-paths miss these cues.[3] All the same, they're perfectly lucid about what they are doing. Their heads are clear. If anything, their hearts are clouded. Of course, in reality it has nothing to do with their hearts. Their brains are the problem.

Tania Singer (2007), a cognitive neuroscientist at the University of Zurich, set out to identify the parts of the brain underlying empathy. Two areas of the brain appeared to stand out: the *anterior insula* and the *anterior cingulate cortex*. When a subject was given a mild electric shock, these two areas were active – in addition to the part of the brain that registers pain: the *somatosensory cortices*. When, instead, the subject's loved one was given the electric shock, the somatosensory cortices were quiet while the anterior insula and anterior cingulate cortex remained active. Independent studies have shown that these areas are critical for emotional regulation and conflict resolution, respectively. The neuropsychiatrist Laurence Tancredi (2005) describes the anterior cingulate as the brain's "Mediator" since it is responsible for problem-solving and emotional self-control. The anterior insula, deep inside the brain, alerts the organism to impending danger. From a neuroscientific perspective, then, empathy is the coordination of brain systems regulating emotion and decision-making. We get emotional information from cues in our environment (our spouse screams in pain), and this engages the rational part of the mind in forming a plan for action. In psychopaths, activity in these areas is decreased. Hence, their ability to process emotions is impaired; psycho-paths are readily distracted and receive insufficient emotional input. The cues that psychopaths receive from the environment are not treated as emotional cues and so do not influence behavior in the way they do for the rest of us.[4]

At the center of many neuroscientific discussions of morality is *inhi-bition*. Morally successful individuals can control themselves, even in particularly trying times. Psychopaths are notoriously deficient on this front. What studies of the brain reveal is that the ability to inhibit one's darker impulses comes from a delicate balance among several areas: among others, the hippocampus, the anterior cingulate cortex, and the amygdala. Like the anterior cingulate cortex, the hippocampus plays a critical role in regulating aggression. So if the hippocampus is damaged or is diminished in size, activity from the emotional centers of the brain goes unchecked, resulting in impulsive and sometimes aggressive behavior. This is true for much of the frontal lobe of the brain: it *damps down* signals from the emotional centers of the brain. On the other hand, unchecked aggression can be the result, not of a diminished hippocampus or frontal lobe, but an *overactive* amygdala. The amygdala, what Tancredi calls the brain's "Guard Dog," assesses threats from the outside world. It governs the threat-response system, what we think of as the "fight or flee" response. Individuals with a hypersensitive amygdala, therefore, regularly perceive threats where the rest of us do not. Such individuals are generally more paranoid than the rest of us. At sufficient levels, perceived threats will overpower the inhibitory work of even developmentally normal frontal lobes.

Research on the brain does not, in itself, settle the question of morality's evolution. What it does show is that the brain contains systems that appear to be necessary for registering the distress of others, and this seems necessary for successful moral behavior (at least for creatures like us). Emotions or affective responses matter. According to Joshua Greene, "there is an important dissociation between affective and 'cognitive' contributions to social/moral decision-making and that the importance of the affective contributions has been underestimated by those who think of moral judgment primarily as a reasoning process" (2005: 341–2). As we know, the development of these systems depends in large part on one's genes. This does not mean that one's environment has no influence on brain structure; in point of fact, early childhood experiences (most notably, traumatic experiences) can alter critical brain connections in ways that can last a lifetime. Still, a child does not *learn* to grow an amygdala or *choose* not to develop fully her anterior cingulate cortex. The genetic code, written into every nucleus of every cell of her body, instructs her body to produce quite specific structures responsible for quite specific tasks. When these instructions are garbled or misinterpreted, the results are telling. A 2002 study by the National Institute of Health (Miller 2002), for example, demonstrated that a single gene alteration can alter the brain's response to emotionally charged situations by altering the performance of the amygdala. Individuals with the genetic variant experience greater levels of fear, the response to which is either excessive withdrawal or excessive aggression.

As I hinted above, distress-sensitivity by itself only vaguely resembles the mature moral sense. For one thing, my feeling bad in response to *your* feeling bad is perfectly compatible with not caring about your welfare; after all, if I don't want to feel bad any more, I can just remove myself from your presence! But this is hardly what we think when we think of empathic responses.

What's missing here is a sense of what things are like *for you* – that is, how things are from your perspective. To achieve this feat, however, requires the ability to grasp (among other things) the fact that you have beliefs and feelings and desires not unlike the beliefs and feelings and desires that I have. We take this for granted now. It's second nature for you and I to think that people do things for *reasons*, where these involve things like beliefs and desires. For example, we might explain Beatrice's getting up and going to the refrigerator and taking out an apple and eating it by appealing to Beatrice's *desire* for an apple and her *belief* that the fridge contains an apple. (What else could explain Beatrice's action if it isn't some combination of beliefs and desires? Alien mind control?) Though this kind of "mind-reading" comes easy for you and I, we can't let this blind us to the fact that, at some point, we *developed* this ability. It's doubtful we popped out of the womb all wet and warm, pondering the profound sense of awe our parents must have been experiencing at that moment.

5.2 Mind-Reading

As it turns out, "mind-reading" is a skill that develops quite naturally in children around the age of 4. We know this because kids at that age – but not typically before – can pass what's known as the "false belief test." In the classic version of the test (Wimmer and Perner 1983), a child watches Maxi the Puppet place a piece of chocolate in a hatbox and then leave. While Maxi is away, Maxi's mother moves the chocolate from the hatbox to the cupboard. When Maxi returns, the show is interrupted and the child is asked: Where will Maxi look for the piece of chocolate? If a child is younger than 4, she will most likely say *the cupboard*, exhibiting a failure to grasp that

Maxi has beliefs (in this case, at least one false one) that are different from her own. For a child younger than 4, the world is typically seen through only one set of eyes: her own. But 4 years of age appears to mark a turning point: 4-year-olds tend to give the correct answer: *the hatbox*. This indicates that a child has come to distinguish her own beliefs from the (apparent) beliefs of another. She realizes that others can think and presumably feel differently than her. She develops, in short, *a theory of mind*, a theory that explains the behavior of others.

This in turn opens up the range of responses a child can have to the people around her. Prior to this realization, there is no real meaning to what a child is responding to; it's as if others emit an electric signal that distresses the child. But with the realization that others have feelings (and desires and beliefs) like her own, a child can suddenly give meaning to what she's feeling: I feel bad *because he feels bad*. And this can be achieved without confusing who is feeling what. Moreover, the ability to grasp what others are thinking and feeling sharpens a child's evaluations of more complicated moral situations, as the following example demonstrates.

A stranger asks Jones how to get to a particular restaurant. Jones intends to give the stranger the *correct* directions, but accidentally sends the stranger in the wrong direction. When Smith is asked (by a different stranger) how to get to a particular restaurant, Smith intends to *mislead* the stranger, but accidentally sends the stranger in the correct direction. What's interesting is that, when children are asked who is "naughtier," their answers vary according to their age – and, presumably, their maturing moral sense. 4-year-olds tend to judge that Jones is naughtier than Smith, apparently placing greater weight on the *consequences* of one's actions rather than on one's intentions. 5- and 6-year-olds progressively tend to say that Smith is naughtier than Jones. According to a recent team of Harvard psychologists, "what develops then is not just a 'theory of mind,' or the ability to represent the mental states of others, but the ability to integrate this information with information about consequences in the context of moral judgment" (Young et al. 2007: 8235). For the developing child, right and wrong begins to go beyond what merely happens. It begins to involve what people *intend* to happen.

This same team of psychologists set out bolster these results by peering into the brain. Do the systems of the brain underlying belief attribution, they asked, *also* underlie moral judgment? Independent studies of the brain have revealed that the right temporoparietal junction (RTPJ) is critically involved in making assessments of others' mental states. Was the RTPJ also active when individuals judged that some act was right or wrong? Apparently so. If someone caused no harm but *intended* to cause harm (as Smith did), subjects' judgments were "harsh, made on the basis of [the actor's] beliefs alone, and associated with enhanced recruitment of circuitry involved in belief attribution." When harm was unintentional, subjects did not exhibit the same pattern of brain activity. The authors conclude that: "Moral judgment may therefore represent the product of two distinct and at times competing processes, one responsible for representing harmful outcomes and another for representing beliefs and intentions" (Young et al. 2007: 8239)

This is in line with the rough picture that has so far been developing. From a very young age, children are attuned to the emotions of others (particularly those emotions associated with distress). Indeed, the brain appears to contain systems crucial to this ability, for when they malfunction, we observe (let's just say) *sub-standard* moral behavior. But mature moral judgments go beyond merely registering the distress of others. It appears that a crucial part of the moral puzzle is perspective-taking. Indeed, the philosopher Jonathan Deigh argues that a full grasp of right and wrong requires *mature empathy*, where this involves "taking this other person's perspective and imagining the feelings of frustration and anger" (1996: 175). Before a child comes to grasp the role that intentions play in moral judgment (which requires, among other things, a grasp of intentions themselves), the child tends to say that causing harm is sufficient for "being naughty." As his understanding of other minds develops, however, he's more and more likely to take into account an actor's *intentions*, reflecting a growing tendency to integrate information about intentions with information about harm in generating moral judgments that approximate judgments adults make.

It might seem that this is the place to wrap up this neat and tidy little story. Unfortunately, things are not so neat and tidy. In fact, one of the most talked-about studies of childhood moral development complicates the account just offered. According to the work of philosopher Shaun Nichols (2004), a child's moral competency does *not* rely so critically on perspective-taking after all. In the next section, we consider why.

5.3 "Them's the Rules"

Consider for a moment all the rules that children are told to follow. "Don't talk with your mouth full." "Share your toys." "Don't hit your sister." "Raise your hand in class if you want to speak." "Don't pick your nose." "Put your dishes in the sink." "Keep your promises." "Don't whine." "Don't lie." "Don't spit." "Shoes off the bed." "Elbows off the table." "Be nice." Caregivers direct these rules at their charges without any real regard to age or understanding. Moreover, they're directed at children with widely varying levels of intensity. Lying, spitting, whining, hitting – there's no telling how a parent will respond. Dropping their child off at daycare in the morning, parents pat their child on the head, sweetly telling him to *be nice*. But later that same day the parents treat food-throwing as the final straw, bursting into a rage and sending the child into "time out." Caregivers make no attempt to separate rules into one kind or another. As far as kids are concerned, rules don't come with labels; kids are just expected to follow them.

But on reflection, we – as theorists – *can* separate these rules into kinds. *Conventional rules*, as they're sometimes called, get their authority from some convention or practice or person. Raising your hand in class is a rule that gets its meaning and authority from conventions associated with school; putting your dishes away gets its meaning and authority from conventions associated with the family; not picking your nose gets its meaning and authority from conventions associated with etiquette; and so on. *Moral rules*, on the other hand, do not seem to depend on conventions. They appear to be authority-independent. They're treated as more serious, "generalizable," and unconditionally obligatory (recall our discussion of morality from §3.1. When we justify following them, we're likely to appeal to such things as justice, a person's welfare, and rights. Now here's the surprising thing: despite the indiscriminate way rules are presented to children, they nevertheless grasp the distinction between conventional rules and moral rules. Here's how we know.

In the mid-1980s the psychologist Eliot Turiel (1983) and his colleagues conducted experiments (which have been replicated numerous times in different settings) asking children as young as 3 to consider some hypothetical situations involving rule-changes. For example, children are told to imagine their teacher saying: "Today, if you want to talk in class, you do *not* have to raise your hand." Children are then asked, "Would it be OK if today you talked in class without raising your hand?" With no hesitation, children say *yes*. Similarly, children say it would be OK to throw food if their parents said it would be OK to throw food.

But then children are asked to imagine their teacher saying: "Today, if you want to hit your friend in the face, you may do so." In this case, children *almost never* say it would be OK to hit their friend, even with their teacher's permission. Most children – asked to imagine a parent saying: "Today, it would OK for you to lie to your brother" – will nevertheless *deny* that it would be OK to lie to your brother. In a dramatic display of this distinction, the psychologist Larry Nucci asked Amish children to imagine a situation in which God made no rule against working on Sunday: 100 percent of the children said that, under those circumstances, it would be OK to work on Sunday. By contrast, when the children were asked to imagine a situation in which God made no rule against hitting others, 80 percent of the children said that, under those circumstances, hitting others would nevertheless *not* be OK (Nucci et al. 1983).

The most immediate implication of this research is this: very young children seem to grasp the difference between conventional rules (e.g., raise your hand before speaking) and moral rules (e.g., don't hit others). Children seem to recognize that some rules can be suspended by an authority (e.g., food-throwing) and some rules cannot (e.g., no hitting). And what's so striking about this is that children recognize this difference *despite* the fact that the difference is not at all apparent in their upbringing. (We'll come back to this point shortly.)

Shaun Nichols (2004) has drawn attention to another important implication of Turiel's work: many of the children who display an understanding of the difference between conventional and moral rules *fail* the "false belief" test. These are, after all, 3-year-olds. But if a child can grasp that some rules are authority-independent, generalizable, and unconditionally obligatory *without* recognizing the mental states of others, then maybe moral competency does not require perspective-taking, as we previously thought. According to Nichols, the rules children regard as authority-independent, generalizable, and serious "constitute an important core of moral judgment" (2004: 7). But if these same children have not developed a proper "theory of mind," then maybe a theory of mind is not necessary for core moral judgments. Maybe the rules of morality are even more basic to our psychology than we thought. Perhaps there is a core of moral knowledge or competency that is *innate*.

5.4 Moral Innateness and the Linguistic Analogy

One of the more lively debates now going on among moral psychologists concerns just this question of innateness. To what extent, if any, is morality innate? Answering this question of course requires straightening out two things: what is *morality* and what is *innateness*? The first of these questions was addressed in §3.1, where (following Richard Joyce) we proposed a list of conditions that a creature must meet in order to be considered moral. Nichols is prepared to accept a slightly less demanding set of requirements. For him, a child who insists that it would *not* be OK to hit your friend even if the teacher said it was OK is morally competent. On Joyce's account, we would need to know more about the child in order to deem her morally competent. For our purposes, we do not decide on the issue here: the results are worth discussing in either case.

The concept of innateness plays a role in a range of disciplines – biology, psychology, philosophy. It's no surprise then that the concept gets handled in different ways depending on which discipline employs it. In some places (e.g., biology), the concept is sometimes understood to mean "environmental invariance," as in: "a trait is innate just in case it reliably develops across varying environments." In other places (e.g., psychology), the concept is sometimes used to mean "not acquired via a psychological process." Fortunately, we can explore some of the data without having to enter into this fight over definitions, for the data appear to suggest innateness according to most definitions.

But the case for moral innateness – at least according to recent defenders – begins in another neighborhood, one that has received a lot of attention in the last forty years: *linguistics,* that is, the study of language. To get things rolling, let's try a little interactive linguistics. Consider the following sentence:

(1) *John said that Bill would feed himself.*

In (1) must the word "himself" refer to John or Bill? Or could it refer to either of them or someone altogether different? (Lest there are any doubts, answers are revealed in note 5.) Try this sentence:

(2) *John told Bill that he would feed himself.*

In (2) must the word "himself" refer to John or Bill? Or could it refer to either of them or someone altogether different? (Take all the time you need.) How about the following:

(3) *John said that Bill saw him.*

In (3) must the word "him" refer to Bill or John? Or could it refer to either of them or someone altogether different? Try converting the following declarative into an imperative – that is, into a question:

(4) *The boy who is happy is missing.*

In (4) is the correct imperative "Is the boy who happy is missing?" or "Is the boy who is happy missing?" Convert this last one into an imperative:

(5) *The duck is sad that the chicken is missing.*

In (5) is the correct imperative "Is the duck sad that the chicken is missing?" or "Is the duck is sad that the chicken missing?"

Unless this chapter is putting you to sleep or you suffer from a specific language deficit, none of these inferences required much thought.[5] But this is not what impresses linguists. What impresses linguists is not how *we* perform on them, but how *4-year-olds* perform on them. 4-year-olds perform nearly flawlessly on these sorts of questions. Take the following example.

Experimenters introduce 4-year-olds to a puppet. They tell the children to ask the puppet if the boy who is happy is missing. Remember that this is a sentence no child has ever heard before, and its structure is also probably very new to children – a sentence with embedded auxiliary verbs (i.e. "is"). Now children have probably heard plenty of people transform declaratives, such as "The cat was in the hat," into imperatives: "Was the cat in the hat?" Much less common to a child's ear are transformations of these more complex sentences. So surely *some* children, when they're asked to transform the sentence "The boy who is happy is missing," are going to say: "Is the boy who happy is missing?" After all, there are *two* auxiliary verbs to choose from; surely some kid is going to move the first one to the beginning of the sentence instead of the second. But 4-year-olds almost *never* do this. They always hit upon the correct transformation.

OK, maybe children are just lucky. Maybe they take a chance (all of them!) and plump for a rule that says that in transforming declaratives with embedded auxiliaries into imperatives, always choose the *last* auxiliary verb to move to the beginning of the sentence. To test this, experimenters give these same 4-year-olds this sentence: "The duck is sad that the chicken is missing." Now if children really are using the *Last Auxiliary Verb* rule, then we should hear them say: "Is the duck is sad that the chicken missing?" But this word salad almost never comes out of children's mouths. Somehow they know that, in *this* sentence, it's the first auxiliary verb that should be moved to the front of the sentence – not the second. How do children know this? How did they come upon this rule? Besides, what *is* the grammatical rule that governs these transformations? (Think you're so smart? Name it.)

This is just one of a host of examples that demonstrate that, as the psycholinguist Steven Pinker argues, "children deserve most of the credit for the language they acquire." Indeed, Pinker goes further: "we can show that they know things they could not have been taught" (1994: 40). But this immediately raises the question: If children know things about language that they could not have been taught, then where does this knowledge come from? You guessed it: they're born with it. Pinker offers this little analogy:

> People know how to talk in more or less the sense that spiders know how to spin webs. Web-spinning was not invented by some unsung spider genius and does not depend on having had the right education or on having an aptitude for architecture or the construction trades. Rather, spiders spin spider webs because they have spider brains, which give them the urge to spin and the competence to succeed. (Pinker 1994: 18)

According to Pinker, our brains are wired for language. Language is "an instinct." It's worth repeating, however, that linguists feel driven to this position because children know things that they could not plausibly acquire from their environment. This is why the argument that drives these linguists is referred to as the *poverty of stimulus argument*: the linguistic stimulus to which children are exposed is too impoverished to explain what children know about language. So what does this have to do with morality?

The answer is this: we have a *moral* instinct, just as we have a language instinct. And the reason for believing this is (you see it coming?) a *moral* poverty of stimulus argument: the moral stimulus to which children are exposed is too impoverished to explain what children know about morality. The philosopher and legal scholar John Mikhail (2009) was the first to rigorously push this idea. According to Mikhail, the moral/conventional studies made famous by Turiel offer the most persuasive case for an innate morality. Turiel showed that children as young as 3 make the distinction between moral rules and conventional rules. But, argued Mikhail, to explain children's capacity to make this distinction, we should expect one of three things: (a) children were *trained* by their caregivers to make the distinction; (b) children *learned* to make the distinction by studying their environment; or (c) children develop the capability by way of *innate* processes. (Note the parallel with language. To explain, for example, children's capacity to correctly transform declaratives with embedded auxiliaries into imperatives, we should expect one of three corresponding things: (a) training, (b) learning, or (c) innateness.)

Well, it's pretty clear that caregivers do not explicitly train their children in how to make the distinction between moral rules and conventional rules. Most caregivers have probably never even considered this distinction. It also seems implausible that children have learned the distinction by studying their environment. Recall that caregivers make no effort to distinguish moral rules from conventional rules. What the child hears is "Don't do that!" – whether that's throwing food or telling a lie. And it can't be that moral rules are treated as more serious than conventional rules, since the consequences for breaking some conventional rules can be just as severe as (or even *more* severe than) those for breaking moral rules. It may depend on the caregiver; it may depend on the day of the week. This leaves (c), the view that children develop the capability by way of innate processes.

But Turiel's work is not the only evidence cited by supporters of innateness. Children also appear to recognize another sort of distinction. For example, a child is told: "If today is Saturday, then tomorrow must be Sunday." Suppose that the child is told that tomorrow is *not* Sunday. Could today be Saturday? Children as young as 4 reliably say *No*. But then a child is told: "If Sam goes outside, then Sam must wear a hat." The child is then told that Sam is not wearing a hat. Could Sam possibly be outside? Despite the identical structure of these two judgments (If p is F, then q *must be* G), kids somehow recognize that, yes, Sam *could be* outside. How? Sam is being naughty! The distinction here has to do with conditionals – that is, if/then statements. We call conditionals like "If today is Saturday, then tomorrow must be Sunday" *indicative* since (very roughly) they indicate what is the case. When we say that Sunday must follow Saturday, we're reporting a conceptual necessity. On the other hand, conditionals like "If Sam goes outside, then he must wear a hat" are called *deontic* since (very roughly) they concern *duties*.

As in the case of the moral/conventional distinction, children seem to grasp this difference *despite* the fact that the difference is not at all apparent in their upbringing. How often do parents stop to spell out the difference between the "must" of necessity (as in "Bachelors *must* be unmarried") and the "must" of duty (as in "You *must* return what belongs to others")? And yet, kids get it. How could this be, ask supporters of innateness, if this knowledge were *not* innate?

Children also seem capable of appreciating the difference *intentions* make. I touched on this in the previous section. Consider some further evidence. A child is told that if Sam goes outside, Sam must wear a hat. The child is then shown four images depicting Sam. In the first image, Sam is inside without his hat on. In the second image, Sam is inside with his hat on. In the third image, Sam is outside without his hat on. In the fourth image, Sam is outside without his hat on, but his hat is being blown off by a gust of wind. The child is then asked: which image(s) show Sam being *naughty*? Now since images 3 and 4 *both* depict Sam outside without his hat on, we would expect that some kids would say that Sam is being naughty in both images, that some kids would say that Sam is being naughty in image 3, and that some kids would say that Sam is being naughty in image 4. But the evidence does not show this. Instead, almost all children aged 4 and over say that Sam is being naughty *only* in image 3. Children evidently realize that being naughty requires *intentionally* being naughty. Since the wind causes Sam to lose his hat in image 4, he is not intentionally outside without his hat on. So Sam is not being naughty in that image. These results hold up even in places where it's rarely cold enough to need hats.

As in the case of language, these results reveal that children possess a rich understanding of morality – despite what appears to be a very limited exposure to moral discourse. But if, argue moral psychologists, what comes out of children is far more sophisticated that what goes in, then there must be a body of knowledge already inside children. Moral knowledge (or at least a core of it) is innate.

That said, it's worth repeating that even if morality is innate, this does *not* entail that morality is an evolutionary adaptation. Stepping back, we should underline that moral nativism, like linguistic nativism, is a story about what's present in humans from the beginning (so to speak). Adaptationism is a story about *how* what's present in humans got there. This means that one could accept moral nativism, but deny that morality is an adaptation. One could argue, for example, that morality is a by-product of other cognitive systems, that is, an *exaptation* (see §1.1. Or, for that matter, one could argue that God placed the knowledge in us at birth. At any rate, it's important to keep our options open as the evidence comes in. If the adaptation story sketched in the previous chapter does not in the final analysis receive the evidence it needs, we may decide to reject it. But this doesn't at the same time force us to reject moral nativism. We might find the evidence on that front compelling. Or we might not.

The hypothesis of moral innateness seems convincing when our attention is focused on what a small set of children know from a very young age. But what happens when we widen our focus? Recall from chapter 4 the variety of moral views we see in other cultures. Acts of killing that we find appalling are acceptable in other parts of the world – if not demanded; in most Western cultures, women are treated equally under the law, a practice that strikes some cultures as morally abhorrent. But doesn't moral variation across cultures mark an obstacle for the hypothesis of moral innateness? After all, if the instinct for morality is present in all humans, shouldn't we observe similar moral views wherever we find humans? This question has prompted some moral psychologists to pull back somewhat from the moral innateness hypothesis.

5.5 Switchboards, Biases, and Affective Resonances

In making the case for linguistic nativism, I sidestepped a rather glaring fact: last time I checked, people speak different languages! But if language is innate, then shouldn't we expect to see everyone speaking the *same* language? No one doubts that the development of two arms and two legs is innate. And sure enough, humans around the globe have two arms and two legs. So how can linguistic nativists claim that language is innate if there are nearly 7,000 different languages spoken around the globe?

The answer requires getting clear on *what exactly* is innate. According to linguistic nativists (following Chomsky), native or natural languages – i.e., the language we actually speak and have learned from our parents – are not innate. What *is* innate, according to linguistic nativists, is the *grammar* underlying all these languages. For one of the striking discoveries of the last fifty years is that all natural languages share some common universals. Chomsky dubbed this deep similarity *Universal Grammar*. One way to appreciate the point is to imagine the space of logically possible languages (computer languages, for example); think of all the wild syntactic rules governing how to turn sounds into meanings that we could come up with. The amazing thing, say linguists, is that all natural languages spoken by humans fall into only a tiny, tiny sliver of that logical space. This is not to suggest, of course, that there aren't vast differences separating different languages. But these differences, it turns out, are only on the surface. Beneath the surface, the differences are negligible. And one way to think about these differences is in terms of switches or parameters. It will help to consider some examples.

Put crudely, what makes English English and not Italian, say, has to do in large part with how the switches are set. For example, Italian speakers (even young children) recognize that the sentences

(1) Io vado al cinema.
(2) Vado al cinema.

are both acceptable. Both express the proposition that I am going to the cinema. But in English, while the sentence

(3) I am going to the cinema.

is acceptable, the sentence

(4) Am going to the cinema.

is not. The reason is that in English – but not in Italian – the subject of the sentence must be pronounced. Linguists refer to this constraint as the *Null Subject Parameter*. Every known language is either Subject Optional (as in Italian) or Subject Obligatory (as in English). For known languages, this exhausts the possibilities. Over the last forty years, linguists have identified many such parameters. In almost all cases, the parameter has but two settings.

Identifying these parameters and how they are set helps us sharpen the linguistic nativist's claim. What the child brings into the world, argues the nativist, is this Universal Grammar "switchboard." What the child acquires from her environment is information about how those switches are to be set. Are the people in my environment regularly pronouncing the subject of declarative sentences or not? The language faculty is supposedly sensitive to this information (below the level of a child's awareness) and makes the necessary setting. What the child does *not* have to learn independently is that sentences have subjects and these subjects are either pronounced or not. That part of her education is over before she begins.

This view of language, say moral nativists, provides a model for how we should understand moral development. Like Mikhail, the psychologist Marc Hauser has been vigorously pushing this idea. According to Hauser, just as a child's grammaticality judgments emerge from a universal linguistic grammar whose parameters are set by local conditions, the child's moral judgments emerge from a "universal moral grammar, replete with shared principles and culturally switchable parameters" (2006: 43). What the child inherits, in short, is a moral switchboard. What the child picks us from her environment is how to set each of the many parameters that make up a moral system. If Hauser is correct, "every newborn child could build a finite but large number of moral systems. When a child builds a particular moral system, it is because the local culture has set the parameters in a particular system" (2006: 298). Hauser sees numerous examples of cross-cultural universals tweaked by distinct cultural norms.

Take killing. According to Hauser, a child is already equipped with a principle that prohibits harming others. A child does not have to learn that harming others is forbidden. What a child must learn are the exceptions, if any. Are there many exceptions to the general prohibition? Or only a few?

In some environments, killing other people is regarded as almost universally prohibited. With the exception of self-defense or maybe capital punishment, killing others is presented to the child as *never* OK. In this environment the switch would be set at ALWAYS PROHIBITED. In other environments the moral status of killing is much more complicated. It appears to be a function of several sub-parameters. Is the person to be killed a member of my tribe? Is the person female? Has this person offended my family's honor? Has this person humiliated me? In environments like this, the switch is much lower, at SOMETIMES PROHIBITED. But it's part of the nativist's claim that the moral switchboard puts constraints on possible judgments – for example, there is no setting for NEVER PROHIBITED. Among the thousands of human cultures studied to date, not a single one exhibits an indifference to harming or killing others. The variation we see appears to be constrained in predictable ways. Analogously, there are many settings on the language "switchboard" that we will not observe since they are disallowed by the rules of Universal Grammar.[6] According to Hauser, "our biology imposes constraints on the pattern of violence, allowing for some options but not others" (2006: 132).

Hauser believes that similar stories can be told about justice, fairness, incest, and infanticide. In all these cases, it appears that humans everywhere (from a very young age) possess an innate sense of what's required and what's forbidden. The variation we observe is explained by parametric variation tweaked by distinct cultures.

But Hauser's principles-and-parameters view of moral development is a bit too rich for some tastes. The philosopher Chandra Sripada is prepared to offer a *kind* of nativist story, but it's far less imposing than the one suggested by Hauser. Sripada's dispute with Hauser concerns what the data force us to accept. *Linguistic* nativists believe we're forced to accept the view that language is innate by reflecting on how difficult the language-learning task is for kids. (Recall our discussion in the previous section.) Sripada is willing to accept this view of language. But unlike Hauser, Sripada does not think that the data force us to accept the principles-and-parameters model of moral development. Why? Because the *moral*-learning task is not nearly so difficult. Moral norms, notes Sripada, are not "far removed from experience in the same manner as the hierarchical tree structures and recursive rules of human grammars" (Sripada 2008: 328). After all, kids are being told by their caregivers what they can and cannot do quite regularly. So while there may be some distinctions requiring explanation (e.g., the moral rule/conventional rule distinction), the moral-learning task confronting children is not nearly as daunting as the language-learning task. Also, in the former case, kids have the advantage of having a language with which caregivers can *instruct* kids on what is right and wrong. Not so in the case of language. Finally, Sripada is concerned that the cross-cultural variation in moral norms is simply too great to be accounted for by the Hauser story. It must be the case then that children come into the world with more flexibility than Hauser supposes.

In place of the principles-and-parameters model, Sripada proposes what he calls the *Innate Bias Model* of moral development. This model allows for more flexibility in moral development because it attributes less to the moral mind. What children possess innately, according to Sripada, are certain *biases* or *dispositions to favor* some norms over others. In other words, human minds are hard-wired to find some social rules more attractive than others. This smoothly explains the moral similarities we observe across different cultures. Sripada cites incest as an example.

There's good evidence that humans possess an innate aversion to engaging in sex with anyone with whom they have spent prolonged periods of their childhood. We refer to this as the *Westermarck aversion*, after the Finnish sociologist Edward Westermarck who first proposed the mechanism. But note that an innate aversion to incest is not the same thing as an innate *moral prohibition* on incest. (Hauser is prepared to argue that children possess an innate moral prohibition on incest.) According to Sripada, the innate aversion will lead to a sort of group disgust in reaction to an act of incest. And this group disgust will lead over time "to the emergence of new moral norms that forbid the offending action" (2008: 336). The Westermarck aversion is just one example of an innate aversion to a given practice that "would enhance the 'attractiveness' of a moral norm" forbidding that practice. If this story is correct, moral prohibitions on killing, stealing, lying, and so on, grew out of innate aversions shared by every member of the group.

The philosopher Shaun Nichols has argued for something quite similar: "Normative claims [some of which will be moral claims] that are 'affect-backed,' that prohibit an action that is emotionally upsetting, will be better remembered than non-affect-backed normative claims" (2004: 128). Memory plays a special role here for Nichols. For norms that are remembered enjoy *cultural survival*, and this explains the near-universality of moral thought. According to Nichols, what we see in the moral domain is not so much the work of biological evolution as of *cultural* evolution. Cultural evolution involves the selection of *ideas* – not genes. (Richard Dawkins dubbed these units of selection *memes*.) Which ideas get selected? Whichever ideas happen to survive and spread to the minds of others.[7]

Suppose an idea is backed by a strong emotion. Take our response to rotting meat. *Disgusting!* Someone floats the idea that rotting meat contains invisible spirits that seek to invade our bodies. In certain environments, that idea would make a certain kind of sense. It would make, if you will, powerful *emotional* sense. In any event, the norm "Do not eat rotting meat" enjoys potent emotional support. Thus it's not hard to imagine that, like a good jingle, once you hear it, you can't help but remember it. You're more likely to tell others, and they, like you, immediately resonate to the idea. And so on until the idea becomes firmly embedded in our culture. So it's no surprise that someone (like Mikhail or Hauser) might *think* that morality is innate: after all, it *does* seem to show up in every culture. But that's misreading the evidence, according to Nichols and Sripada. Morality is not innate. Specific biases or (as Nichols describes them) "affective resonances" are innate. The connections between biases and morality are forged by one's environment – in particular, the transmission of emotionally powerful ideas.

One advantage of this view is that innate biases do not strictly rule out the acceptance of quite exotic rules. To be averse to a given rule (e.g., "killing innocent humans") does not mean that you can't accept it. It may just require increased cultural pressure. The pressures of conforming to your environment, along with repeated exposures to the stimulus, may suppress – if not ultimately extinguish – whatever innate aversion you possess toward some practice. So the accounts offered by Sripada and Nichols appear to have the resources to explain the key data. They can explain, first, how it is that children rapidly develop a "moral grammar" despite having no formal training. Second, they can explain both the moral similarities and the extreme moral differences across the globe.

5.6 Non-Nativist Doubts

But even this conservative view of morality is too much for the philosopher Jesse Prinz. Prinz is not convinced that non-nativist accounts of morality cannot account for the data just mentioned. A less negative way of putting the same point: Prinz thinks the data are perfectly compatible with a non-nativist story. Let's begin with the case of so-called moral universals.

According to Prinz (2008b: 372), the moral nativist has to show at least three things to prove her case. First, she must show that there really are similar moral rules that appear in all cultures. This would be equivalent to showing that there is a Universal Moral Grammar, akin to the Universal Grammar posited by Chomsky. Second, the nativist must show that there are no plausible *non-nativist* ways of explaining those universal moral rules. If a non-nativist story can adequately explain the data, then unless there is some *other* reason that we must accept nativism, we should go with the simpler story: children learn the rules of morality in the same way that they learn so many other aspects of life. Finally, the nativist must show that the innate machinery responsible for making moral judgments is *specific* to morality; that is, she must show that this machinery is not the result of (merely) innate general-purpose cognitive mechanisms. After all, non-nativists like Prinz are not opposed to the idea that certain general-purpose learning mechanisms are innate. It's hard to see kids learn *anything* without some inborn capacity to form theories about their experiences. Despite the efforts of nativists like Hauser and Sripada, Prinz doubts that the nativist can show *any* of these things – much less *all* of them.

As far as the existence of universal moral rules goes, Prinz thinks the evidence is "depressingly weak" (2008b: 373). A little tour through the world's cultures quickly reveals that, for example, the *toleration of harm* is "as common as its *prohibition*." Take the Yanamomo of the Amazon region, or the Ilongot of Luzon, or the highland tribes of New Guinea, or the Aztecs, or even sub-cultures within large-scale industrial societies: all reveal quite permissive attitudes toward violence. Some people are not only not averse to killing others; they celebrate it. Of course we like to think that pretty much everyone judges that harming others is wrong. But an honest appraisal of the world's people, says Prinz, casts serious doubt on the idea that there is a universal moral prohibition on harming others.

It may be responded that all cultures prohibit harm for no good reason. But the non-nativist can readily account for this universality. What good, asks Prinz, is harming someone if it serves no personal end? Indeed, it's often the case that harming others brings with it steep social costs. Children learn early on that misbehaving has its consequences. So to explain the (alleged) fact that all cultures prohibit harm for no good reason does not require positing an innate moral system. All it requires is the capacity to learn which things elicit negative reactions in others and perhaps the disposition to avoid those things. But this is a far cry from an innate morality. Prinz is prepared to accept the notion that we are biologically disposed to care about each other. He's also prepared to accept the idea that there may be "universal constraints on stable societies." But these dispositions do not require an innate moral sensibility.

But what of the moral poverty of the stimulus argument? Recall that the non-nativist has to explain how it is that children distinguish between moral rules and conventional rules without the aid of explicit training. According to Prinz, it's quite possible that children can learn the distinction without the aid of explicit training. He cites evidence that suggests that caregivers *do* in fact exhibit different styles of "disciplinary intervention" depending on the kind of rules at issue. When it comes to enforcing moral rules, caregivers use "power assertions" and appeals to rights. When it comes to enforcing conventional rules, caregivers reason with children and appeal to "social order." If this is right, then the data do not force us to accept moral nativism after all.

5.7 Conclusion

The science of virtue and vice has barely moved beyond its infancy. What we *do* know about how humans come to have the moral beliefs and emotions they have is overshadowed by what we do *not* know. The focus on child development remains intense. The dispute that separates the moral nativist from the moral non-nativist hinges critically on (a) what the child knows at a young age and, more importantly, (b) the possible paths that could have plausibly led to that knowledge. If closer investigation reveals that a child's moral knowledge is quite rudimentary – that is, it's nothing like the kind of highly sophisticated knowledge that grounds human language – then the nativist's case begins to look weak. But if that knowledge is as rich as moral nativists claim, then the pressure is on the non-nativist to show how a child could have arrived at such knowledge. This may require observing very closely the natural social environments of children. But such observations face steep obstacles. For one thing, it would require three to four years of intense observation because – remember – the nativist's claim is that the child has not been exposed to enough moral stimuli to form the kind of judgments she comes to form. But the only way to know this is to observe *everything* a child has been exposed to during her upbringing. Moreover, scientific observations are often intrusive. What we need to see is the *natural* environment, and this may be hard to do. If you know scientists are observing your behavior, this may alter, perhaps unconsciously, how you behave.

Returning to themes that occupied us in the earlier parts of the chapter, we can at least feel more comfortable about the basics. Nobody seriously maintains that humans come into the world utterly blank – morally or otherwise. Even most non-nativists accept the idea that we're hard-wired to respond to the distress of others. A bit more controversial is the idea that we're hard-wired to develop, at around the age of 4, the ability to take on the perspective of others. It's clear that children come to use this information to make more sophisticated moral judgments, judgments that appear to be sensitive to an agent's intentions.

But the claim that morality (properly understood) is a product of evolution depends critically on the question of nativism. Is there enough evidence to show that moral thinking is innate? To show this, researchers must continue to study *what* children know and *how* they came to know it. This line of research rests on the reasonable assumption that if children possess a body of knowledge that did not come from their environment, then it must be innate. Another approach to the question of nativism is cross-cultural: Is there a Universal Moral Grammar that cuts across the human family? This line of research rests on the (perhaps shakier) assumption that traits that appear in all cultures, despite local differences, arise from a common human developmental program. Of course, even if both lines of research were to deliver powerful evidence in support of nativism, the case for the evolution of morality would remain incomplete. Is there enough evidence to show that morality was *selected for*? Belly-buttons, after all, were not selected for, but every person in every culture, despite their upbringing, has one. Maybe morality was a by-product of, say, bigger brains. Maybe morality was instilled in us by some supernatural power. The upshot of all this is that we're nowhere close to a settled view of the matter. The science of virtue and vice has yet to issue its final verdict.

We have reached the end of part I. Our journey has taken us from Darwin and selfish genes to ancient human communities to modern boys and girls in their first struggles with morality. Guiding us along the way has been the idea that morality is in our genes, that the same forces that shaped the structure of the human heart shaped the structure of the moral mind. In part II, our interest turns from how we think about right and wrong to the nature of right and wrong itself. Do the forces of Darwinian selection not only explain why we might judge that, say, premeditated murder is wrong, but also *justify* our judgment that it's is wrong? Can biology tell us what is good, what is bad? Should we guide our lives in accordance with evolutionary principles? These are some of the questions we'll tackle in the next part.

Further Reading

Boehm, C. (2000) Conflict and the Evolution of Social Control. *Journal of Consciousness Studies*, 7, 1–2: 79–101.

Carruthers, Peter, Stephen Laurence, and Stephen Stich (eds.) (2005/6) *The Innate Mind*, vols. 1 and 2 (Oxford University Press).

Chomsky, Noam and Carlos Peregrín Otero (2004) *Language and Politics* (AK Press).

Cima, Maaike, Franca Tonnaer, and Marc Hauser (2010) Psychopaths Know Right from Wrong But Don't Care. *Social, Cognitive, and Affective Neuroscience.* Advanced access: http://scan.oxfordjournals.org/content/early/2010/01/06/scan.nsp051.full.

De Waal, Frans (2005) *Our Inner Ape* (Riverhead).

De Waal, Frans (2006) *Primates and Philosophers: How Morality Evolved* (Princeton University Press).

Eisenberg, Nancy and Paul Henry Mussen (1989) *The Roots of Prosocial Behavior in Children*. Cambridge Studies in Social and Emotional Development (Cambridge University Press).

Haidt, Jonathan (2006) *The Happiness Hypothesis: Finding Modern Truth in Ancient Wisdom* (Basic Books).

Hauser, Marc (2006) *Moral Minds: How Nature Designed our Universal Sense of Right and Wrong* (Ecco).

Mikhail, John (2009) The Poverty of the Moral Stimulus. In W. Sinnott-Armstrong (ed.), *Moral Psychology: The Evolution of Morality*, vol. 1 (MIT Press).

Nichols, Shaun (2004) *Sentimental Rules: On the Natural Foundations of Moral Judgment* (Oxford University Press).

Pinker, Steven. (1994) *The Language Instinct: How the Mind Creates Language* (Morris).

Sinnott-Armstrong, Walter (ed.) (2008) *Moral Psychology: The Evolution of Morality*, vol. 1 (MIT Press).

Tancredi, Laurence (2005) *Hard-Wired Behavior: What Neuroscience Reveals about Morality* (Cambridge University Press).

Warneken, F. and M. Tomasello (2007) Helping and Cooperation at 14 Months of Age. *Infancy*, 11, 271–94.

Part II

From "What Is" to "What Ought To Be": Moral Philosophy after Darwin

The truly dangerous aspect of Darwin's idea is its seductiveness.
(*Daniel Dennett, Darwin's Dangerous Idea*)

The move is effortless. We make it half a dozen times a day. And it's almost always unconscious. We hear "all natural," "nature's own," "naturally grown," and we think *good*. Why? To say it's because we're suspicious of the *artificial* only reignites the question: Why do we regard what's natural as better for us than what is artificial or unnatural? Maybe we assume that our bodies (and our minds?) evolved under, if you will, "all-natural conditions." So if we are the product of nature, it only makes sense that we should use "natural" products, no? We assume a kind of harmony must exist between the conditions that led to our being the way we are and the kind of things that can support our being the way we want to be.

Innovation is no doubt exciting. But too much innovation too quickly unnerves us. Consider some responses to genetically modified foods. Or cosmetic surgery. Violations of nature! When *in vitro* fertilization became a viable reproductive option in the 1970s there was (and in some corners there remains) a critical backlash. Some of the criticism was measured: Do we know what the long-term health risks are? Will the public discriminate against "test-tube babies"? But some of the criticism went much deeper: Do we know how this affects our very humanity? Arguably, the issue that inflames the most passionate response of this kind is human cloning. The bioethicist Leon Kass does not dawdle around the edges, but goes right for the heart of the matter: "We are repelled by the prospect of human cloning . . . because we intuit and feel, immediately and without argument,

An Introduction to Evolutionary Ethics, by Scott M. James. © 2011 Scott M. James

the violation of things that we rightfully hold dear. We *sense* that cloning represents a profound defilement of *our given nature*" (1997: 21). The political philosopher Michael Sandel invokes a similar kind of argument in his case against genetic enhancement. According to Sandel, the "danger" of genetic enhancement ultimately lies in the human attitudes that prompt it: "they represent a kind of *hyperagency* – a Promethean aspiration to remake nature, including human nature, to serve our purposes and satisfy our desires" (2004: 893). Like those who draw a connection between "all natural" and good, Sandel and Kass both assume that what is natural and what is good are closely aligned.

This sets the stage for the second phase of our inquiry: What is the relationship between values and nature? Between what is good and bad, on the one hand, and what is natural, on the other? And it's a short step from here to this question: What's the relationship between the natural forces that led to our species' existence and morality? Is it possible that some of the products of human evolution – not only things like competition, but also cooperation and love – also determine what is morally right? This question is independent of the one that occupied us in the previous chapters. For even if human moral thought was *not* selected for, we might still insist that *biological imperatives determine moral imperatives*. In the next several chapters we will explore the checkered history of this idea. The point of this exploration is primarily pedagogical: the lessons we learn from the early failures of evolutionary ethics directly influence its current shape. Anyone who has even a passing familiarity with evolutionary ethics knows of its bad odor. Some, for example, will recognize its association with some of the most abhorrent social movements of recent memory: for example Nazism. The extent to which evolutionary theory influenced the social policies of early twentieth-century totalitarian regimes remains a hotly contested issue among historians. But our task is not historical so much as philosophical. Our task is get clear on why almost all efforts to use evolution as a guide to how we ought to behave are misbegotten. The move from "all natural" to "all good" is dangerously confused.

Darwin's discovery was, first and foremost, a *biological* discovery. And that's how most people regard it today. It's an idea that circulates among biologists and among more daring social scientists. Darwin himself made no serious effort to see his idea as anything but a biological discovery, a description of how species evolve. He even mocked the idea that his discovery represented a *prescription*, that is, guidance on how we ought to live our lives. Herbert Spencer had no such reservations. He was the first (and, arguably, the most enthusiastic) philosopher to regard Darwin's discovery as a *moral* discovery. The term *Social Darwinism* has come to be associated with the view that evolution by natural selection provides moral or practical guidance on how we ought to live our lives.

A contemporary of Darwin, Spencer was optimistic about the natural progression of the human race. As we'll see in chapter 7, the publication of Darwin's *Origin of Species* confirmed what Spencer had suspected: that social harmony is our natural state. It is where evolution naturally leads. And because it is our natural state, it is morally desirable. The idea that our natural state constitutes what is right still resonates today, whether we're talking about cloning or hair coloring. After all, to say that something *goes against nature* amounts to a criticism. At the time of Spencer's writing, Darwin's discovery represented the first *scientific* explanation of why going against nature was wrong. And who wants to argue with science?

Of course Spencer would have had more success had he gotten the science right. But, as we'll see, he didn't. Evolution by natural selection does not work in the way Spencer had assumed, so it's no wonder that Spencer went astray. In chapter 7 we review the first of two separate but related attacks on the supposed connection between rightness and nature. According to the first criticism (sometimes referred to as *Hume's Law*, after the Scottish philosopher David Hume), no moral claim follows logically from purely non-moral claims. Insofar as Spencer believed evolution *by itself* justified conducting our lives in this or that way, his thinking was fallacious. In chapter 8, we consider a related criticism (the so-called *Naturalistic Fallacy*) introduced by the philosopher G.E. Moore: any attempt to identify goodness with some other property (like social harmony) is bound to fail. According to Moore, goodness cannot be reduced to anything more basic since it *is* basic. For most philosophers, Hume's Law and the Naturalistic Fallacy decidedly closed the door on Social Darwinism. There was nothing more to say. If that's what E.O. Wilson meant by "biologicizing ethics," then there was no good reason to remove ethics "from the hands of philosophers" since biology is simply not in the moral rule-giving business.

More recent philosophical thinking has perhaps been a bit more open-minded. In chapter 9 we revisit Moore and Hume. We put their criticisms under the microscope to see if in fact they're as fatal as some believe. As we'll see, some philosophers doubt that Hume and Moore showed what they claimed to show. Some offer ways of bridging the so-called *Is/Ought Gap*. Hume's Law, it's argued, *can* be broken. Others suspect that Moore's Naturalistic Fallacy is itself a fallacy, pointing to cases where his argument gives the incorrect answer. If these philosophers are right, then Social Darwinism may, in the end, live to fight another day. Of course, to remove two objections to a view does not in itself make that view correct. Even in the absence of explicit criticisms, defenders of Social Darwinism still owe us an argument as to why we should think the view is plausible, if not correct. Arguably, that argument has yet to materialize.

More recently, evolutionary ethics has taken on a different cast. As we'll see in chapters 10 and 11, contemporary philosophers have drawn a different lesson from Darwin: "biologicizing ethics" means reducing ethics to an illusion. Ethics (like beauty) is only in the eyes of the beholder, according to these philosophers. We *believe* that right and wrong are objective – or real. But we have evolution to thank for that, not the (so-called) objective moral order. On this approach, we don't believe that right and wrong are objective because we apprehend the *real* moral order. We believe it only because evolution has tricked us into believing it. In chapter 12, I'll suggest some possible ways to resist this line of attack. This is an important undertaking. For to take evolution seriously, while at the same time maintaining that some acts are objectively immoral, requires responding to this anti-realist argument. Some philosophers don't believe you can have it both ways. I'll lay out some options for those who believe you can.

6

Social Harmony: The Good, the Bad, and the Biologically Ugly

The poverty of the incapable, the distresses that come upon the impru-
dent, the starvation of the idle, and those shoulderings aside of the weak
by the strong, which leave so many "in shallows and in miseries" are the
decrees of a large, far-seeing benevolence.
                        (Herbert Spencer, The Principles of Ethics)

It is chauvinistic to treat humans as though they were the end point of
evolution. They are only one of millions of end products – one tiny twig.
                  (Richard Dawkins, interview in the New Statesman)

In this chapter we review the temptations and mistakes of early evolutionary
ethics. The aim is to clear out of the way some common misperceptions
about what contemporary philosophers are doing when they claim to be
doing evolutionary ethics.

6.1 From the Great Chain of Being, to the Tree of Life, to Morality

In the cartoon version of human evolution, single-celled organisms evolved
into multi-celled organisms. Multi-celled organisms evolved into fish that
eventually waddled out onto a beach somewhere. Walking fish became
reptiles that became little mammals. Little mammals became bigger mammals. Bigger mammals moved into the trees. Then out of the trees. They
stood on two legs, lost their hair, and, finally, their posture straightening,
they walked grandly out of the forests and onto the broad boulevards of
London, distinguished, refined, and never short on conversation.

An Introduction to Evolutionary Ethics, by Scott M. James. © 2011 Scott M. James

Much of this of course is misleading. (For one thing, individuals don't evolve, populations do.) But the basics are sound. Not only did some of our ancestors swing from trees, but some swam in oceans. Indeed, there is an unbroken genetic chain that goes all the way back to the lowliest plankton and beyond.

The point I want to begin with here is that this cartoon version of evolution by natural selection encourages a distorted picture of the evolutionary process. That is, when we take the "long view" of things, it's difficult to resist the picture of a steady *progression* from the less complex to the more complex. From micro-organisms like protists to sponges, from sponges to sand dollars, from sand dollars to lamprey eels, from lamprey eels to tuna, from tuna to turtles, from turtles to weasels, from weasels to zebras, from zebras to apes, from apes to humans, the progression seems unmistakable. And it's not merely progression in size. Weasels are more cunning by a mile than redwoods. The social hierarchies governing ape interactions are more sophisticated than the hierarchies governing zebra interactions.

You've probably seen the medieval depiction of humanity's place in the universe: the Great Chain of Being (Figure 6.1). At the bottom are minerals and plants – not much fun to be around. But as you work your way up, organisms take on greater and greater sophistication. Of course, in the traditional hierarchy, God sits at the top, like an angel perched atop a Christmas tree. We're no angels, but we're not far behind. Darwin's ideas no doubt upset this picture in some ways. But in other ways it appeared to be a scientific *vindication* of this order: humans remain *above* the rest of the natural world. Consider how the Great Chain of Being became the Tree of Life (Figure 6.2). While the Tree of Life depicted the interconnections (or, as biologists would put it, the *phylogenetic* relations) among organisms in a way that the Great Chain did not, it preserved the *vertical* hierarchy of life. Indeed, humanity wholly replaces God in the 1879 depiction by the great German naturalist Ernest Haeckel. We have not gotten away from the idea, so grandly expressed in first book of the Old Testament, that humans still have "dominion over the fish of the sea, and over the fowl of the air, and over the cattle, and over all the earth, and over every creeping thing that creepeth upon the earth."

And, frankly, the intuition is seductive. Recall the last time you took a plane ride. Looking out across the landscape, what did you see? Which species had left its mark? Deer didn't come together to build those roads; woodpeckers didn't build those subdivisions. Those are not

Figure 6.1   The Great Chain of Being as proposed by Aristotle *From the* Rhetorica Christiana *by Didacus Valades, 1579*

baboons in those medical research facilities or in those processing plants or in those universities. Think about it. How many dogs do you know that can put a human (OK, a dog) on the moon? Ever seen a cat compose a sonata? A mole, a sonnet? Elephants are no doubt forces to be reckoned with, but name one bridge, one tunnel, one stadium – hell, one *lean-to* – that they single-handedly designed and constructed. It's true we can't fly like birds. But who needs to fly like a bird when we can fly like VIPs – at much faster speeds and with complimentary nuts? We're pretty poor swimmers when you put us next to the mackerel, but I've never met a mackerel who had the idea of taking

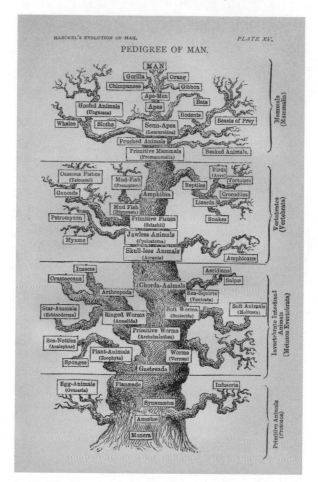

Figure 6.2 Haeckel's Tree of Life, from *The Evolution of Man*

160,000 gross tons of material and building a cruise-liner that can carry 5,000 friends.

The force of this idea – the idea that humans are evolutionarily special – gets added strength by considering not just what we do, but what we do *not* do. Infanticide is not a routine part of our family structure, as it is for countless other species, including pigs and mice, lions and monkeys. Humans of course commit infanticide, but we regard the rare instances as abominations. How about killing and *eating* our offspring? Even our most reviled sociopaths don't go *that* far. But cannibalistic infanticide is fairly common among chimpanzees, cats, elephants, dogs, baboons, bears, and lions. Also, humans are, generally speaking, pair-bonding: we stick with our mates "for better, for worse, for richer, for poorer, in sickness and in health." In the rest of the animal world, with only a few exceptions it's pretty much love the one you're with.

If we didn't know any better, we would not hesitate to draw the conclusion that humans have evolved into "higher" beings. Who could deny that we are stunningly complex, adaptive, and capable of profound self-sacrifice? We are "enlightened" – at least in this sense: we harnessed the power of reason to do such things as extend our lifespan (by some forty or fifty *years* according to some accounts), improve our health, explore the far corners of the planet and beyond, develop the arts, and establish laws and covenants, systems of trade and commerce. We are compassionate. We *feel* a deep connection to others. We want to work together, even in our limited ways. The roads and hospitals, banks and performance halls, parliaments and parks, were all made possible by *cooperation*, by the spirit of joint action. But these, noted Spencer, are the products of the "last stage of evolution." Humans are distinct in that they have achieved a kind of social harmony that facilitates the production of such great wonders.

These observations alone invited early evolutionary theorists to think that natural selection tends toward "higher forms." This is not to say that there couldn't be forms higher than humans. The future may in fact hold a more advanced, more evolved race of creatures, the members of which possess an even greater share of reason, compassion, and (perhaps) artistic sensibility. But, here, now, humans carry the mantle. If (as Spencer believed) evolution "favors" traits that increase the length and comfort of an individual's life, then humans are evolution's poster-children. According to Spencer, key to humanity's preeminence is *conduct* – how we treat our neighbor. What we see when we turn from the animals to humans is a moral sensibility that places a check on selfish conduct. This in turn promotes "permanently peaceful" communities. Having secured for ourselves such communities, we can then turn our attention to other ways of increasing the length and quality of our lives.

It's at this point that Spencer made the decisive move. He reasoned that if a type of conduct is crucial for the maintenance of social harmony, why should we not identify that conduct as *good* – as *right*? Spencer could see no reason why:

> The conduct to which we apply the name good, is the relatively *more evolved* conduct; and bad is the name we apply to conduct which is relatively *less evolved* ... Moreover, just as we saw that evolution becomes the highest possible when the conduct simultaneously achieves the greatest totality of life in self, in offspring, and in fellow-men; so here we see that the conduct called good rises to the conduct conceived as best, when it fulfills all three classes at the same time. (2004/1879: 25)

So there it is. From the Great Chain of Being, through the Tree of Life, to morality itself. Darwin's ideas, argued Spencer, revealed not only how we came to be the creatures that we are, but how we *ought to be*. Morality runs parallel to the Tree of Life. Just as organisms reach ever skyward in complexity, sophistication, and compassion, humans (having achieved the highest level of evolution) *ought* to reach ever skyward, where life is longer and more pleasant. If evolution naturally directs organisms to extend and enhance their lives, surely it makes sense to call the conduct that does just this *good* or *right*. And surely it makes sense to call conduct that does the reverse *bad* or *wrong*.

6.2 Uprooting the Tree of Life

Where has this line of thinking gone wrong? It may be harder to tell than you think. After all, plenty of thinkers were (and some still are) seduced by these ideas.

As it happens, this line of thinking commits two fundamental mistakes. The first consists of a basic misunderstanding of the evolutionary process itself. Any practicing biologist should recognize it. The second mistake is a distinctly philosophical mistake. By this I mean that our *concepts* are confused. A closer inspection of the structure of our concepts reveals that we cannot move from one set of ideas to another in the way that Spencer thought. In the remaining part of this chapter I'll take up the biological mistake. In chapter 7 we'll turn to the philosophical mistake.

In chapter 1, I described Darwin's contribution to biology – evolution by natural selection – as a "very simple, very elegant idea." Perhaps I overstated the case. Elegant, to be sure. But given the tendency to misconstrue both the idea and its implications, I might wish to take back the "simple" part. What gets in the way here are the terms *adapt, select, function, purpose*. They imply agency; they imply a sort of guiding force, as if nature is being shaped according to some cosmic plan. Even Dawkins' (1986) efforts to clarify – he suggested "blind watchmaker" – mislead. Darwin himself was aware of how easily his ideas could be mishandled. After the publication of *Origin* he lamented to his friend Charles Lyell: "I must be a very bad explainer ... I suppose 'natural selection' was a bad term" (Desmond and Moore 1991: 492). To help smooth the way for his revolutionary ideas, Darwin began *Origin* by discussing how humans have domesticated and selected varieties of plants and animals for their own ends, a choice that now seems to have only added to the misunderstanding.

To fully understand the implications of Darwin's idea one has to embrace a kind of *mindlessness*. This is not some Buddhist imperative. It is what makes Darwin's idea truly breathtaking. For, according to the theory of Darwinian natural selection, the organisms that crowd the planet today (setting aside the domesticated ones) are here as a result of a mindless process, a process that requires absolutely no foresight. An early critic of Darwin hit the nail on the head: "Absolute Ignorance is the Artificer." (Of course this anonymous critic failed to understand the theory and so took this fact as evidence that Darwin was mistaken – if not utterly mad.) Natural selection is not selection at all insofar as this implies a selector. Natural selection is best thought of as a *sorting* process. But of course without a *sorter*.

If you will, think of the environment as a great sieve, through which only those individuals who happen to have useful traits pass. These traits come to be thought of as adaptations. But, at the outset, which traits ultimately become adaptations is quite unpredictable – for at least two reasons. First, the variations in form that may make a difference to an organism are the result of *random genetic mutation*, in combination with environmental input.[1] Second, variations that improve an organism's fitness in one environment may be disastrous in another (for example, an individual's thicker fur that might be helpful in colder climates might be harmful in warmer climates). The upshot is that mindlessness undermines any hope of anticipating how the course of evolution may play out. More to the point, the evolution of creatures that look like us – let alone think and feel and desire like us – could not have been anticipated. Humans are no more biologically inevitable than three-toed sloths, or cacti. "We are glorious accidents of an unpredictable process with no drive to complexity," wrote the late paleontologist Stephen Jay Gould (1996: 216).

Gould famously invited us to imagine "rewinding the tape of life" back some 530 million years, well before most familiar organisms had evolved. If we were to let the tape play out again, what are the chances, Gould asked, of *homo sapiens* once again appearing on the scene? Vanishingly small. The cast of characters populating the world, according to Gould, would have been wildly different. And we would have been nowhere to be seen. Think of matters this way. If you were to get into your car in New York City and drive for a month, taking random lefts and rights, random on-ramps and off-ramps, what are the chances that you would end up in, say, Dallas, Texas? Probably about as good as ending up in *any city whatsoever*. Of course, in our case, we did end up in Dallas (so to speak). But start all over, and where would you end up? It's anyone's guess. That's Gould's point.

But what does this point have to do with Spencer? Well, it appears that Spencer thought that humans were in fact the necessary endpoint of Darwinian natural selection. On Spencer's understanding of evolution, rewinding the tape of life and letting it play out again would eventually bring us back to the human race, in all its distinguished glory. After all, for Spencer, evolution *progresses* – from simpler to more complex forms. And we are the most complex. The truth of course is that evolution doesn't progress. Says Gould:

> The fact of evolutionary change through time doesn't represent progress as we know it. Progress is not inevitable. Much of evolution is downward in terms of morphological complexity, rather than upward. We're not marching toward some greater thing. The actual history of life is awfully damn curious in the light of our usual expectation that there's some predictable drive toward a generally increasing complexity in time. If that's so, life certainly took its time about it: five-sixths of the history of life is the story of single-celled creatures only. (1996: 52)

So much for the inevitable drive to complexity. We cannot look to evolution as a process whose very point is the development of complex organisms like us. To describe a trait as "more evolved," as Spencer does, implies *next to nothing* about its structure, its complexity, or whatever. From a biological standpoint, it's not even clear what that expression means. Are bacteria more evolved than humans? After all, some bacteria have been evolving for 4 *billion* years – 10,000 times longer than the period of modern human evolution! Is it the *rate* of evolution that makes a creature "more evolved"? If so, then viruses stand miles ahead of us. The proteins of the influenza virus, for example, evolve about a *million* times

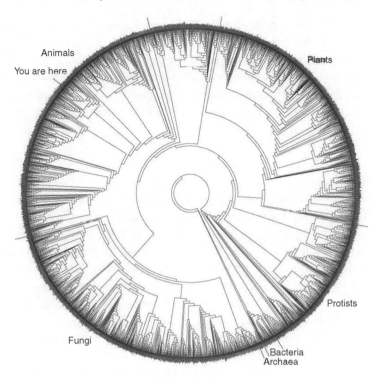

Figure 6.3   Simple Tree of Life   *From D. Sadava, H.C. Heller, G.H. Orians, W.K. Purves, and D.M. Hillis, Life: The Science of Biology, 8th edn. Sinauer Associates and W.H. Freeman, 2008.*

faster than human proteins. To paraphrase Richard Dawkins' observation that forms the epigraph to this chapter, humans (to take our favorite example) are not the *point* of evolution; we are merely its product. There is no point to evolution.

If we have to attach a special metaphor to the process of evolution, it shouldn't be "upward." It should probably be "outward" – as in the way a bush grows. Or, better yet, as a wheel. Biologists David M. Hillis, Derrick Zwickl, and Robin Gutell, of the University of Texas, developed a tree of life based on a small subunit of rRNA sequence taken from about 3,000 species throughout the tree of life (which, as it turns out, amounts to only about 0.18 percent of all known species). Figure 6.3 is a simplified version of the Hillis et al. illustration. According to this depiction of life, mammals, our favorite biological class of organisms, figure as just another class on the wheel – no "higher" or "lower" than ferns or flatworms. We just occupy a different spoke (or twig of the evolutionary bush). We have no *biological* reason to regard our species as anything particularly special. We're good at some things, to be sure. But we're also terrible at other things. And of course there's no guarantee that our rather pretentious presence on the planet will last. We showed up late to the party (billions of years after it started) and it's very likely we'll leave early (mess with the global thermostat too much in one direction and we're goners).

At any rate, all this spells trouble for Spencer. So long as Spencer's argument depends on the assumption that the human species represents a pinnacle in evolutionary design, it fails. We simply cannot assert that humans occupy a place higher up on the evolutionary scale for the simple reason that there is no such scale. In the biological realm, no such value orderings are possible. In our little niche we've done pretty well. But it would take an entire library to list all of the organisms that have done just as well or better than us in their little niches. What this means, then, is that although the kind of conduct that improved and extended our lives (kindness, charity, tolerance, fairness) may have worked for *us* in *this* niche, that's only a historical accident. In other niches, such conduct may not have improved and extended our lives. And in many other possible worlds, we do not even exist – and in many of those worlds, neither does such conduct.

But this is only the beginning of the problems with Spencer and what has come to be called Social Darwinism. For *even if* it turned out (miraculously) that biologists are wrong about the structure of Darwinian evolution, *even if* evolution did tend to progress in complexity and design, Spencer would be no better off. As we'll see in the next chapter, the move from biology to values is fraught with obstacles. More specifically, any attempt to justify how things *ought to be* on the basis of how things *are* is, according to philosophers, doomed.

Further Reading

Brockman, John (1995) *The Third Culture: Beyond the Scientific Revolution* (Touchstone).

Dennett, Daniel C. (1995) *Darwin's Dangerous Idea: Evolution and the Meanings of Life* (Simon & Schuster).

Gould, Stephen J. (1992) *The Panda's Thumb* (Norton).

Rachels, James (1990) *Created from Animals: The Moral Implications of Darwinism* (Oxford University Press).

Ruse, Michael (1986) *Taking Darwin Seriously: A Naturalistic Approach to Philosophy* (Oxford University Press).

Sadava, D., H.C. Heller, G.H. Orians, W.K. Purves, and D.M. Hillis (2008) *Life: The Science of Biology*, 8th edn. (Sinauer Associates and W.H. Freeman).

Spencer, Herbert (2004/1879) *The Principles of Ethics* (University Press of the Pacific).

Thomson, Paul (ed.) (1995) Issues in Evolutionary Ethics (SUNY Press).

7

Hume's Law

I have received, in a Manchester newspaper, a rather good squib, showing that I have proved "might is right."
(*Charles Darwin, Life and Letters*)

But as Authors do not commonly use this precaution, I shall presume to recommend it to the Readers; and am persuaded, that this small attention would subvert all the vulgar systems of morality.
(*David Hume, A Treatise on Human Nature*)

What if Spencer had been correct about Darwinian evolution? What if human beings really did represent the pinnacle of evolution by natural selection? What if evolution, truly possessed of a "far-seeing benevolence," did in fact weed out of the population those that failed to embody industriousness, prudence, temperance, kindness, generosity, and the rest? In this imaginary world, could we then say with confidence that morality had found its natural foundation? That we *ought* to strive to embody those traits? Or that our fundamental moral obligation is to promote social harmony since this is the direction in which evolution naturally leads? Could we at least say that we ought, generally speaking, to follow nature's lead?

The answer, in short, is *No*. Spencer's case is not improved by ignoring the fact that evolution does not tend toward morally "higher" beings. Those who want to use evolution (or, for that matter, any "natural" process) for the purposes of showing that, for example, "might is right" face a steep philosophical climb. For, to put it cryptically, you can't get from the *is* of biology to the *ought* of morality. There are two (related) reasons why. Both have to do with our concepts.

One reason goes back to the Scottish philosopher David Hume. According to Hume, no claim(s) about how things *are* logically entail how things *ought*

---

to be. A conceptual gap divides these two realms. Our aim in this chapter is to get clear on what Hume meant. The other reason derives from the work of G.E. Moore. According to Moore, talk of what is good (or right or wrong, etc.) cannot be reduced to talk of the natural world. For slightly different reasons, Moore, too, thought that a conceptual gap divides these two realms.

Together Hume and Moore are the Godzilla to Spencer's King Kong (or, maybe, the Alien to Spencer's Predator). To many contemporary philosophers, evolutionary ethics represents just this battle between Social Darwinists like Spencer and critics like Moore. The history of this debate suggests that when philosophers took a hard look at the hypotheses of the Social Darwinists, it is assumed that they put those hypotheses to bed, once and for all. Moore and Hume crushed the Social Darwinists. The truth of course is messier than that, as it always is. But there can be no doubt that the march toward a "biological ethics" hit sizable walls in Hume and Moore. In this chapter we'll begin with Hume and what some call – rather grandly – Hume's Law. In the next chapter we'll turn our attention to Moore.

7.1 Deductively Valid Arguments

Let's begin with a little refresher lesson in logic. Suppose it is true (as I think it is) that all humans are mortal. Suppose it is also true that Beatrice is human. On the basis of these two truths can we infer anything else about Beatrice? Of course. Beatrice is *mortal*. If all humans are mortal and Beatrice is human, *then it must be the case* that Beatrice is mortal. How could it not? (I defy you to imagine a world where all humans are mortal, Beatrice is human, *but* Beatrice is not mortal. You can't do it – at least without doing damage to yourself. So long as you are not changing the meaning of the words, Beatrice's morality is guaranteed. It's logically necessary.)

We can represent the argument I just offered this way:

1   All humans are mortal.
2   Beatrice is human.
3   Therefore, Beatrice is mortal.

This is what logicians call a *deductively valid argument*, meaning that if the premises (1 and 2) are true, then the conclusion (3) *must be* true. Asserting the premises but denying the conclusion is a contradiction. By and large, analytic philosophers aim to construct valid arguments. The reason is obvious: if philosophers can convince their readers that the premises are true, then the conclusion is guaranteed. It comes for free. Invalid arguments leave philosophers in a vulnerable position, for a critic can rightfully say: I can accept all your premises, but I need not accept your conclusion. For all anyone knows, your conclusion is false *even though* all your premises are true. If your goal is to construct airtight systems of philosophy, valid arguments are the gold standard. Anything less leaves the door open to skepticism.

So let's apply this lesson to morality. Suppose I give you the following argument:

1   Jones kills Beatrice.
2   Jones wanted to kill Beatrice.
3   Beatrice did not want to die.
4   Beatrice's death is harmful to Beatrice.
5   Beatrice's death is harmful to all who care about Beatrice.
6   Therefore, Jones *should not* have killed Beatrice.

This argument seems pretty convincing. We have someone who desires to kill another human being and does so. Surely Jones shouldn't have done what he did. But is the argument valid? That is, can we accept all the premises, but *deny* the conclusion?

Take a minute, fire up your imagination, and imagine a world in which it's *true* that Jones, who desires to kill Beatrice, kills Beatrice, but it's *false* that Jones shouldn't have done what he did. Can you think of a case?

In case your imagination is slow to fire up, here are three cases that show this argument is invalid: (a) Jones is trying to prevent Beatrice from killing him; (b) Beatrice is an enemy soldier on a battlefield, and she is threatening Jones' platoon; and (c) Jones, as a member of a state execution team, is executing Beatrice for raping and murdering five children. In all of these cases, the premises are assumed to be true, but it is at least arguable that the conclusion is false. At the very least, we can see that the conclusion is not *necessary*. That is, there's no contradiction in accepting the premises but denying the conclusion.

Suppose, however, we were to add to premises 1 to 6 above the following:

5a   Beatrice is innocent of any crime.
5b   Beatrice is not an enemy soldier.
5c   Beatrice is not attempting to kill Jones.

Would we be logically required to assert, then, that Jones *should not* have killed Beatrice? Well, what if, by some cosmic coincidence, the brake lines of Jones' car malfunction as Jones is approaching a busy intersection, an intersection that Beatrice, on foot, happens to be crossing? Despite his attempt to swerve, Jones nevertheless kills Beatrice. It would be highly dubious to say that Jones' action was wrong. And since events conspired against Jones, it would be beside the point to say that Jones shouldn't have done what he did.

Come on, you say. *Let's not get cute.* Take this case: Jones wants to kill Beatrice, and so he picks up a gun and shoots her point-blank in the head. End of story. Surely we wouldn't say, under *these* circumstances, that Jones should have done this, that his action was not immoral. Surely this is a valid argument if there ever was one.

We have to be careful here. It's one thing to ask whether or not Jones' action is wrong. Pretty clearly it is. But it's another thing altogether to ask whether the argument to that conclusion is deductively valid. To say it is would be to say that asserting the premises but denying the conclusion amounts to a *contradiction*. It's not enough to produce premises that make the conclusion highly likely. That's not a valid argument. Consider this argument as an example:

1 The chances that this lottery ticket will win tomorrow's drawing are 1 in 43,887,609,870.
2 This is a non-fraudulent ticket.
3 Therefore, this ticket will *not win* tomorrow's drawing.

Would it be a contradiction to accept the premises, but deny the conclusion? Not at all. As the holder of this ticket, you might be accused of being a hopeless optimist if you doubted the conclusion, but you aren't *contradicting* yourself. It's of course very, very, *very* unlikely that your ticket will win, but it's not guaranteed to lose. After all, if your ticket does win, what do we say? That the universe suddenly contradicted itself? The lesson here is that, in determining whether an argument is valid, it must be the case that the premises make the conclusion *necessary*, that there is no possibility whatsoever of the premises being true but the conclusion false.

Returning to our revised example involving Jones, we can see that accepting the premises but denying the conclusion is not a contradiction, even though it might seem highly unlikely that Jones' action is *not* wrong.

It's not like asserting that all humans are mortal and Beatrice is human but *denying* that Beatrice is mortal. That's not merely unlikely, that's impossible! In Jones' case, we cannot be guaranteed that some highly remote possibility may undermine the conclusion. But even setting aside exotic cases, we must not confuse asserting a contradiction and doubting what seems morally obvious. We might accuse someone who doubts the wrongness of Jones' action of being morally obtuse or excessively cautious. But that's not the same as accusing them of making a logical error: someone who denied Beatrice's mortality (despite accepting the facts that humans are mortal and Beatrice is human) would be making a logical error.

To get as much traction on this issue as possible, step back and think about what you are saying when you say: "Jones should *A*." (Replace *A* with an activity of your choice: *eat chocolate cake, play badminton, keep his promise.*) In saying that Jones should *A* you recognize, at least implicitly, that this is entirely compatible with Jones *not A*-ing – whether it be in the past or now. In fact, saying that Jones should *A* is compatible with Jones never ever *A*-ing – as long as Jones lives. But you could still stick by your judgment. You might still insist that Jones should *A*. The reason is that utterances like "Jones should *A*" express a very particular kind of relation between, in this case, Jones and *A*-ing: it's a *recommendation* or a *command*. It's already accepted that this is not the way things are now (after all, if Jones kept his promises, there would be no need to insist that Jones keep his promises, right?). But what does this mean? It's means that saying how things *are*, as a matter of fact, is fundamentally different from saying how things *should* be. But if this is true, then is it any wonder that saying only how things are does not logically entail how things should be? Extending this idea further, it seems we could know everything about how the world is, but still not know how the world ought to be. Knowing how things ought to be requires more than just a grasp of (true) descriptions; it requires a grasp of *prescriptions*.[1]

7.2 You Can't Get Out What You Don't Put In

So does all this mean that there can't be deductively valid moral arguments? It might seem like that's the conclusion to draw from all this. But it's not. As I'll show presently, constructing deductively valid arguments is actually quite simple. In one sense, the solution was there all along. Consider:

1   No one *should* ever deliberately kill another innocent human being.
2   Beatrice is an innocent human being.
3   Therefore, no one *should* deliberately kill Beatrice.

Take a minute to consider the premises. Admittedly, premise (1) is a pretty blunt instrument. It doesn't, for example, discriminate between soldiers and civilians. But, for the sake of the argument, imagine that it's true. And imagine that Beatrice is in fact innocent. Can you imagine a case in which (1) and (2) are true, but the conclusion is *false*? After a moment's reflection, you should see that that's impossible. So long as you accept the premises (and don't change the meaning of the words), it should be clear that the premises make the conclusion *necessary*.

How did we pull this off? What was missing in our earlier moral arguments that prevented us from deriving a logically necessary conclusion? The answer is clear: in our earlier attempts, none of the premises asserted what *should* be the case; they merely asserted what *is* the case. And that's the problem. Arguments that attempt to infer a "should" from purely "is" premises are invariably invalid. An argument that attempts to derive a "should" conclusion must contain at least one "should" premise. If you don't put one in, you can't get one out. As we saw above, there appears to be a fundamental gap separating asserting what *is* the case from asserting what *should be* the case. And this gap implies that we cannot derive claims about what should be the case (e.g., Jones *should not* kill Beatrice) from claims *only* about what *is* the case (e.g., Beatrice's death would be harmful to Beatrice). To make such derivations, we need to add at least one claim about what should be the case ("No one should ever kill humans").

Philosophers have come to describe this as the fact/value distinction. The world, apparently, contains facts and values – and one is not reducible to the other. One way of expressing a value is a prescription, a statement about what should or ought to be the case. This, according to the fact/value distinction, is distinct from expressing a fact, a statement about how things, as a matter of fact, are.

7.3 "Of the Last Consequence"

What does this have to do with the philosopher David Hume? (And what does this have to do with evolution? We'll get to evolution in the next section.) Well, we have Hume to thank for first noting this distinction between fact and value. In one of the great philosophical tracts of Western philosophy, *A Treatise on Human Nature*, Hume observes:

> In every system of morality, which I have hitherto met with, I have always remark'd, that the author proceeds for some time in the ordinary ways of reasoning, and establishes the being of a God, or makes observations concerning human affairs; when all of a sudden I am surpriz'd to find, that instead of the usual copulations of propositions, is, and is not, I meet with no proposition that is not connected with an ought, or an ought not. This change is imperceptible; but is however, of the last consequence. For as this ought, or ought not, expresses some new relation or affirmation, 'tis necessary that it shou'd be observ'd and explain'd; and at the same time that a reason should be given; for what seems altogether inconceivable, how this new relation can be a deduction from others, which are entirely different from it. (Hume 2009/ 1882: part 1, §1)

In our terms, Hume recognized that statements of fact "are entirely different from" statements of value. And he was the first to note the illicit move from is-statements (or "copulations of propositions, is and is not") to ought-statements. Though imperceptible, the move is "of the last consequence," which is to say: *very important.*

If true, "Hume's Law" would place a critical constraint on any future moral theorizing: to establish a claim about what you ought morally to do, you have to presuppose at least one *other* claim about what ought morally to be done. And to defend *that* claim, you have to presuppose *another* claim about what ought morally to be done. And so on. One implication of this seems to be that moral theorizing (to the extent that theorizing is possible) is going to be forever autonomous, that is to say, a field of study whose laws and connections must, in the end, remain within the sphere of value. This should immediately suggest consequences for Social Darwinism.

7.4 Blocking the Move from Might to Right

Darwin expressed amusement at the idea that his theory entailed that "might is right." It's not clear whether Darwin had Hume in mind here, but Darwin had certainly read Hume and was influenced by Hume's writings.[2] In any case, Darwin was echoing in his amusement the observation Hume had made a century before: describing how things are is not the same as saying how things *ought to be.* But there can be no doubt that others missed the distinction. Consider one of Spencer's more pointed critiques of the way the state intervenes on behalf of the less fortunate. And note his assumption about the direction of "the natural order of things":

> Blind to the fact that under the natural order of things, society is constantly excreting its unhealthy, imbecile, slow, vacillating, faithless members, these unthinking, though well-meaning, men advocate an interference which not only stops the purifying process but even increases the vitiation – absolutely encourages the multiplication of the reckless and incompetent by offering them an unfailing provision, and *discourages* the multiplication of the competent and provident by heightening the prospective difficulty of maintaining a family. (Spencer 1851: 151)

According to Spencer, those who would advocate stepping in to assist the "incompetent" are disrupting the "purifying process" that is natural selection. To achieve its highest state, its most evolved form, the human race ought to let natural selection follow its course, as merciless as it may seem. Nature knows best. This is the core of Social Darwinism. That, on this view, is how nature works – and it's a good thing. We saw in the last chapter, that nature does not work in that way. In many "near-possible worlds" natural selection does not purify (in the sense that Spencer meant); it contaminates. It produces creatures that are unfailingly cruel and unfaithful and lazy. English gentlemen are not at all the inevitable product of evolutionary forces.

But even if we set this aside, even if Spencer got that part right, he fell afoul of Hume's Law when he tried to infer, from those premises alone, that that's how things ought to be. Suppose it's true that natural selection tends, as a matter of fact, to produce humans who are fair and industrious. Suppose natural selection, left to its own devices, tends to eliminate those who do not show generosity or kindness. Suppose natural selection works toward a species that realizes, as far as possible, social harmony. Suppose all this is true. Suppose, that is, that that is how things are and how things have been. All of our efforts in this chapter have been aimed at *blocking* the move from these premises (alone) to: we *ought* to be fair and honest, generous and kind; we *ought* to promote social harmony. So long as the Social Darwinist does not include among the premises an ought-claim (or normative claim), none of these ought-claims follows. According to Hume, "a reason should be given ... how this new relation can be a deduction from the others." With no such reason offered, the Social Darwinist does not close the gap.

Of course, if the Social Darwinist does include a premise about how we ought to promote those qualities that lead to social harmony, then the deduction might go through. But in this case, it's not clear what role Darwin's ideas play in the Social Darwinist's argument. After all, the conclusion would follow even if we dropped all the business about natural selection designing creatures to be generous and the like.

To be clear, this is as true for the traits we value (like fairness and honesty) as for the traits we do not value (like indifference to suffering). Critics of Social Darwinism often point to the morally repugnant traits it endorsed. Spencer's remarks above promote a pretty uncaring attitude toward the less fortunate. This is tough love – just without the love. It's sacrificing the disenfranchised for the perfection of the human race. But after studying Hume's criticism, we can see that the problem with Social Darwinism goes deeper than this. It's not that Social Darwinism endorses traits we don't like; it's *how* Social Darwinism *arrives* at them. The path is corrupt. But if the path is corrupted for traits we don't like, the same will be true for traits that we do like. So even we could show that nature in fact tends toward virtues like justice and empathy, we could not use this fact alone to show that these are the virtues we ought to adopt.

7.5 Darwinism and Preserving the Human Species

Herbert Spencer was perhaps the first Darwinian guilty of violating Hume's Law (or running into Hume's *Guillotine*, to borrow Max Black's famous phrase). But Spencer was hardly the last. In the Introduction to this book I began our discussion by citing E.O. Wilson's suggestion that ethics be "biologicized." Part of what Wilson had in mind was the project we outlined in part I: explaining how natural selection gave rise to the human moral sense. But Wilson was not content to leave matters there. This project should, according to Wilson, lead the way to a "biology of ethics, which will make possible the selection of a more deeply understood and enduring code of moral values" (1978: 196). And what sorts of values should appear in this more enduring code? Wilson offers the following: "In the beginning the new ethicists will want to ponder the cardinal value of the survival of human genes in the form of a common pool over generations." The philosopher Philip Kitcher interprets this as the fundamental ethical principle: "Human beings should do whatever may be required to ensure the survival of a common gene pool for *Homo sapiens*" (1985: 445).

If this is the principle Wilson intends to defend, the obvious next question is: What justifies this principle? That is, what are the premises that supposedly lead to this principle? It's fairly clear from looking at Wilson's discussion that the premises are purely biological, purely descriptive. For example, Wilson notes with alarm that few "persons realize the true consequences of the dissolving action of sexual reproduction and the corresponding unimportance of 'lines' of descent." But nowhere among the premises Wilson uses to justify his fundamental ethical principle is there a value statement – nothing about what we *should* do. If this in fact is the structure of Wilson's argument, then it is no better than Spencer's, even though it aims at a different (and perhaps laudatory) conclusion. The lesson is the same: we cannot derive a claim about what we ought to do, morally speaking, simply from claims describing facts about the evolutionary process.

7.6 Conclusion

I'm often struck by how many students believe that we have a moral obligation to act in ways that preserve the human species. And this isn't the simple-minded "species-ism" one might expect. It takes into account our dependence on the environment and encourages the preservation of endangered species. When I ask these students why they believe we have such a moral duty, they say something to the effect that that's how evolution works. That is how nature intends things. And we should respect that. Our discussion should make it clear why this line of thinking is mistaken. It may be that we *do* have a moral obligation to preserve the human species (at what cost, who knows?), but such an obligation cannot be derived from purely biological premises. It might be that we should preserve the human species because in doing so we promote human happiness and, morally speaking, it's ultimately human happiness that we should promote. Or maybe humans are best equipped to reduce suffering (whomever experiences it) and, morally speaking, it's ultimately suffering that should be reduced. In any event, to reach the desired conclusion about preserving the human species, Hume's Law requires the addition of a value-statement. Moving from what is the case to what ought to be the case is simply a conceptual mistake. It's the philosophical equivalent of pulling the rabbit out of the empty hat. Either we believe in magic or we reject the move as a clever deception. Hume recognized the deception, even if latter-day Darwinians fail to. In the next chapter, we consider a closely related point: any attempt to reduce moral claims to naturalistic claims commits what has come to be called the Naturalistic Fallacy. Though this fallacy is motivated by slightly different considerations, its implication for Social Darwinism is the same: no claims about what we ought, morally speaking, to do can ever be derived from biology alone. Unlike Hume's Law, however, the Naturalistic Fallacy has lost some of its force since G.E. Moore first introduced it. In chapter 9 we'll gauge the extent to which Hume's Law and the Naturalistic Fallacy succeed in demolishing any hopes of connecting ethics to biology. Some philosophers think that although the more flat-footed project of Social Darwinism does not survive Hume's and Moore's attacks, a more supple and modest project might. We'll look at what this might mean in chapter 9.

Further Reading

Hume, David (2009/1882) *A Treatise on Human Nature* (General Books LLC).
Kitcher, Philip (1985) *Vaulting Ambition: Sociobiology and the Quest for Human Nature* (MIT Press).
Rachels, James (1990) *Created from Animals: The Moral Implications of Darwinism* (Oxford University Press).
Spencer, Herbert (2004/1879) *The Principles of Ethics* (University Press of the Pacific).
Thomson, Paul (ed.) (1995) *Issues in Evolutionary Ethics* (SUNY Press).
Wilson, E.O. (1978) *On Human Nature* (Harvard University Press).

8

Moore's Naturalistic Fallacy

If I am asked, "What is good?" my answer is that good is good, and that is the end of the matter.

(G.E. Moore, *Principia Ethica*)

I noted in chapter 7 that one of the implications of Hume's Law was the *autonomy* of moral theory. If no moral conclusion (i.e., a claim about what *ought* to be the case) follows deductively from purely descriptive claims (i.e., claims about what *is* the case), then every moral claim must rest on some other moral claim – assuming it is not self-supporting. This seems to imply that moral theory must always look "within itself" for justification. Hume had his own ways of spelling this out (and it wasn't good news for those hoping to ground a "science of morals"). In the twentieth century G.E. Moore developed a different set of arguments designed to reveal explicitly why morality was autonomous. And in Moore's sights was Herbert Spencer. Moore left little doubt as to what his opinion of the Social Darwinist project was. He accepted Darwin's ideas insofar as they applied to fields *outside* moral theory, but he strongly rejected any effort to use Darwin's ideas to justify a system of morality. In fact, Moore's argument went further. If successful, the argument promised to show that no attempt to identify moral properties with naturalistic properties *could possibly* succeed. The gap between (natural) facts and values is not merely hard to bridge; it's unbridgeable.

Of course an argument that purports to establish a claim like that immediately arouses philosophers' suspicions, and in the next chapter we'll consider the possibility that maybe Moore bit off more than he could chew. In the meantime, we'll take apart Moore's argument to see how it works. To get the ball rolling, I'm going to repeat the strategy I employed in the previous chapter: I'm going to start with an analogy.

An Introduction to Evolutionary Ethics, by Scott M. James. © 2011 Scott M. James

8.1 The Open Question Test

Let's take an old philosophical chestnut: the concept of *bachelor*. By definition, bachelors are unmarried, marriageable males. Once you grasp the concept of bachelor, you know that if Smith is a bachelor, then Smith is (among other things) unmarried. That's part of what it *means* to be a bachelor. Thus, for someone who truly understands what it means to be a bachelor, it would be nonsensical to ask: Even though Smith is a bachelor, is he unmarried?[1] *Huh?* To establish that Smith is a bachelor is to *close* any question of Smith's marital status. After all, given that the concept of *bachelor* contains in part the concept of *unmarried*, the question amounts to little more than this: Even though Smith is unmarried, is he unmarried? Someone who asks this question is experiencing the cortical equivalent of a hard-drive crash. (Or he's trying to make a philosophical point.)

This little excursion into bachelorhood should reveal then the following lesson. (I'll start with a kind of formal definition.) If A is truly defined in terms of A's having some property P, then we cannot intelligibly ask of something X: "X is A, but does it have P?" In other words, if A just *means* (in part) having P, then it should *not* be an open question whether something that is A has P. Since bachelor is defined in terms of unmarried (marriageable) male, assuming we grasp the concept of bachelor, we cannot intelligibly ask "Is some bachelor unmarried?" That's not an open question.

So the Open Question Test, as we might call it, is a way to determine whether or not a concept is truly defined in more basic terms. That is, if you want to know whether or not A is just another way of saying having property P, then perform the Open Question Test. So, for example, X is a triangle, but does it have three sides? Since this is not an open question, we can feel confident that triangle is truly defined (in part) by having three sides. Three-sidedness is, if you will, a *necessary* property of triangles: you can't be a triangle and *not* have three sides. Y is a horse, but is Y a mammal? Again, not an open question. Thus we can say that being a horse is truly defined (in part) in terms of being a mammal. Being a mammal is a necessary property of being a horse.

How about this one? Z is a fruit, but is Z sweet? Unlike the previous examples, this question is open. It's a perfectly intelligible question. We can perfectly well imagine biting into a piece of fruit but it's not being sweet (imagine biting into a green tomato). Thus we can conclude that sweetness is not a necessary property of being a fruit. The Open Question Test, therefore, apparently allows us to understand how our concepts fit together, how some are built into others. Furthermore, it seems to give us an insight into the *very nature* of a given concept. You want to know what justice is? Or mind? Or causality? Propose a property and ask whether something that has that property really deserves to be called just. Or a mind, or whatever.

If this makes sense to you, then you're 90 percent of the way toward understanding Moore's attack on naturalist conceptions of ethics – which would include, most prominently, Social Darwinism. For at the heart of Moore's attack is this Open Question Test.

8.2 Failing the Open Question Test: Desiring to Desire

Moore's official position, noted above, is that "good is good, and that is the end of the matter." If you didn't know that Moore was a philosopher (in very good standing), you might think that these were the words of an impatient parent lecturing his child. But Moore believed that he had earned the right to say this. Moore believed that *good* (as in goodness) was a "simple notion," meaning that it cannot be reduced or broken down into simpler components. And he believed this because, with respect to goodness, no property could pass the Open Question Test. If no property can pass the Open Question Test, such that we cannot break down goodness into simpler parts, well, then, it appears that "good is good." And that's that.

Here's Moore: "whatever definition may be offered, it may always, be asked, with significance, of the complex so defined, whether it is itself good" (1903: 15). Moore begins with a conception of good popular at the time: that which we desire to desire. On this conception, goodness is a kind of *second-order* property. We desire all kinds of things, but this isn't enough to deserve the label "good." Being good is not identical to being merely desirable. The reason is that some of the things we desire, we don't desire to desire. Take cocaine or sleeping all day or a sixth donut. We may have strong desires for such things. But we probably also wish that we didn't have those desires. That is, we don't desire to desire a sixth donut. We wish such a desire would leave us be. On the other hand, those things that, on reflection, we *would* desire to desire seem worthy of being called good. At least this was the view of some philosophers around the turn of the last century. The concept of good is nothing more than the concept of that which we desire to desire.

So does this conception of good pass the Open Question Test? Moore thinks the answer is obvious:

> if we carry the investigation further, and ask ourselves "Is it good to desire to desire A?" it is apparent, on a little reflection, that this question is itself as intelligible, as the original question, "Is A good?" – that we are, in fact, now asking for exactly the same information about the desire to desire A, for which we formerly asked with regard to A itself. (1903: 16)

In other words, it is an open question whether it is good that I desire to desire A. We can intelligibly wonder whether such a desiring is good. Indeed, we can come up with a case that confirms our doubts. Perhaps by dint of some gross misinformation, Debra believes that smoking actually *improves* her health. So not only does she desire this cigarette, she *desires to desire* this cigarette since she believes it will improve her health. But here we have a case in which having the property desiring to desire A is not good. According to Moore, the fact that we can pull these two notions apart shows "that we have two different notions before our mind." Thus, goodness is *not* that which we desire to desire.

8.3 Failing the Open Question Test: Spencer

Does the Social Darwinist proposal fare any better? Let's look back at one of Spencer's suggestions: "The conduct to which we apply the name good, is the relatively *more evolved* conduct; and bad is the name we apply to conduct which is relatively *less evolved*" (2004/1879: 25, emphasis in original). The Open Question Test, then, would have us ask: A is more evolved than B, but is A *good*? As we saw in chapter 7, it's not at all obvious what "A is more evolved than B" is supposed to mean. But Spencer has something particular in mind: "Just as we saw that evolution becomes the highest possible when the conduct simultaneously achieves *the greatest totality of life in self*, in *offspring*, and in *fellow-men*; so here we see that the conduct called good rises to the conduct conceived as best, when it fulfills all three classes at the same time" (2004/1879: 25–6). One way to paraphrase this might be: good is that which increases the overall quantity and quality of the human species.

So now we ask: An action X increases the overall quantity and quality of the human species, but is X *good*? Can we intelligibly ask this question? Is it an open question? Or, is this question like asking: Adam is a bachelor, but is he unmarried? It seems fairly clear that it *is* an open question. It does not seem confused. Indeed, like we did above, we can even come up with a case that seems to confirm our doubts. Suppose that there is no other way to test a new AIDS vaccine apart from exposing healthy humans to the deadly syndrome. But suppose that no one consents to being exposed to the syndrome. Imagine then that the government secretly rounds up homeless individuals in major cities and successfully performs the necessary experiments on them. An effective AIDS vaccine is thus produced. To be sure, those few homeless individuals that survive the experiments are exterminated to prevent public backlash.

So I ask you, was the decision to use those homeless people in that way *good*? (Before you answer, put yourself in the shoes of those homeless individuals for just a minute.) If you're like me, the answer seems plainly *No*. But even if you're wrestling with an answer, this merely confirms Moore's point: it's an *open* question! That's all Moore needs to do to undermine Spencer's proposal.

8.4 Failing the Open Question Test: Wilson

Things don't look any better for E.O. Wilson's proposal, the one we considered in the last chapter: "Human beings should do whatever may be required to ensure the survival of a common gene pool for *Homo sapiens*." An action Y ensures the survival of a common gene pool for *Homo sapiens*, but is Y good? Again, this question seems perfectly intelligible. It seems reasonable for us to want to hear some cases in order to determine whether or not this definition stands, but that's just to admit that the goodness of such hypothetical cases is an open question.

The philosopher Philip Kitcher (1985) has us imagine a case in which, according to unimpeachable scientific evidence, our species will become extinct in twenty generations unless we reduce the world's population by 90 percent. Since almost no one volunteers to end her life for the sake of preserving the human species, would it be good to kill off 90 percent of the population against their will? At the risk of gross understatement, let me just say: the goodness of that proposal is *not obvious*. It is (you'll agree) a very open question.

8.5 Conclusion

To be clear, we're not denying that acting in ways that support the human species is usually good. Nor are we denying that acting in ways that increase both the quantity and quality of human life is usually good. We can apply the concept of good to many different activities. These are good. Moore's point is more subtle. According to Moore, whenever the phrase "is good" figures in a sentence, it is being used to *describe* something as having a certain property, never to *identify* goodness with something more basic. As philosophers will say, the "is" is the "is" of *predication*, not identity, where predicates (is green, is stinky, is over five feet tall) attach to subjects. This point is not so complicated as it sounds.

When I say that carrot cake is good, I'm saying that the cake has a certain property – in this case, goodness. What I am *not* doing (and what no one would suspect me of doing) is *identifying* goodness with carrot cake – that is, asserting that to be good is just to be carrot cake. (That would be the "is" of identity, as in: Spiderman is Peter Parker. They're one and the same dude.) This would have the absurd result that sex has the property of being carrot cake and reading a stimulating book has the property of being carrot cake and so on. The difference is the difference between "Spiderman is Peter Parker" (*identity*) and "Spiderman is agile" (*predication*). On Moore's picture, "is good" is always being used in the latter way.

On the basis of the Open Question Test, Moore concludes that any proposition that asserts that such-and-such is good must be understood as ascribing to such-and-such the property of being good – not identifying goodness with some more basic thing. To think otherwise is to commit the Naturalistic Fallacy. Says Moore: "Far too many philosophers have thought that when they named these other properties they were actually defining good; that these properties, in fact, were simply not 'other,' but absolutely and entirely the same with goodness" (1903: 62). They're mistaken. Social Darwinism, for all its revolutionary aspirations, falls into the same trap as any moral view that proposes to reduce goodness or rightness to something simpler. Not gonna happen, says Moore. Good is good, and "that is the end of the matter."

Further Reading

Kitcher, Philip (1985) Vaulting Ambition: Sociobiology and the Quest for Human Nature (MIT Press).

Moore, G.E. (1903) Principia Ethica (Cambridge University Press).

Stratton-Lake, Phillip (2003) Ethical Intuitionism: Re-Evaluations (Oxford University Press).

Warnock, Mary (1966) Ethics Since 1900 (Oxford University Press).

9

Rethinking Moore and Hume

Fans of horror films have come to expect that signs of a villain's demise are almost always premature. It's always a bad sign when the hero drops his weapon after battle and slumps to the ground in exhaustion, his back to the motionless villain. We know it's not over. So long as there's some chance (remote as it may be) that the villain is not dead, we don't move from our seats. And the next shot is invariably a hand twitching or an eye fluttering open. Here we go again . . .

Well, you guessed it: there's life left in Social Darwinism. The reason is not so much that the view has undergone a makeover, but that the attacks on the view have been questioned. In the absence of fatal counter-arguments, we have to acknowledge that there's some chance (remote as it may be) that the view is not dead. So, yes, you're stuck in your seat for at least little while longer. In this chapter, we'll raise questions about Moore's Open Question Test and reconsider Hume's Law. Will these attacks-on-the-attacks put Social Darwinism back on a solid footing? Probably not. But intellectual honesty requires us to be forthcoming about the limitations of the objections to Social Darwinism. Let me start with Moore.

9.1 Some Preliminary Doubts about the Open Question Test

How good is the Open Question Test? On the one hand, it seemed to deliver the right verdict when it came to bachelors and triangles and fruit. "An object is a triangle, but does it have three sides?" is not an open question.

An Introduction to Evolutionary Ethics, by Scott M. James. © 2011 Scott M. James

We're therefore supposed to conclude that triangles are identical with three-sided objects. *Check.* "An object is a piece of fruit, but is it sweet?" *is* an open question. We're therefore supposed to conclude that pieces of fruit are not identical with sweet things. Again, *check.* So far so good. But let's move outside our comfort zone a bit.

Imagine how a member of a primitive tribe in Africa might conduct the Open Question Test. Rumors have circulated within the tribe that water is really this more basic group of substances called H_2O. Having never seen this more basic group of substances, this tribesperson is dubious, but she's willing to pursue the matter in the interest of truth. She's familiar with Moore's Open Question Test (don't ask how) and knows that this test can reveal important identities in nature. So she collects a cup of water and asks herself this question: "This is water, but is it H_2O?" For all she knows, water might be H_2O, but her task is simpler than this. All she has to do is determine whether or not this question is *open*. That is, could there be any doubt about this substance's constituents?

In other words, is the question about water like this one: "Grace is my sister, but is she female?" Or is it like this one: "This is fruit, but is it sweet?" Well, this is easy. Her question about water seems like the latter. It's most definitely an open question. This is a serious problem for the Open Question Test. Here's why.

If Moore is right, then this tribesperson has determined that water is not in fact H_2O. And she's justified in believing that these two substances are not identical. But, wait, they *are* identical! The tribesperson is just mistaken. The Open Question Test has delivered the *wrong* answer. Less exotic examples can work just as well. Try this one.

Suppose that I tell you that Jay-Z is really just Sean Carter. To determine whether or not I'm speaking the truth, you run the Open Question Test. You pull up an image of Jay-Z (just to be sure) and ask: "This is Jay-Z, but is he Sean Carter?" Well, that may well seem like an open question to you. You could quite easily imagine that that person (Jay-Z) is *not* Sean Carter. So, on the basis of the Open Question Test, you are allowed to conclude that Jay-Z is not one and the same person as Sean Carter. But I'm here to tell you: Jay-Z *is* Sean Carter. Those are two names for the same guy. The point, however, is that the Open Question Test leads us in the wrong direction, by allowing us to conclude that the two are not identical. All this raises the question: if the Open Question Test does not test for identities, what does it test for? After all, there seem to be at least a handful of cases it gets *right*.

9.2 What Things Mean vs. What Things Are

Philosophers have diagnosed the above situation in a variety of ways, but at the heart of the matter seems to be a failure to distinguish between the relationship that exists between words and the relationship that exists between – well, things. Take any two terms (or words), A and B. One thing we can do is ask about their *semantic* relationship, that is, the relationship between what A means and what B means. Take "bachelor" and "unmarried." As we all know, part of what it means to be a bachelor is to be unmarried. Your understanding of bachelorhood is built out of simpler conceptual components. So here we could say (if, that is, we wanted to in press our friends at a party) that the concept of bachelor is *semantically reducible* to unmarried (marriageable) male. Being a bachelor is *nothing more than* being an unmarried (marriageable) male. They're identical. Examples like this are tempting. They tempt us into believing that A cannot be identical to B unless there is an appropriate *meaning* relationship that connects the two. But this is not the only kind of relationship that exists between terms A and B.

We can also ask after their *ontological* relationship. That is, we can ask whether A is the same as B as a matter of *mind-independent existence*. This latter notion is just a philosopher's way of identifying things as they are, independently of the way we think about them. For example, this book's existence does not depend on your thinking it exists or desiring that it exists or caring that it exists. Even if all sentient life were suddenly to end at this moment, this book would not suddenly disappear. Why? Because its existence is part of what we call a mind-independent existence. (Santa Claus, alas, is *not* part of this mind-independent existence. If everyone stopped thinking about him, Santa Claus would not exist.) As an example of ontological relationships, take "water" and "H_2O." The former is ontologically reducible to the latter. Thanks to the work of nineteenth-century chemists, we know that water is nothing other than H_2O. They're identical.

But here's the really important point. Just because an ontological relationship (like identity) holds for two terms (like water and H_2O) does not entail that a semantic relationship holds between those two terms. Arguably, this is what Moore failed to note. Just because water *is* (as a matter of fact) H_2O does not entail that water *means* H_2O. Clearly it does not. If it did, then we'd have to say that young children and primitive tribes (not to mention *everyone* prior to the discovery of the atomic constituents of water) do not know what "water" means. But that's absurd. Surely they grasp the concept (wet, clear, potable, liquid, etc.) What they fail to understand is what water *really is*. But failing to understand that does not disqualify them from understanding the word. Let me state the general point as clearly as I can: A can be identical to B even though A does not *mean* in part B – even though, that is, A is not semantically reducible to B.[1]

9.3 Implications for Social Darwinism

The implications for Social Darwinism should be pretty obvious. Insofar as Social Darwinism attempts to establish a *semantic* relationship between, say, conduct that promotes social harmony and conduct that is morally good, the attempt fails. It's at least arguable that the latter does not *mean* the former. By claiming that "the conduct to which we apply the *name* good" (emphasis added) is "the relatively *more evolved* conduct" (2004/1879: 25), Spencer seems to open himself to this interpretation. He seems to be asserting a kind of semantic relationship between the two. But if Social Darwinism is being put forward as a claim about the *ontological* relationship between morally good conduct and evolution, then the view escapes Moore's criticism. That is, if it's being claimed that "morally good conduct" *is*, as a matter of mind-independent existence, "more evolved conduct," then the view is not obviously mistaken. For in this case, it's a claim about what morally good conduct is, not a claim about what the concept "morally good conduct" *means*.

Now how would a Social Darwinist go about establishing this claim? Great question. At this point, we have no reason to believe that the Social Darwinist can succeed here. Insofar as our deeply held moral commitments provide data that a moral theory must explain, Social Darwinism has an uphill climb. For as we saw in the last chapter, some "more evolved" conduct or conduct that's good for the overall species does not comport with our deeply held moral commitments (e.g., killing off 90 percent of the population without their consent). Until Social Darwinism can convince us to give up these commitments, the view is stalled. But if our criticism of the Open Question Test is on track, then neither is the view fatally flawed.

9.4 Forays across the Is/Ought Gap: Searle

The philosopher John Searle believes (*pace* Hume) that we *can* span the Is/ Ought Gap. He believes that we can construct a deductively valid argument whose premises describe only how things *are*, but whose conclusion dictates how things *ought to be*. Here's his argument (1964):

1   Jones uttered the words, "I hereby promise to pay you, Smith, five dollars."
2   Jones promised to pay Smith five dollars.
3   Jones placed himself under (undertook) an obligation to pay Smith five dollars.
4   Jones is under an obligation to pay Smith five dollars.
5   Therefore, Jones ought to pay Smith five dollars.

According to Searle, the premises are purely factual. The conclusion, however, is moral. Apparently, how things are in this case deductively entail how things ought to be. How does Searle pull off this (apparent) deduction? He relies on the institution of promise-making. For creatures like us, uttering the words "I promise" is sufficient to place one under a certain kind of obligation, the obligation to do what one promises. But to be under an obligation to do what one promises entails that one *ought* to do what one promises. Because Hume overlooked the existence of "normative in-stitutions" (that is, institutions that have rules somehow built into them), he imagined an unbridgeable gap between fact and value. If Searle is right, Hume suffered from a failure of imagination.

But is Searle right? Have we really deduced a moral conclusion from purely descriptive premises? Things are actually more complicated than they appear. The philosopher J.L. Mackie (1977) argues that the introduc-tion of institutions like promise-making poses a dilemma for Searle. On the one hand, we can evaluate the institution of promise-making from *outside* the institution, as an alien might do. From such a perspective, the alien would need to be told of the following rule:

1a If one utters the words "I promise that I will *x*" from *within* the institution, one has *within* the institution promised to *x*.

What the alien thus learns is that this rule holds within the institution. It's like being told that when you're playing chess, a pawn can be promoted to queen when it reaches the opposite side of the board. Similar rules will need to be explained to the alien in order for him to deduce (4) from (2) – and (5) from (4). According to Mackie, then, when the alien concludes that Jones ought to pay Smith five dollars, he has *not* in fact deduced a moral claim from purely factual claims. Instead, what he has deduced is yet another factual claim. It's a *description* of what Jones ought to do *within that institution*, according to the rules that have been explained to him. What doesn't follow is the claim that Jones ought pay Smith *full stop*. When I say that my pawn ought to be promoted to a queen because it's reached the opposite side of the board, what I've said is actually shorthand for saying that my pawn ought to be promoted according to the rules that are part of the institution of chess.

On the other hand, if we were to evaluate the argument from *within* the institution, then reaching the conclusion will require accepting (as premises) certain "ought" statements. For example, "One ought to conclude, on the basis of uttering the words 'I promise to *x*,' that one has promised to *x*." In effect, one is smuggling in an inference rule. And rules, by their nature, tell us what we *ought* to do. If this is right, then the argument indeed derives an "ought" conclusion but at the price of relying on "ought" premises.

As you might imagine, this response to Searle prompted further counter-responses, which in turn prompted further counter-counter-responses until the thread of the dispute has been unwound and tangled. For our purposes, it is enough to say that Hume's Law may not have closed the door on getting from facts to values. Indeed, a cottage industry, straddling several sub-disciplines in philosophy, has taken on the supposed fact/value distinction. Some have argued that science – a field that supposedly trades only in facts – secretly trades in values. Others argue that values will ultimately prove to be illusory, so no (true) moral claim follows from *any* set of premises.

9.5 Forays across the Is/Ought Gap: Rachels

The philosopher James Rachels (1990) takes a more modest approach to Hume's Law. Instead of attempting to bridge the gap *deductively*, Rachels wonders why we can't settle for something slightly less conclusive. Recall that Hume's Law is aimed at arguments that purport to be deductive, that is, arguments whose conclusions *must* be true if the premises are true. But deductive arguments are not the only game in town. And thank goodness, for if we tried to restrict ourselves to deductive reasoning, life would quickly come to a grinding halt. Consider this argument:

1   Most cars stop at red lights.
2   Safely crossing this street requires that cars stop at the red light.
3   Therefore, I can safely cross this street.

So, can I cross the street? Well, if we're restricting ourselves to deductive reasoning, then *No*. The truth of the premises does not guarantee the truth of the conclusion (cars sometime run red lights). If no claim was justified that didn't follow deductively from a set of premises, then no jury should ever return a guilty verdict, no scientific theory should ever be accepted, no street should ever be crossed, and so on. Indeed, apart from a few boring claims about bachelors and triangles, and apart from some mathematical propositions, we should be skeptical of just about every claim that comes to mind.

But this is ridiculous. Surely we are justified in believing in claims that are based on non-deductive reasoning (even if there remains some theoretical mystery about *how* justification is conferred in these cases[2]). Justification in these other sorts of cases is not logical entailment. Instead, justification amounts to evidence or support. The evidence may not be airtight (as one gets with logical deduction), but it's evidence all the same. Juries are told to consider whether there is any *reasonable doubt* that the accused committed the crime. Suppose you knew that Smith's fingerprints were found at the crime scene, that Smith had the relevant motive, that he confessed to the crime, that seven independent witnesses all claimed to have seen Smith commit the crime. You would have compelling evidence that Smith committed the crime. Is Smith's guilt *logically entailed* by those facts? No. It's logically possible that Smith didn't commit the crime (think: elaborate conspiracy). But it would be highly *unreasonable* to believe that Smith didn't commit the crime, given what you know. Philosophers refer to this kind of argument as *abductive* or, more plainly, inference to the best explanation.

Inductive arguments move from premises about observed cases (e.g., "All observed swans are white") to a conclusion about unobserved cases ("*All* swans are white"). Take our earlier example: You're justified in believing that the next car that approaches the red light will stop (largely) on the basis that cars have stopped at red lights in the past. You would thus have good reason for believing that it's OK to cross the road. Still, inductive arguments, like abductive arguments, do not guarantee the truth of their conclusion. But that doesn't necessarily make believing in the conclusion unreasonable. In this case, *not* believing in the conclusion would be unreasonable. So what we see here is that deductive reasoning is not the only form of reasoning we might use in forming our beliefs.

How does all this bear on Hume's Law? Well, Hume's Law (as it is traditionally understood) applies only to deductive arguments. So grant him that point. But, as Rachels puts it, Hume "was surely mistaken that to think that the point 'subverts all the vulgar systems of morality' ... Traditional morality is not subverted because in fact it never depended on taking the matching moral idea as a strict logical deduction" (1990: 97). Non-moral (or factual) claims "provide good reason for accepting" certain moral claims.

In Rachels' case, the moral claim happens to fall at the other end of the spectrum from Spencer: humans should *not* be accorded special moral status. They do not, in other words, deserve special moral treatment simply because of their species membership. The argument in support of this claim, says Rachels, consists of entirely factual claims. In particular, it consists of two *negative* claims: first, it is *not* the case that we are made in the image of God and, second, we are *not* "uniquely rational animals." The reason Rachels considers himself an evolutionary ethicist is because he believes the support for *these* claims comes from evolutionary theory. Rachels has turned Spencer on his head. Both claim to follow evolution wherever it leads. But whereas Spencer saw evolution leading to humanity's preeminence, Rachels sees evolution as undermining humanity's preeminence. For Rachels, this means "traditional morality" must be abandoned: humans should not be treated as having greater significance than other animals.

Though its moral stance has been flipped (and though Spencer is no doubt turning in his grave), this is a kind of Social Darwinism. Call it Social Darwinism 2.0. It deserves to be called Social Darwinism because Rachels believes that what we ought to do is supported exclusively by what we are – that is, the way evolution has shaped us. His extended discussion of Hume makes it clear that he intends to do exactly what Hume says you can't do.

Things are, I'm afraid, more complicated than Rachels seem to think. At least, that's my impression. I'd like to argue that getting to the moral claim appears to rely on premises Rachels accepts but resists stating openly. Consider how Rachels characterizes his own general argumentative strategy:

> The doctrine of human dignity says that humans merit a level of moral concern wholly different from that accorded to mere animals; *for this to be true, there would have to be some big, morally significant difference between them.* Therefore, any adequate defense of human dignity would require some conception of human beings as radically different from other mere animals. But that is precisely what evolutionary theory calls into question. (1990: 171–2, emphasis added)

Why have I italicized part of the passage? Is Rachels mistaken about the need for "some big, morally significant difference?" No. In fact, most of us would say he's *exactly right*. We shouldn't treat individuals differently unless there's some morally significant difference between them. For example, it would be wrong to rescue little Jack from drowning *but then refuse* to rescue little Jill only because little Jill is female. One's gender is not a morally significant difference between Jack and Jill – at least in this case.

So why have I drawn attention to Rachels' use of this general moral claim? Because he seems to think he needs it in order to get to his desired conclusion, namely, that humans should not be accorded special moral status. In other words, Rachels seems to be using that claim as one of the premises in his argument. In order to justify the claim that humans should not be accorded special moral status, he's assuming not only that they are not made in God's image and that they are not uniquely rational, but that we should not treat individuals differently unless there's some morally significant difference between them. And since plenty of people doubt his claim about human dignity, he's correct in thinking he needs that assumption.

If this analysis is on track, then Rachels has not done what he thinks he has done. He has not derived a moral claim from purely non-moral premises. He has derived a moral claim from some factual claims *and* at least one moral claim, namely, a claim about what justifies different moral treatment. Despite explicitly resisting the need for a deductive argument, Rachels can't help but fall back on a deductive argument. But can you blame him? He wants to convince you of his conclusion, and what better, more convincing, way to do that than with a deductive argument? Such arguments leave no room for doubt.

9.6 Conclusion

Getting from how things are to how things ought to be remains a tricky business – whether we're talking about evolution or some other empirical account of humanity. A moral code based solely on biology, despite what critics of Moore and Hume say, is still a long way off. On the one hand, we might concede that Moore missed an important distinction, one that separates (roughly) how terms relate to other terms and how terms relate to the world. But this just leaves the Social Darwinist with the task of figuring out how to show that our moral concepts really do fall out of evolutionary theory. Even without insisting on a semantic relation, we can see that this task will not easily be met. On the other hand, we can admit that there may be non-deductive arguments, consisting solely of factual claims, that lead to moral claims, but arguments like Rachels' are convincing only because they're deductive arguments in disguise. We find them compelling (if we do) only because they close the logical gap between what is and what should be.

In the next chapter our discussion turns to more contemporary efforts to connect evolution and ethics. Unlike the work of traditional Social Darwinists, contemporary evolutionary ethicists are using the evolutionary story not to prop up a moral system, but to destroy it. "New wave" evolutionary ethicists have turned Social Darwinism on its head. For they assert that the story of human evolution shows that there are, ultimately, no objective moral duties. The argument for this claim, along with various responses, will occupy us in the remaining chapters.

Further Reading

Black, Max (1964) The Gap Between "Is" and "Should." The Philosophical Review, 73/2: 165–81.
Mackie, J.L. (1977) *Ethics: Inventing Right and Wrong* (Viking).
Moore, G.E. (1903) *Principia Ethica* (Cambridge University Press).

Rachels, James (1990) *Created from Animals: The Moral Implications of Darwinism* (Oxford University Press).

Searle, John R. (1964) How to Derive "Ought" from "Is". Philosophical Review, 73: 43–58.

Stratton-Lake, Phillip (2003) *Ethical Intuitionism: Re-Evaluations* (Oxford University Press).

Thomson, Paul (ed.) (1995) *Issues in Evolutionary Ethics* (SUNY Press).

10

Evolutionary Anti-Realism:
Early Efforts

A major attraction to my position in my eyes is that one simply cannot be guilty of committing the naturalistic fallacy or violating the is/ought barrier, because one is simply not in the justification business at all.
(Michael Ruse, "Evolution and Ethics")

Stephen Morgan and Johanna Justin-Jinich met at a New York University summer course in 2007. How it began is not clear, but Stephen started sending Johanna harassing e-mails. Johanna in turn complained to the authorities. But Stephen disappeared, apparently returning to his home in Colorado, and the matter appeared to resolve itself. Then, on May 6, 2009, Stephen returned to Connecticut where Johanna was a student. Events unfolded this way:

> Mr. Morgan walked into a campus bookstore about 1 p.m. Wednesday, then toward the Red and Black Cafe, where Ms. Justin-Jinich worked. He was a bearded, menacing figure on the overhead surveillance camera, a dark gun in his right hand swinging at his side, and something else hidden behind him in his left hand. It was a long-stranded wig and he put it on, the baldish man undergoing a bizarre transformation as he confronted her, raised the gun and opened fire, a point-blank, seven-shot execution, officials said. Ms. Justin-Jinich fell, mortally wounded. (*New York Times*, A1, May 8, 2009)

There are a number of questions we might ask about this series of events. For example, we might seek to answer *psychological* questions, questions about Stephen's mental health, and the causal factors that led to his actions. We might seek to answer *legal* questions, questions about the legality of his actions prior to the shooting. We might want to know whether his mental health might figure in his legal defense (was he criminally insane at the time of the killing?). We might seek to answer *sociological* questions, questions about the social environment that contributed to Stephen's avowed anti-Semitism (Johanna was Jewish). All of these questions would be worth pursuing. And we have some idea about how to go about pursuing them.

Take, for example, questions about Stephen's mental health. We might look to psychologists who have developed clinical measures for psychopathy, thus allowing us to say (with greater or lesser accuracy) that Stephen *was* a psychopath based on, for example, his responses to a battery of personality tests. Perhaps images of his brain might reveal the neurophysiological signature of psychopathy. At any rate, we have some idea (perhaps mistaken) about *what would make it true* that Stephen was a psychopath. Or, we have some idea (perhaps mistaken) about *what would make it true* that Stephen violated Section 1109b of the United States Federal criminal code. In all these instances, we can offer in more or less basic terms the *truth-conditions* for judgments about his mental state or the illegality of his actions or whatever.

But these are not the questions we're interested in. Suppose I say (and I don't think I'm going out on a limb with this one) that what Stephen did was wrong. His actions were *seriously immoral.* It might thus be asked: What makes it true that Stephen's actions were immoral? Now this question is not posed as a skeptical question, as if maybe we're not sure if shooting someone seven times, at point-blank range, is wrong. The question is posed, instead, as a theoretical question, a question we might ask in hopes of learning about the nature of morality itself. What is it about the world that makes the judgment that his actions were wrong *true*? What in (or out of) the world do we point to? What are the basic terms that make up the *truth-conditions* for that moral judgment?

With regard to judgments about Stephen's mental health, it's at least pretty clear. We might point to past behavior or Stephen's personality test results. Maybe we point to fMRI scans of Stephen's brain. With regard to judgments about the illegality of Stephen's actions, we might point to publicly accessible criminal codes and evidence of how Stephen behaved. But with regard to judgments about the *morality* of Stephen's behavior, what do we point to? What, if anything, justifies the claim that what Stephen did was seriously immoral? And how does that justification fit together with everything else we know about the world? In particular, the *natural* world?

What, if anything, does wrongness have to do with, say, neurons or gravity or electrons? Are there objective standards to which we can appeal to in trying to determine which moral judgments (if any) are correct? If Stephen were to claim that his actions were *not* wrong, could we show that Stephen is making a *factual* mistake, a mistake not unlike the claim that the earth is flat or that $23 + 6 = 30$?

These sorts of questions are at the heart of the field known as *metaethics*. Metaethics, broadly understood, is the study of moral concepts, what these concepts mean, and how they hang together with other concepts (such as electrons); furthermore, metaethicists investigate the ultimate justification or foundation (if any) for moral judgments. This is not the study of what you ought to do (e.g., "You should not kill others"). This is the study of what, if anything, *justifies* claims about what you ought to do. It is a metaphysical discipline. For it seeks to uncover the ultimate reality or nature of moral properties such as wrongness, rightness, and goodness. Now how does this study make contact with evolution?

Let's go back to the beginning. Recall that the shot across the bow was Wilson's claim that ethics ought to be "removed temporarily from the hands of the philosophers and '*biologicized*.'" This challenge, however, allowed for several different interpretations. In part I of this book we explored the possibility that Darwinian selection played a central role in explaining why we happen to have this tendency to make moral judgments. "Biologicizing" ethics was a task for moral psychologists. In that part of the book, we purposely avoided passing judgment on the whether these moral judgments were *justified*.

In recent chapters we have looked at efforts to justify some moral claims by appeal to Darwinian selection. Social Darwinism, in Spencer's hands at least, was an attempt to "biologicize" ethics by showing that social harmony is good because it's what natural selection tends toward. But as we saw, these attempts face serious obstacles. Indeed, given the apparent decisiveness of Hume's and Moore's objections, "traditional evolutionary ethics ground to a complete stop," as the philosopher Michael Ruse describes it. If we accept Hume's and Moore's objections, then the obvious conclusion to draw is that *morality really is autonomous*. That is, disciplines outside of moral philosophy can offer no insight into the nature of morality. Moral theory must solve its problems (if it can) only on its own terms.

So we might reasonably wonder why we are plunging once again into the question of morality's justification in the context of evolution. Didn't we show that this was a waste of time? Even if the speculative story sketched in part I of this book is correct, the question of how we ought, morally speaking, to live our lives remains wide open. Nothing about morality's justification has been settled. The philosopher James Rachels amplifies this point with an analogy.

> Imagine that someone proposed eliminating the study of mathematics, and replacing it with systematic study of the biological basis of mathematical thinking. They might argue that, after all, our mathematical beliefs are the products of our brains working in certain ways, and an evolutionary account might explain why we developed the mathematical capacities we have. Thus "mathobiology" could replace mathematics. (1990: 78)

But this sounds funny. True, it seems plausible that our ability to perform mathematical calculations had certain biological advantages. (For example, Ogg observes three saber-tooth tigers going into a cave; he then observes two coming out. When Ogg thinks it's safe to go into the cave, Ogg does the human species a favor: he removes himself from the gene pool. Score one for mathematical thinking.) But accepting this story as plausible doesn't seem to drive us to the conclusion that mathematics is dispensable. That seems strange. Why? "The proposal is strange," says Rachels, "because mathematics is an autonomous subject with its own internal standards of proof and discovery." Imagine a mathematician trying to solve Fermat's Theorem by studying the activity of the hypothalamus. She's not going to get very far.

Similar results are supposed to follow for morality. If we want to know whether abortion is wrong or whether torture is ever morally justified, or if we want to know what it is that made Stephen Morgan's act of killing seriously immoral, it would be nonsensical to speculate about human evolution, or observe how the amygdala and occipital lobes communicate. This line of objection looks impeccable. In fact, as Ruse notes, this is how "matters have rested for three-quarters of a century."

But things are once again stirring. Beginning in the 1970s, philosophers and biologists glimpsed a new way of understanding the relationship between evolution and morality. This new way does not require taking on Moore or Hume directly. As far as these philosophers are concerned, Hume and Moore were correct. Any attempt to vindicate moral claims on the basis of evolution is bound to fail. But why, these philosophers ask, must we seek to *vindicate* moral claims?

According to this new approach, evolution in fact *does* yield important moral conclusions, but not the kinds of conclusions that would have comforted Spencer or Rachels. Instead of seeking to *vindicate* or *justify* certain moral principles (e.g., that social harmony is to be promoted, or that non-human animals deserve the same moral treatment as humans), this new approach to evolutionary ethics seeks to *undermine* morality. What evolution shows is *not* that this or that way of acting is morally preferred. Instead, evolution (in combination with certain philosophical principles) shows that *there is no morally preferable way of acting at all*. On this version of evolutionary ethics, Darwinian evolution does not support; it destroys.

To be clear, the conclusions it seeks to establish are *metaethical*. This means that we are drawing conclusions about moral *concepts* themselves and what they refer (or, in this case, *don't refer*) to. If this recent sort of view – what I'll call *evolutionary anti-realism* – is correct, then whatever else we say about Stephen Morgan's actions on May 6, 2009, we cannot say that they were *objectively* wrong. The reason is: *nothing* is objectively wrong. And the reason nothing is objectively wrong follows from an argument that appeals specifically to our evolutionary past. Certain premises of that argument have appeared before in the history of moral philosophy. But others were unavailable until more recently, when the picture of human evolution began to come into focus. In this chapter we'll begin by looking at early efforts to undermine morality, an effort mounted by E.O. Wilson and Michael Ruse. In chapter 11 we'll see how this early effort has been extended, by looking at recent arguments by the philosophers Richard Joyce and Sharon Street. In chapter 12 we'll consider how the skeptic might respond to these arguments. At least three different kinds of proposals have been recently floated.

10.1 This Is Your Brain on God

In the mid-1990s Michael Persinger, a Canadian neuropsychologist, found God – just not where most people expected (Hitt 1999). Michael Persinger applied mild electromagnetic bursts (called Thomas Pulses) to the right temporal lobe of subjects' brains. Subjects reported having powerful "religious experiences," involving more often than not a "sensed presence." For some, the sensed presence was God, for others it was Mohammed. Avowed agnostics suspected UFOs. Various theories have emerged as to why the brain interprets these electromagnetic bursts in the way it does. But whatever the final theory looks like, it appears that Michael Persinger has found God *in the brain*.

Now some marveled at this neat little neuropsychological splash, but nevertheless ignored the ripples. Others, however, sensed a philosophical lesson here. (And it is this lesson that will interest us in the coming chapters, so indulge me.) Why might this neuropsychological discovery – if, indeed, it stands up to review – trouble believers? Why should some neuropsychologist tickling temporal lobes in Canada threaten my belief (let's say) in God? The following is one way of spelling out the threat.

Suppose that *ultimately* the case for God's existence comes down to the religious experiences of individual believers. Suppose, that is, that the evidence for God's existence does not ultimately rest on anything other than these "transcendental" experiences. (I can't imagine that this assumption will go unchallenged. For now, though, we're just trying to spell out a threat.) Let's also suppose that each of these experiences is merely the result of increased activity in subjects' temporal lobes. This activity can be artificially induced (as Persinger has done) or naturally induced by varying electromagnetic fields in the environment. In either case – and this is the point – we can fully explain these religious experiences *without* having to appeal to a (mind-independent) supernatural being. We don't need God's existence to explain anything in need of explaining. Therefore, *if* the evidence for God's existence ultimately comes down to these experiences, and *if* these experiences can be explained without remainder as mere "side-effects" of run-of-the-mill activities of the brain, then what reason do you have for believing in God's existence? What justification do you have for such a belief? If this threat is for real, the answer is, *None*.

Two points of clarification. First, you might continue to believe in God's existence, but this belief will have been shown to be irrational. Think of it as an epistemic hangover. The point of the threat is not to show that we don't or won't continue to believe in God, just as the point of an optical illusion is not to show that your eye won't be fooled again. The point is to show that such a belief is unjustified, given the neuroscientific data. Second, even if the threat is real, God may nonetheless exist. Again, the threat is about knowledge – what you ought to believe given the evidence – not about the nature of the world per se. You have no reason to believe that there is a teacup orbiting Pluto, but (for all that anyone knows) it could be the case that a teacup is orbiting Pluto. Call this a cosmic coincidence.

If you were able to get traction on this example, you'll be primed for what's about to come. In the case of evolutionary ethics, Darwin's discovery plays the role of the "Persinger effect." But let's begin with some preliminaries.

10.2 Preliminaries

Evolution has fooled you. If (the people I'm calling) evolutionary anti-realists needed a bumper sticker, this would be it. According to evolutionary anti-realism, there are no objective moral standards, but your believing that there are is a trick of evolution. If evolutionary anti-realism is correct, then while we will, in all likelihood, continue to judge that certain actions are immoral, our judgments will be *false*, strictly speaking. To be sure, calling an action immoral may have a purpose. We might want to shame someone or punish her, and in so doing we might appeal to the (alleged) fact that she behaved immorally. But to the extent that we are interested in truth, our judgments do not track the way the world really is. Morality, on this view, is a convenient fiction.

The situation is not unlike what may be the case with respect to appeals to God. We might appeal to God – his mercy, his wrath, his wisdom – in trying to shape others' behavior. Believing that God will reward or punish you in the afterlife will very likely have a tremendous impact on how you behave. (Ask most 6-year-olds.) But if there is no God, then of course any judgment about how you ought to behave that depends on God (e.g., "You should not steal because God prohibits it") is false. There may be a reason not to steal, but it can't be because God prohibits it. Maybe the risk of getting caught is not worth the minor gain. Maybe you'll feel bad about yourself.

Matters are the same for the evolutionary anti-realists. If their view is ultimately vindicated, then the judgment that "You should not steal because it's wrong" is, strictly speaking, false. The property that supposedly justifies the imperative not to steal (i.e., wrongness) is missing from the world – in the same way that God is missing from the world in our previous example.

Evolutionary anti-realism is a species of *moral anti-realism*, and moral anti-realism is not new. Philosophers have been flirting with the view for thousands of years. What is new is the claim that evolution by natural selection *explains* why our believing in an objective morality is not justified. This was an (alleged) insight that was not possible before Darwin's discovery. Over the course of these three chapters, we're going to look at how this claim has, er, evolved. More specifically, we're going to look at how *defenses* of this view have evolved.

I do not believe I am overstating the case when I say that among contemporary philosophers interested in the intersection of evolution and morality, evolutionary anti-realism has become – at least in print – a popular view. There is by no means unanimity. Still, the number of philosophers defending the view appears to comfortably exceed the number of those critical of the view. This is somewhat striking because the earliest efforts to defend this view were, to put it charitably, rocky. Part of the problem lay in keeping evolutionary anti-realism separate from closely related views. In this next section, we'll look E.O. Wilson's attempts to articulate something approximating evolutionary anti-realism. Matters were greatly clarified by the philosopher Michael Ruse, as we'll see in §10.4.

10.3 Wilson

E.O. Wilson has appeared in several places in our discussion. I'm afraid we've not always treated his contributions kindly. I have noted at regular intervals the mistakes Wilson made. But picking out the flaws of early pioneers is an easy business; we have the luxury of hindsight. To be fair, Wilson deserves more: no contemporary thinker has done more than Wilson to bring evolutionary theory to bear on human affairs. He is, after all, the father of sociobiology, the precursor of evolutionary psychology (see §1.4). In his 1975 book *Sociobiology: The New Synthesis*, Wilson laid out a program of study that has revolutionized our understanding of human beings: it is not merely our bodies that carry natural selection's mark, but our minds as well.

Of course, the seeds of this idea did not originate with Wilson. As we've seen, Darwin set in motion ideas that led naturally to human affairs. No doubt some of the early opposition to Darwin came from the recognition that if Darwin was right, we would have to admit that humans – in both body and mind – would eventually have to succumb to an evolutionary explanation. This was a radical idea to express, and Darwin went out of his way *not* to express it. Thomas Huxley, Darwin's most vocal defender during Darwin's life, explicitly *denied* the idea. While admitting that "no absolute structural line of demarcation" exists between "the animal world" and ourselves, Huxley left little doubt what his position on humans was: "no one is more strongly convinced than I am of the vastness of the gulf between civilized man and the brutes; or is more certain that whether *from* them or not, he is assuredly not *of* them" (1863: 234). What, then, makes us so special? You guessed it: "the conscience of good and evil." While some of Darwin's intellectual descendants may have doubted Huxley's claim, no one openly expressed these doubts. Until 1975.

In 1975 E.O. Wilson boldly took the step that most had been anticipating. Toward the beginning of *Sociobiology*, Wilson made the following claim:

> The biologist, who's concerned with questions of physiology and evolutionary history, realizes that self-knowledge is constrained and shaped by the emotional control centers in the hypothalamus and limbic system of the brain. These centers flood our consciousness with all the emotions – hate, love, guilt, fear, and others – that are consulted by ethical philosophers who wish to intuit the standards of good and evil. What, we are then compelled to ask, made the hypothalamus and limbic system? They evolved by natural selection. *That simple biological statement must be pursued to explain ethics and ethical philosophers ... at all depths.* (1975: 3)

Whatever you want to call Wilson, you can't call him shy. He's going after big fish, fish that would seem to belong in other people's nets. According to Wilson, once we understand the natural selection of certain brain systems, *we will understand all of morality* (and, as an added bonus, moral philosophers).

Now as I've been at pains to point out, claims like these are dangerously vague. You should be asking yourself now: *What part of morality* will we be able to explain? How we evolved to think morally? How we ought to act? Something else? In these latter parts of *Sociobiology*, Wilson moves carelessly among these different senses. He speculates on how humans came to have moral emotions (what we speculated on in part I). He speculates how evolution might point to "a more deeply understood and enduring code of moral values" (what we have discussed in previous chapters). Then, without much warning, we get this: "It should also be clear that no single set of moral standards can be applied to all human populations, let alone all sex-age classes within each population" (1975: 288). It's hard to see this as anything but a rejection of a universal moral code. There is no objective standard for what we ought to do morally. At best, we have moral relativism.

With time, Wilson sharpened his critique. He joined forces with the biologist Charles Lumsden, and together they complained that "philosophers and theologians have not yet shown us how the final ethical truths will be recognized as things apart from the idiosyncratic development of the human mind" (Lumsden and Wilson 1983: 182–3). To paraphrase, *ethics is all in your head.* Of course, if it's all in your head, then it's not in the world. And if it's not in the world, then there's nothing "out there" for us to grasp – there's nothing to measure our moral judgments against. If I say that your action was unethical, what I've said is no more correct than if you say your action was ethical. The reason is, actions are not, in reality, ethical or unethical. Ethics, like Santa Claus, is a figment of our imagination.

Although Wilson's claim was fairly unambiguous, the same could not be said for the *argument behind* the claim. Wilson showed great enthusiasm for the idea that natural selection played a decisive role in shaping our moral minds. While not as developed as the story we recounted in §3.2 (Wilson did not have the benefit of much recent work in developmental psychology and neuroscience), the idea shared the same basic components. But why should this idea undermine moral objectivity? That is, why should this developmental story about our minds lead us to think that rightness and wrongness are mere figments of the mind? Presumably, there are steps that lead from one idea to the next, but Wilson fails to spell them out – at least in a way that would help us evaluate the truth of evolutionary anti-realism.

10.4 The Argument from Idiosyncrasy

Not long after *Sociobiology* appeared, Wilson teamed up with the philosopher Michael Ruse. The image they presented was that of "philosophers' hands reaching down . . . to grasp the hands of biologists reaching up" (Ruse and Wilson 1986/1994: 430). What their teaming up meant was a more careful treatment of the question of ethical objectivity. And their conclusion was straightforward enough: based on "the scientific interpretation of moral behavior . . . there can be no objective external ethical premises." I take this to be a form of what I've been calling evolutionary anti-realism.

The first argument that Ruse and Wilson introduce I'll call the *Argument from Idiosyncrasy*. It goes like this: the value we ascribe to things like justice and fairness and compassion and tolerance – not to mention the sense of *obligation* that seems to be the hallmark of the ethical realm – arises from cognitive processes that were themselves the "*idiosyncratic* products of the genetic history of [our] species and as such were shaped by the particular regimes of natural selection" (1986/1994: 431). In other words, "ethical premises are the peculiar products of genetic history." The key word here is *idiosyncratic*, which my dictionary defines as an "individualizing characteristic or quality." What Ruse and Wilson are saying is that the thoughts and feelings constitutive of our moral sense happened to favor (in one way or another) the survival of early hominids confronting idiosyncratic problems. (This is not far from the thesis explored in part I.)

Here's where things get interesting. If these cognitive processes were the result of idiosyncratic products of our genetic history, then we could have had *different* cognitive processes, had our genetic history been different. (And recall from chapter 6 that our genetic history could have been substantially different than it was.) But if we could have had different cognitive processes, then we could have had different ethical beliefs. Ruse and Wilson invite us to imagine an "alien intelligent species," whose path of evolution led its members to value "cannibalism, incest, the love of darkness and decay, parricide, and the mutual eating of feces." Members of this species feel passionately that these practices are "natural and correct" – indeed, just as passionately as we feel that justice and compassion are "natural and correct." Obviously, their "moral values" cannot be translated into ours and vice versa. From this, Ruse and Wilson conclude that "no abstract moral principles exist outside the particular nature of individual species" (1986/1994: 431). It just so happens that killing people for fun is wrong for creatures like us, but the status of this claim is like the status of the claim that sleep is an important part of our mental health. It didn't have to be this way, and in fact features of our species could change that render the claim false. Let's turn now to Ruse and Wilson's second argument: the *Argument from Redundancy*.

10.5 The Argument from Redundancy

Let me come at this argument by way of a quick detour into *epistemology* (that is, the philosophical study of knowledge). You believe that at this very minute you are reading a book. Indeed, you might insist on something stronger: you *know* that you are reading a book at this very minute. Asked to justify your belief, you might cite your perceptual experiences – how it *feels* in your hands, how it *looks* under different lighting, perhaps even how it *smells* and *tastes*. All these perceptual experiences are best explained by the fact that there is a mind-independent book that you are at this very minute reading. It's really there (or here) and you're detecting it.

Moreover, your belief is connected in an important way to the following *counterfactual* (that is, how things *could have been*): had you not been reading this book at this very minute you would not have believed that you were. Had you not been reading this book at this very minute, you would not be having the perceptual experiences cited above. If you tried to spell this out, you might say that you stand in a particular kind of causal relation to the book, such that the book *causes* you to feel and see the way you do. And if you did not stand in this causal relation to the book, you wouldn't be having those experiences. The point is: if it *was* the case that you would believe that you are reading a book at this very minute *whether or not you were actually reading a book* at this very minute, then this would undermine your justification for believing the book really exists. Why? Well, your belief is no longer evidence that you're reading a book at this very minute. Your belief has been disconnected from the book's (alleged) existence.

Mixing my metaphors, I would offer this. Imagine that there's a short-circuit in the dashboard display panel of your car that causes an "engine warning" light to go off and on arbitrarily. Imagine further that the light is in no way connected to the engine itself. So the next time the light goes on, there's no reason to believe that there *really is* an engine problem – even though that's what we normally think. Believing so is (as we might say) redundant. We already know everything that needs to be known about why the light is going on. The light goes on whether or not there's an engine problem. Of course, there *could* be an engine problem, but that would be a total coincidence. And as far as believing it goes, we would need evidence from a source other than the engine warning light itself. Likewise in the case of the book: if you would believe that you were reading a book at this very minute whether or not you were, then – in the absence of evidence from a source other than the belief itself – there's no justification for believing that there really is a book in front of you now.

This is the thrust of Ruse and Wilson's Argument from Redundancy: "The evolutionary explanation makes the objective morality redundant, for even if external ethical premises did not exist, we would go on thinking about right and wrong in the way that we do" (1986/1994: 431). Like the dashboard warning light, our moral sense "goes on" not because we are registering some independent moral realm. It "goes on" because it was installed by a process that rewarded survival and reproduction – nothing more. In other words, the point is not to detect a separate realm of moral facts. The point is *reproductive success*. In Ruse and Wilson's language, we would come to believe that some acts are immoral *whether or not* those acts really were immoral, given the facts of Darwinian evolution. This moves us in the direction of a theme that underlies most arguments for evolutionary anti-realism: explaining the *causes* behind our tendency to make moral judgments undermines any *reason* to believe in an objective morality. Let's spend time on this idea.

10.6 Causation, Justification, and ... a Rotting Corpse

Suppose the long-winded story we told in part I is correct. Suppose, that is, that the reason we tend to judge that some acts are wrong is fully explained by that tendency's impact on individual fitness: those who think and behave morally, generally speaking, make more babies (than those who don't make such judgments). If this is correct, then our moral beliefs are not the result of responding to a separate moral realm. Instead, our moral beliefs are the result of a causal process unconnected to any moral realm at all. And what does this imply? Well, once we have a causal story that does not require the existence of morality, then what reason do we have to seek out a *justification* for our moral judgments? Apparently none. In this case, once we know what caused our moral judgments, there's no need to investigate whether those judgments are *true*. To do so is to confuse causation and justification. With the help of (yet another) analogy I think we can get straight on this difference between what I'll call the *Explanatory Project* and the *Justificatory Project*. As Ruse emphasizes, offering an explanation of our moral sense (the Explanatory Project) makes justifying moral principles (the Justificatory Project) "inappropriate" or unnecessary.

Imagine stumbling upon a rotting corpse in a city alleyway. "Oh, *gross!* Disgusting!" Your response would be immediate and involuntary. And I would wager that individuals in every culture on the planet would have just the same response to a rotting corpse. I would even wager that small children would react similarly. Now what best explains this uniformity of response? As a matter of human psychology, why are humans so prone to these "gross-judgments" in response to rotting corpses? If the question is posed at the level of the species, the answer is not hard to come by. An Explanatory Project that addresses our "gross-judgments" should be easy to complete.

We know now quite a lot about the parasites and bacteria associated with rotting corpses, so physical proximity to them can be a serious health hazard. And so it was hundreds of thousands of years ago. This then would have been an adaptive problem faced by our distant ancestors: how to avoid rotting corpses. But the solution is obvious. That early ancestor (who most likely pre-dated hominids) who was innately equipped with the tendency to regard corpses as "gross" out-reproduced his neighbors who did not have that tendency, all else being equal. Equipping early humans with a tendency to regard some things as gross would have been cheap and highly effective. Completing this Explanatory Project would require spelling out how our "gross-judgments" are particularly attuned to certain perceptual cues, but there's nothing terribly mysterious about how this might go. We would not need to know anything about grossness *itself*, for the simple reason that "grossness" itself is not the issue. That, we might say, is a useful fiction. The issue is explaining the causal process that triggers those judgments. All we need to do is assign a team of cognitive psychologists to the task of explaining the causes behind our judgments.

But now imagine this. Imagine that you aren't alone when you come upon that rotting corpse. A friend sees (and smells) what you see (and smell). But, quite remarkably, your friend does *not* respond as you do. She looks curiously at the corpse as you recoil in disgust. Perplexed, you ask your friend: Don't you think that that's gross? She responds flatly: "No." No seriously, you say, that's *gross!* "No, it's interesting," she replies. Your friend appears to be sincere. But clearly she's made a mistake, you think. And so you point out to her (in case she missed it) the putrefying flesh, the rancid odor, the blind, busy work of maggots. "Yes, I see all that, but I don't find it gross," she says. You're dumbfounded. She's clearly mistaken, you think. She's made an *error*. There's something about the scene that she has failed to grasp, namely, that that corpse is gross. The corpse has the property *being gross*, and your friend – despite perceiving its *other* properties: its odor, its appearance – has failed to perceive *that* property.

So you attempt to *justify* your judgment, to show why your judgment that the corpse is in fact gross is *true* while her judgment (that it's not gross) is false. You accept the evolutionary account of why people tend to make the judgments they make in response to rotting corpses, but you think there's an additional account, an account of what *justifies* the judgments that something is gross. This account can help decide who's correct and who's incorrect in their "gross-judgments." Here we can hire a team of "grossologists" (from – where else? – the Department of Grossology) to determine whether or not grossness is objectively present in the corpse. This would be the Justificatory Project.

All this of course is silly. The Justificatory Project in this case is wrongheaded. What makes the project wrongheaded is that, on reflection, "gross-judgments" are not the kind of things that need justification. Furthermore, we don't think of them as the kind of things that can really be true or false. They're really just a matter of taste – or should I say *dis*taste? They're not like judging that the Eiffel Tower is 180 meters tall or that the United Nations is ineffective. In these cases, we have some idea of what the world would have to be like in order for the judgment to accurately represent the world. But "gross-judgments" are not like this. When you judge that some object is gross, there's no need to spend too much time investigating the object, as if by looking closely enough (perhaps under a microscope) we'll detect that elusive property of grossness and thus justify your judgment. A better use of our time would be to investigate *you*. What is it about you – your genetic makeup, your upbringing, and so on – that *explains* why you made that judgment? After all, you could have had an unusual experience as a child that explains, for example, why you find spaghetti gross. Regarding our earlier example, your friend could be a forensic pathologist with a long history of examining corpses, and this would explain why she doesn't find the rotting corpse gross.

Recall the upshot of the Explanatory Project. We can explain all that needs to be explained about our "gross-judgments" without ever having to assume there *really are* things with a special property – grossness – that humans are uniquely capable of perceiving. Thus, there's no reason to go hunting for reasons why our "gross-judgments" are true. Since we know everything we need to know about why the judgment is made, we need not bother with asking: But is the judgment justified? Did the person have sufficient grounds for thinking the judgment true? In the case of evolution and ethics, the Explanatory Project makes the Justificatory Project inappropriate. Here's how Ruse makes the point: "sometimes when one has given a causal analysis of why someone believes something, one has shown that the call for reasoned justification is inappropriate – there is none" (1998: 124). This is the same point Ruse was making more than ten years earlier (1986: 102): "All one can offer is a causal argument to show why we hold ethical beliefs. But once such an argument is offered, we can see that that is all that is needed."

10.7 Conclusion

Wilson and Ruse have revived evolutionary ethics, but not at all in the shape that Spencer (and perhaps Rachels) imagined. The critical response

to Spencer gave the impression that evolution had no bearing on substantive ethical issues. The domain of *what is* cannot influence *what ought
to be*. And so it was thought that evolutionary ethics perished in a blaze of
bad philosophy. Ruse jokes that all one needed to do was "murmur the
magical phrase 'naturalistic fallacy'" in order to turn the page and move on
to another topic.

But Wilson and Ruse envisioned a new relationship between evolution
and ethics. Spencer thought that evolution *supports* ethics. Wilson and Ruse
think evolution *destroys* ethics (at least in the sense that ethics consists in
objective rules). The change in approach to evolutionary ethics is best
reflected in the following:

> The evolutionist is no longer attempting to derive morality from factual
> foundations. His/her claim now is that there are no foundations of
> any sort from which to derive morality ... Since, clearly, ethics is not
> nonexistent, the evolutionist locates our moral feelings simply in the
> subjective nature of human psychology. At this level, morality has no
> more (and no less) status than that of the terror we feel at the unknown –
> another emotion which undoubtedly has good biological value. (Ruse
> 1986: 102)

To support their view, Wilson and Ruse offer several arguments.
According to the Argument from Idiosyncrasy, our moral beliefs are
the result of an idiosyncratic process, and had that process been
different, our moral standards would have been different. But one
implication of moral objectivity is the idea that moral standards do
not change. What's wrong is wrong – no matter what your beliefs and
background. According to the Argument from Redundancy, believing in
the objectivity of ethics is redundant since we would believe in the
objectivity of ethics *whether or not* ethics was in fact objective. This can
be further understood by distinguishing the *causal* processes that led to
our moral beliefs, on the one hand, from the (alleged) *justification* of
those beliefs, on the other. Ruse argues that understanding the causal
processes makes justifying our moral beliefs unnecessary. There are no
objective moral properties in the world – just as there are no objective
gross properties in the world. We believe and talk as if there are, but this
can be explained without referring to such things. Our explanation need
only point out biological and environmental causes. Evolution has, in
the end, fooled us.

Further Reading

Sober, Elliott (ed.) (1994) *Conceptual Issues in Evolutionary Biology*, 2nd edn. (MIT Press).

Wilson, E.O. (1975) *Sociobiology: The New Synthesis* (Harvard University Press).

11

Contemporary Evolutionary Anti-Realism

The availability of a non-moral genealogy appears to leave us with no reason to think that any of our moral beliefs are true.
(*Richard Joyce, The Evolution of Morality*)

In 2006 Richard Joyce published a book-long defense of evolutionary anti-realism, arguably the most comprehensive to date. The structure of that book parallels the structure of this book. He begins by defending the "provisional and to a degree speculative" hypothesis that human morality is innate. This is the hypothesis we explored in part I. Joyce then asks what the philosophical significance of this hypothesis is. Does it *vindicate* morality, as Spencer[1] supposed? Or does it *undermine* it? Joyce defends the latter hypothesis. Like Ruse, Joyce denies that morality has an objective basis. Joyce's discussion of evolutionary anti-realism is the most recent and most thorough, so it's worth spending some time piecing together his argument. In chapter 12 we'll consider some responses to Joyce's argument.

11.1 Napoleon Pills

To motivate his argument for evolutionary anti-realism, Joyce conjures up the following thought-experiment. Imagine that there exists a pill that, if taken, will cause you to believe that Napoleon *lost* the battle of Waterloo. And imagine that there exists a pill that, if taken, will cause you to believe that Napoleon *won* the battle of Waterloo. Finally,

An Introduction to Evolutionary Ethics, by Scott M. James. © 2011 Scott M. James

imagine that there exist corresponding antidotes. So, for example, if you were to take the "Napoleon lost the battle" *antidote* (after having taken the pill that causes the belief that Napoleon lost the battle), you would no longer believe that Napoleon lost the battle of Waterloo. You wouldn't believe that it's *false* that Napoleon lost the battle. Rather, you would neither believe nor disbelieve that Napoleon lost that battle. You would be agnostic. (Incidentally, these pills leave the rest of your beliefs intact.)

Now imagine that you become convinced that, as a young person, *you* were surreptitiously given the pill that causes the belief that Napoleon lost the battle of Waterloo. Let's say that you have unimpeachable evidence that you yourself were slipped that pill (suppose your family physician produces medical records under the threat of legal action). Of course, you assume that you "learned" that Napoleon supposedly lost that battle in school, but you can't honestly say how you came to have this belief. What is clear now, however, is that (a) you believe that Napoleon lost the battle of Waterloo and (b) this belief was caused by taking the relevant pill. Take a second to let this sink in.

The question Joyce poses at this point is this: *Should you take the antidote?* Should you take the pill that extinguishes the belief that Napoleon lost the battle of Waterloo? In case there's any question about your motives, let's make it clear that (as you do now) you have a standing interest in having justified true beliefs – or, if you prefer, knowledge. So, should you take the antidote? Joyce thinks *of course*. At the very least, your belief that Napoleon lost the battle of Waterloo should be "placed on the dubious list." You should be agnostic about Napoleon's efforts at Waterloo. Should you believe that Napoleon *won* at Waterloo? No. According to Joyce, you should withhold all judgments regarding Napoleon at Waterloo. You are not justified in holding any belief regarding *what really happened* at Waterloo.

Why? What lesson is this example supposed to uncover? Joyce thinks the lesson is this: "on some occasions knowledge of a belief's origins can undermine it" (2006: 179). As in Joyce's example, if a belief does not originate in the "normal" way, we ought not to accept it. What do we mean by "normal"?

Let's unpack the lesson this way: if the belief that p (where p just stands for some proposition like "Napoleon lost the battle of Waterloo" or "Today is Monday" or "Two plus two equals four") is not caused directly or indirectly by *the fact that p*, then you are not justified in holding that belief. This is not the most perspicacious definition but it'll do for now. In Joyce's example, your belief that Napoleon lost at Waterloo was not caused by directly perceiving the event (obviously), but nor was it caused indirectly – by, say, a chain of testimony linking you to the event. Instead, your belief about Napoleon was caused by something *entirely unrelated* to the (alleged) fact. It was caused by a pill. This should short-circuit your confidence in the belief's truth.[2] Here we have a situation in which knowledge of the origins of the belief undermines it. So to the extent that you care about having true beliefs, you should care about the fact that your belief about Napoleon was caused by something other than the (alleged) fact itself. Hence, you should take the antidote.

If Joyce is right about all this, what follows about morality? Well, suppose it's true that our moral beliefs were caused, by and large, by the long processes of Darwinian selection. But we have learned in chapters 6 to 10 that these processes were not guided by what is morally better or morally worse. Our explanations of why we have the moral beliefs we do, do not refer to the moral realm. Our explanations are purely *descriptive*. Darwinian explanations do not indicate how things *ought* to be or identify some forms as *good* or *bad*. As far as our moral minds are concerned, Joyce argues that "the function that natural selection had in mind for moral judgment was [nothing] remotely like *detecting a feature of the world*, but rather something more like *encouraging successful social behavior*" (2006: 131). Contrast this with our visual system. Our visual system was selected for because its apparent purpose (visually detecting objects in our environment) was identical with its actual purpose (visually detecting objects in our environment). In other words, we can't explain why our visual system evolved without mentioning *the actual things we visualized*. Evolution did not fool us into believing there were actual mind-independent objects in our midst. Such objects really are in our midst (the skeptics be damned).

According to Joyce, we *can't* say the same thing about our moral minds. In that case, we *can* explain why our moral system of beliefs evolved without mentioning actions *actually being right or wrong*. In this case, evolution has fooled us.

Let's put all this together. Our moral beliefs were not caused by the (alleged) moral facts, but by processes entirely unrelated to those (alleged) facts. But the example of the Napoleon pills supposedly showed that if the belief that *p* is not caused directly or indirectly by *the fact that p*, then you are not justified in holding that belief. Thus the evolutionary anti-realist's conclusion: as far as our moral beliefs are concerned, we are not justified in believing in them. We should take the morality antidote. We should withhold beliefs about what our moral duties *really are*. Indeed, Joyce suggests that we "keep an open mind about whether there exists anything that is morally right and wrong, [and accept] the possibility that describing the world in moral terms is in the same ballpark as taking horoscopes seriously" (2006: 181).

In all likelihood we'll continue to *use* moral language. But, like Santa Claus language, it will be for purposes other than describing how things really are in the world. That is, we may talk *as if* Santa Claus delivered presents last night, but saying such things won't be construed (at least by those of us old enough to know better) as a bona fide attempt to explain how the presents really appeared. Saying such things, one might argue, is a useful way to perpetuate a valuable cultural tradition. On this analogy, then, moral language might be used for all sorts of things. But if the evolutionary anti-realist is correct, one thing it *cannot* be used for (at least by those who know better) is to describe the way the world really is. In the final analysis, nothing in the world is objectively right or wrong or good or bad. Believing as much is a trick of evolution.

11.2 A Darwinian Dilemma

About the time that Richard Joyce was developing his arguments for evolutionary anti-realism, Sharon Street was developing a line of argument that came, more or less, to the same conclusion. Street drew attention to a dilemma confronting the moral realist. A dilemma in this context means that one has two choices in responding to a challenge, but neither choice looks good. You're damned if you do, damned if you don't. The dilemma, in Street's eyes, has to do with the *relationship* between the evolutionary forces that played a "tremendous role" in shaping our moral minds, on the one hand, and the (alleged) independent moral truths, on the other. The moral realist can either *deny* that there is a relationship or *explain* that relationship. According to Street, neither choice looks promising.

Like Ruse and Joyce, Street moves from speculations about how our moral sense evolved to "what might be said philosophically." And what might be said philosophically, according to Street, is this: "realist theories of value prove unable to accommodate the fact that Darwinian forces have deeply influenced the content of human values" (2006: 109). As such, realist theories of value should be abandoned. Instead, we should adopt *anti-realism*. If anti-realism turns out to be true, then there are no moral facts or truths that hold independently of our attitudes. This means that morality is all in our heads.

The outlines of Street's argument should by now look familiar. She begins with the same set of ideas we rehearsed in part I. She asserts that "natural selection has had a tremendous *direct* influence on ... 'our more basic evaluative tendencies,' and these basic evaluative tendencies, in their turn, have had a major influence on the evaluative judgments we affirm" (2006: 119–20). The processes of evolution have made us *prone* to accepting some moral judgments over others. (Think about our gustatory preferences: we naturally prefer brownies over broccoli.) Echoing a point made by Wilson and Ruse, Street maintains that, had these basic evaluative tendencies been different, the *content* of our evaluative systems (that is, the things we actually value) would have been different. Street is hitching her wagon to the same horse Wilson and Ruse and Joyce (and plenty of others as well) have: evolution shaped our moral minds.

Now what is the moral realist supposed to say in response to this? Remember the moral realist insists that there are moral facts or truths that hold *independently* of what we think or feel or desire, that is, independently of our evaluative attitudes. As a comparison, think of the earth's shape. The earth's roundness does not depend on how you or I or anyone judges the matter. The earth was round before we believed it, and it'll still be round (barring cosmic collisions) even after there's no one around to believe it. Indeed, had the planet been entirely devoid of sentient life, the earth *still* would have been round.[3] Analogously for the moral realist, moral truths hold independently of all our evaluative attitudes. For example, killing others for fun is wrong no matter what anyone happens to believe or feel or desire. It was wrong before we believed it and would have been wrong even if none of us believed it. The challenge to the moral realist, then, is to say what the relationship is between these truths, on the one hand, and the idea that evolution shaped our moral minds, on the other.

The first option is to *deny* that there is any relationship at all. The moral realist might maintain that the evolutionary forces that shaped our moral minds have nothing to do with the existence and structure of these independent moral truths. However, as Street suggests, this seems to imply that these evolutionary forces exerted a "purely distorting influence" on our evaluative judgments. She likens the situation to trying to sail to Bermuda, but leaving yourself entirely at the mercy of the wind and the tides. The wind and the tides are uninterested in where you want to go and, in all likelihood, will push you in the wrong direction. Of course, should you wash up on the shores of Bermuda, this would be a remarkable coincidence to the say the least. What worries Street is that if you accept the premise that evolutionary forces indeed had a tremendous influence on our moral minds, then most of our beliefs about what is right and wrong, good and bad, are "in all likelihood mostly off-track." After all, they're "utterly saturated and contaminated with [an] illegitimate influence" (2006: 122). But it seems quite implausible to say that we're mostly mistaken about the things we take to be good and bad, right and wrong. Surely we have a pretty good handle on these things. According to Street, since denying any relationship at all (between the evolutionary forces that shaped our moral minds and independent moral truths) leads to this skeptical result, the moral realist had better abandon the option. The moral realist ought to tackle the other option. And the other option – you'll recall – is to try to explain what that relationship is.

The most obvious way to explain this relationship is by way of a *tracking account*. On this account, some acts have the objective property of being prohibited, and we evolved a mental faculty to "track" that property. This account is modeled on other mental systems. The reason we have a visual perception system, for example, is because there exist objects in the physical world that happen to reflect ambient light, and our visual perceptual faculty evolved to track those objects. Doing so was biologically beneficial. In the moral case, the reason we are disposed to make moral judgments is because such judgments are, by and large, *true*, and our moral faculty evolved to track those truths. Doing so was biologically beneficial. We reviewed these matters in chapter 3. Being able to recognize what is morally prohibited or morally required, all things being equal, confers greater reproductive advantages on an individual than being unable to recognize such things. Seeing the moral truth, like seeing the edge of a cliff, is good for you – and for your offspring.

It sounds plausible, but plausibility comes cheap, argues Street. The question is whether there is another, more persuasive, account that has all the virtues of the tracking account, but lacks its vices. Is there, in other words, a leaner, more scientifically respectable, account? Street believes there is. In direct competition with other scientific theories of our moral tendencies, the tracking account loses out to what she calls the *adaptive link* account. On the adaptive link account, our moral minds evolved to link certain circumstances with biologically beneficial behavior – and that's it. According to Street, moral judgments evolved not because "they constituted perceptions of independent evaluative truths, but rather because they forged adaptive links between our ancestors' circumstances and their responses to those circumstances" (2006: 127). She likens this tendency to a "reflex mechanism." The mechanism is not in the business of detecting wrongness or rightness, goodness or badness, in the world. Instead, the mechanism merely reinforces a link between situations of a certain kind with responses of a certain kind. An example will help.

Suppose that you recognize that Gertrude has helped you. Let's say that Gertrude shared some of her food with you. This recognition in turn triggers a judgment that you ought to return the favor – that is, you ought to share some of your food with Gertrude when the opportunity arises. And this judgment in turn motivates you to do just that. When the opportunity arises, you *do* share some of your food with her. The crucial question here is this: What is the *function* of the judgment that you ought to return the favor? Is it, as the tracking account maintains, to detect that special moral property (namely, duty) that somehow "gloms onto" the situation? This seems biologically superfluous – not to mention mysterious. Shouldn't we say that the function of the judgment that you ought to return the favor is simply to get you to return the favor? Street thinks so. On the adaptive link account, the point is to move you to act. It's not necessary that you detect the (alleged) moral obligation of returning a favor. It's only necessary that you *act* in a specific way.[4]

There are of course differences between reflex mechanisms and moral judgments, as Street notes. For one thing, moral judgments are presented to you as reasons. For example, that an action is wrong is a reason not to do it. And we have the power to deliberate over these reasons. We can accept them or reject them. But this fact doesn't derail the adaptive link account. After all, the *point* of having these reasons presented to you is that they get you to respond in ways that are biologically adaptive. We're more sophisticated than Venus fly-traps, to be sure, but we're subject to the same evolutionary forces.

The philosophically significant point here is this: the adaptive link account provides all the explanatory power of the tracking account but with fewer components. Better still, the components the adaptive link account dispose of are admittedly *peculiar*: namely, objective rightness and wrongness. The adaptive link account can happily ignore the thorny issue of the truth of moral judgments. Is lying on this occasion *really and truly* immoral? Is killing one person to save three others *really and truly* morally permitted? As far the adaptive link account is concerned, questions like these are, at best, irrelevant. According to Street, the adaptive link account can explain all that we might want to explain about the presence of moral systems in the world, but "without any need to posit a role for evaluative truth" (2006: 129). At worst, such questions are uniformly false. Nothing in the world is immoral or amoral.

The Darwinian Dilemma thus confronting the realist looks insurmountable. Street thinks that the moral realist has "no escape." If the moral realist chooses to deny that there is any relationship between evolution's influence on our moral minds and the independent moral truths, then he has to accept the untenable view that evolution "either pushed us *away from* or pushed us in ways that *bear no relation* to these evaluative truths" (2006: 135). On the other hand, the only available alternative is a tracking account of some kind. But, according to Street, an adaptive link account will always be (empirically and philosophically) preferable to any tracking account.

11.3 Conclusion

The philosopher Philip Kitcher is probably right when he says that "philosophers most interested in the biological basis of morality struggle with issues about objectivity" (2005: 177). What the Darwinian revolution brought to the moral philosophers' table, it now appears, was a story about why we have the moral beliefs we do, and this story dispenses with *objective* morality. In chapter 10 I offered an analogy based on the neuroscientific discoveries of Michael Persinger: insofar as your justification for God's existence rests solely on your religious experiences, your justification founders in the face of the neuropsychological causes of such experiences. Richard Joyce offers the Napoleon pill analogy: insofar as your justification for believing that Napoleon lost the battle of Waterloo is based merely on having the belief, then your justification founders in the face of the discovery that you were given a pill that caused such a belief. According to Street, someone who defends the reality of moral properties must somehow reconcile that belief with the (alleged) fact that evolution exerted a tremendous influence on our disposition to adopt moral beliefs.

Further Reading

Joyce, Richard (2006) *The Evolution of Morality* (MIT Press).

Kitcher, Philip (2005) Biology and Ethics. In D. Copp (ed.), *The Oxford Handbook of Ethics* (Oxford University Press).

Ruse, Michael (1986) *Taking Darwin Seriously: A Naturalistic Approach to Philosophy* (Oxford University Press).

Street, S. (2006) A Darwinian Dilemma for Realist Theories of Value. *Philosophical Studies*, 127: 109–66.

12

Options for the Evolutionary Realist

It's no accident, I think, that philosophers most interested in the biological basis of morality struggle with issues about objectivity.
(Philip Kitcher, "Biology and Ethics")

The evolutionary realist must be, at this point, feeling backed into a corner. The previous two chapters have painted a fairly grim picture for anyone sympathetic to the idea that morality is *real*, that actions can in fact be *objectively* wrong, good, or bad. So what sorts of options are available to someone committed to the idea of moral realism? In this chapter we'll explore four different sorts of options. The first option involves a fairly blunt instrument: denying that evolution played any role in the development of our moral sense. I describe this as "blunt instrument" because it refuses to accommodate the central claim of the evolutionary anti-realist. Instead, it attempts to clear everything off the table and begin anew.

The three other options we'll explore attempt to work within the developmental framework emphasized by the evolutionary anti-realist. They concede, to varying extents, the idea that evolution played *some* role in developing our moral minds. Does this commit the realist to a kind of tracking account, as suggested by Street in the previous chapter? Not exactly. In fact, I think it's fair to say that at least two of these positions – response dependency and virtue ethics – represent the possibility of a *kind of* moral realism that does not require, for its defense, a tracking account. The philosopher Jesse Prinz is prepared to defend *response dependency* as a species of moral realism. On this view, the property *moral wrongness* is like the property *funny* or *disgusting*, in this sense: they dispose subjects to respond in stereotypical ways under normal conditions. Prinz is dubious that evolution played the defining role that the anti-realists we've discussed think it did in shaping our moral minds. Instead, Prinz argues that evolution

---

An Introduction to Evolutionary Ethics, by Scott M. James. © 2011 Scott M. James

is responsible for selecting a core set of emotions that are then shaped in important ways by the environment. Nevertheless, Prinz does assign some role to evolution in the shaping of our moral minds, so his view is not the blunt instrument I described above.

The philosophers William Casebeer and – somewhat tentatively – Philip Kitcher, take a different tack in response to the evolutionary anti-realist. They defend a version of *virtue ethics* in the context of evolution. This means that the focus of moral evaluation is not primarily on action, but on a person's character. The virtue ethicist seeks to answer the question, *What sort of person should I be?* and not (or not in the first instance), *What's my moral duty?* And to answer the question about what sort of person I should be, the contemporary virtue ethicist looks to Darwinian selection. We'll leave the details for later.

Finally, building on the work of others, I have offered a moral constructivist position, according to which moral rightness and wrongness consist in what agents (from a particular standpoint) would accept as rules to govern behavior. Unlike the other options outlined in this chapter, my position is an explicit attempt at a tracking account. I'm prepared to say that the reason we evolved to make moral judgments has precisely to do with the fact that a preponderance of these judgments were *true*. I'll save the details for later.

Before getting started, I should try to say something about the vexed notion of *moral realism*. Like so many other technical terms, moral realism does not have a received meaning among philosophers.[1] Even seeking a minimum conception is difficult. But let me offer this: moral realism is true just in case (1) moral properties (like rightness or wrongness) exist and (2) their existence does not depend on anyone thinking (or desiring or caring) they exist. This is simply an extension of the general definition for realism. Some philosophers insist on something more robust; others are content to accept less. It won't advance our discussion much by cataloguing all these differences – partly because the dispute over moral realism sometimes amounts to little more than a *terminological* dispute. Philosophers say: I understand all the components of your view, but does it deserve the title "realism"? Well, that of course depends on your definition of realism. But one would hope that we are interested in matters more substantial than definitions. For this reason, I propose that we spend our time discussing the details of the views themselves. Whether the view *really* deserves to be called realist we can regard as a secondary concern.

12.1 Option 1: Learning Right from Wrong

Recall that the evolutionary *anti-realist* motivates her case by arguing that our disposition to make moral judgments is *not*, in an important sense, learned. Rather, our moral sense is an evolutionary inheritance. The crux of the anti-realist's metaethical case is that when we examine this evolutionary inheritance, we see that there is no need to appeal to an independent realm of moral facts to explain our moral sense. All we need is the evolutionary story.

One option for the evolutionary *realist* is to deny that our moral sense is an evolutionary inheritance. Barring the possibility that we inherited it from aliens or God, such a denial would imply that we *learned* right from wrong. And if the evolutionary realist can make this case, then she has thereby made room for the possibility that learning right from wrong is in part a matter of learning what the moral facts are. In other words, perhaps the best explanation for why it is that humans come to develop a moral sense must make mention of the moral properties that somehow exist independently of humans. Otherwise, our explanation is incomplete. The evolutionary anti-realist thinks her case is complete because she maintains the evolutionary story explains all that we want explaining. But if the evolutionary story is irrelevant – or, at best, incomplete – then she's mistaken. And the evolutionary realist can then take advantage of the opening by giving an account of moral development that relies on human "interaction" with moral properties.

Two caveats about this option. First, taking this option requires (among other things) a thorough repudiation of the *empirical* case made by the evolutionary anti-realist. Recall the lines of evidence introduced by the anti-realist in chapters 5 and 6. While philosophical speculation no doubt plays a role here, the anti-realist at least attempts to hitch those speculations to a train of research, research that extends from neuroscience to primatology. It is not enough to accuse the anti-realist of making a conceptual error. There is a body of evidence that needs to be dealt with, case by curious case. I do not mean to suggest that such an undertaking is out of the question. In fact, we've already considered just such an undertaking in chapters 5 and 6. My point here is that the option we're discussing requires some very heavy empirical lifting. And no matter how comfortable our philosophical armchairs may be, we cannot expect to this option to pay off unless we get out of our armchair and confront the data.

A second caveat echoes the tone of the first. In my original sketch of the realist's option, I was careful to say that showing that the evolutionary case for moral development is mistaken only "makes room for the possibility of" moral facts. In saying this I meant to imply that the realist's work has only just begun. Making room for the *possibility* that your view is true is a far cry from showing that your view true. To demonstrate the latter requires engaging in a careful examination of how moral judgments (as described at §3.1) are made true by facts about the world that we can all accept. Moral realism gets no special pass when it comes to defending itself.

So in effect option 1 amounts to *stage* 1 of a multi-stage program. Stage 1 is largely an empirical matter, involving as it does a critique of the evolutionary anti-realist's case for the evolution of our moral mind. Stage 2 and beyond is a philosophical matter. It involves linking our conception of moral judgment with facts about the world. In one loose sense, I've just described the work of the philosopher Jesse Prinz. Part of the reason I've decided to treat his work differently, however, will be explained in the next section.

12.2 Option 2: Response Dependency

Jesse Prinz is not convinced that morality is innate. We reviewed his concerns at §5.6. Prinz's leading concern seems to be (as he put it recently) the "absolutely dizzying" variation in moral codes around the world (2008a: 221). He also suggests that the data that Joyce and others point to in defending moral nativism can just as easily be accounted for by a *non-*nativist explanation. In other words, we don't need to posit some special moral "faculty" of the mind in order to explain (for example) cross-cultural similarities or the apparent moral knowledge of children. Still, Prinz is not about to dismiss the role of evolution when it comes to our moral minds.

Prinz believes that we *do* come into the world equipped with a set of capacities that underwrite a moral sense, namely, the capacity to *feel*. For Prinz, emotions are central to morality (he makes his case in *The Emotional Construction of Morals*). And Prinz believes that evolution may play a critical role in explaining why we have the emotions that we do. The so-called moral emotions are constructed out of more basic emotions. So, for example, moral anger is anger that is directed at those who violate rights or commit an injustice. Guilt is sadness directed at *oneself* when one has violated rights or committed an injustice (Prinz 2008b: 69ff.). And insofar as Darwinian pressures are responsible for these affective systems in humans, then evolution and morality are not, on Prinz's view, unrelated.

This, however, might strike you as odd. You might be tempted, for example, to suspect that Prinz's moral psychological view leads seamlessly to evolutionary *anti*-realism. After all, you might argue that if human morality can be explained merely by pointing to the emotional dispositions of creatures like us, then there's no need to appeal to moral facts. Morality is nothing more than the pushes and pulls of our own emotional states. Morality – it would appear – is all in our heads. Prinz thinks the matter is more complicated than this. Indeed, his reasoning leads him to assert that "moral facts are both real and motivating" (2008a: 223). Moral realism has a voice after all.

Now before proponents of moral realism take their victory lap, it's important to understand exactly what this view entails – and what it does *not* entail. For it is especially what the view does not entail that may disappoint some moral realists. First and foremost (in case anyone actually imagined otherwise), moral facts will look nothing like, say, physical facts. They aren't concrete entities that you could put in your pocket or observe under a microscope. No great loss here, since few probably expected moral facts to have *that* kind of status. But, going further, moral facts, on Prinz's view, will also look nothing like numerical facts. Philosophers standardly treat numbers as *abstract* objects, objects that are real, though they do not have a location in space or time. Some moral philosophers like this idea and have sought to model moral facts after numerical facts. But Prinz will not be much comfort here either. His view does not make moral facts out to be anything like numbers. So what, then, is Prinz offering?

Prinz, following the work of other response-dependency theorists, argues that the property *being wrong* is like the property *being funny* in this way: to have this property is just to have the tendency to cause certain responses in observers. We don't want to say, for example, that things are funny because they have some special comedy dust sprinkled on them. Or, in a more academic spirit, that they are instances of an "incongruous relationship" between human intelligence and human habit (as suggested by the philosopher Henri Bergson). Rather, what makes funny things funny is just that they tend to amuse people. That's it. If we go searching for something that *unifies* all these things, at a level *beneath* these typical responses, we'll come up empty-handed, according to response-dependency theorists. Being funny is an example of a *response-dependent* property because what makes it true that a given object (a joke, a person, etc.) is funny depends essentially on the typical *responses* of observers. If most people do not tend to find a particular joke funny, then on this view it's not funny. Other response-dependent properties might include *being delicious, being loathsome, being disgusting.*

Prinz is attracted to this view in part because it squares with the intuition that you can actually be *mistaken* about what's funny or what's delicious. Exotic cases aside, funerals are not funny and rotting meat is not delicious. If you were to judge otherwise, you would be mistaken. However, your mistake would lie *not* in a failure to grasp some deep (comedic or funereal) property, but simply in a failure to assess what tends to make people laugh or what tends to give people gustatory delight.

So what does it mean then to say that *being wrong* is a response-dependent property? Roughly, an action is wrong just in case it is disposed to cause disapprobation (or disapproval) in observers. Just as in the case of humor, if we go searching for something that unifies all immoral acts, at a level beneath typical responses, we'll come up empty-handed. We cannot pick out what is immoral without appealing to how such acts tend to strike observers. In this way, moral judgments can be treated as *truth-apt*, that is, as capable of being true or false. Furthermore, it should be obvious that some moral judgments will indeed be true. For example, the judgment that it is wrong to kill your child for fun is true. So is the judgment that you ought to help others if they have helped you in the past. What makes them true has to do with the kind of responses such acts tend to produce in observers. In this way, Prinz (and other response-dependency theorists) can promote their view as a kind of moral realism. There is, after all, a fact of the matter as to whether stealing your neighbor's car for fun is wrong. And that fact lies outside what you happen to think or desire or whatever.

Admittedly, this brand of realism may not satisfy everyone. Keen readers will be quick to point out that on this view moral facts are suspiciously *contingent* – that is, they could just as easily have been different. Not only that, but Prinz's view looks positively *relativistic*. For relative to a culture where emotional responses tend to be *different*, acts that we regard as impermissible may turn out to be permissible. In modern Western cultures, for example, killing members of another group to promote one's status is greeted with disapprobation. But in some primitive cultures, that very same practice is greeted with approval. If Prinz's view is correct, then that practice is wrong in our culture but not wrong in another culture. After all, nothing in Prinz's view requires that everyone everywhere tends to have the *same* kind of emotional response to the same kind of behavior. Of course, where this is true, there will be moral uniformity. But where it isn't, there will be moral plurality.

Troubling as these implications may be, they do not amount to a criticism of Prinz's view. The thing to keep in mind here is that while Prinz may have promised moral *realism*, he did not promise moral *objectivity*. The former notion implies, very roughly, that there are facts of the matter regarding what you should or should not do, morally speaking. The latter notion implies, very roughly, that those moral facts are not subject to the various attitudes people might take to them. Evidently, on Prinz's view, moral realism does not entail moral objectivity. At any rate, Prinz is driven to this view because it succeeds in accommodating two important ob-servations: first, that emotions are central to moral judgment and, second, that moral views vary across cultures. If this is not what readers had hoped for in a moral realist position, Prinz would surely say that this reflects a problem – not in the view – but in the viewer. Prinz positively embraces relativism (he calls it subjectivism) with the same confidence that he rejects anti-realism.

The responses to Prinz's views are, as of this writing, only beginning to trickle in. We cannot say now how his view will generally be received. Still, we know how at least one evolutionary *anti*-realist – Richard Joyce – feels. But rather than discuss Joyce's replies to Prinz here, I'm going to hold off until the end of the chapter. For Joyce thinks that his replies to Prinz apply, with *equal force*, to the kind of constructivist position I have offered. So for the purposes of continuity, I'd like to first sketch the other two options available to the moral realist before returning to Joyce and his criticisms.

12.3 Option 3: Virtue Ethics Naturalized

The history of moral philosophy – to paint with a *very* broad brush – did not begin with discussions of right and wrong, moral duty, or rights. The search for an analysis of what makes an action immoral would have struck ancient philosophers as odd, if not misguided. From the vantage point of one the most influential ancient philosophers, Aristotle, the fundamental philo-sophical question was, in one sense, much broader than this. We should be asking: *How should I live? What kind of thing(s) should I pursue?* While such questions will no doubt make contact with moral judgments as we've described them, they also reach beyond or beneath them. For Aristotle and latter-day Aristotelians, such questions push us in the direction of asking: *What kind of person should I be? Which traits are good for me to have?* The Greek word for these traits is *arēte*, often translated as "virtue." Thus, *virtue* ethics. By cataloguing the various virtues, we can then say which sorts of traits we ought to develop in ourselves. Virtue ethicists (following Aristotle) often point to traits like honesty, kindness, courage, and temperance. Having these traits, according to Aristotle, is constitutive of the best life. It's good to have them.

But why *these* traits? After all, it's logically possible that the virtues are radically different than we suppose. Perhaps the good life consists of deception, meanness, and greed. (Didn't Gordon Gecko, the fictional hero of the 1987 film *Wall Street*, famously proclaim, "Greed is . . . good?") Here is where the work of the virtue ethicist begins. For we need a compelling reason to think that the better life consists of traits like honesty and generosity and not traits like meanness and greed. What is it about us that makes such traits virtues? How do we know what's good for creatures like us?

Aristotle's answer was refreshingly direct: *function*. Consider: What makes a good hammer *good*? What makes a good pianist *good*? What makes a good computer *good*? No one would attempt to answer these questions by launching an investigation into the microphysical properties of these items, as if each thing had some "goodness" atom in common with the rest. The answer is much closer to the surface. What makes a good hammer good is its ability to pound nails in well, to extract nails easily, and so on. What makes a good pianist good is her ability to play well. What makes a good computer good is its ability to process information quickly and accurately, its ability to store a lot of information, and so on. What can we generalize from these examples? That is, how would you complete the following definition?

For anything *x*, *x* is good if and only if *x* ___.

Well, in each of the above cases, what made a particular item good was its ability *to perform its function well*. A good hammer is made good precisely because it performs its designated function well. A good pianist is good precisely because she performs her designated function well. And so on and so forth.

With this little formula in hand, we can turn to our favorite subject: *us*. What makes a good person *good*? What makes a good (human) life *good*? To answer these questions requires, as per our formula, understanding of our function. Aristotle poses the questions this way:

> Have the carpenter, then, and the tanner certain functions or activities, and has man none? Is he born without a function? Or as eye, hand, foot, and in general each of the parts evidently has a function, may one lay it down that man similarly has a function apart from all these? What then can this be? (1988/350 BCE: Book I, §7)

This is the linchpin of the virtue ethicist's story. If she can put this piece of the puzzle in place, then we can trace a direct line from natural facts to facts about how we ought to live our lives. The method Aristotle uses to identify our function involves searching for that capacity that distinguishes us from other creatures. And according to Aristotle, it is the "life of the rational element" that distinguishes us from other creatures. In other words, our ability to reason and to follow reason. Unlike other creatures, we do not (always) eat the moment we are hungry or fight the moment we are confronted. Instead, we are unique in our ability to *deliberate*, to weigh considerations both for and against a course of action. Perhaps eating (or fighting) now conflicts with other goals. At any rate, what distinguishes us is this capacity to deliberate, to reason. If this is right, then our function is to live a life according to reason. And if this is right, then it follows (according to Aristotle) that what makes a human life good is a life lived according to reason. Now Aristotle unpacks this idea of a life lived according to reason by suggesting that we adopt certain intellectual and social (or moral) virtues, but we can hold off on delving any deeper. We've already hit a few snags.

One concern modern readers have with this line of reasoning has to do with our distinguishing trait. Is it so obvious, they ask, that humans are in fact the *only* organism with the sort of deliberative powers Aristotle cites? It does not appear that higher primates are the thoughtless brutes we may have once thought. But this is not the only problem. Suppose it's true that humans are unique in their ability to reason. What licenses the move from this claim to the claim that reasoning is our *function*? After all, there are surely other characteristics that are unique to humans: for example, walking upright, recursive grammar, hat-wearing. Is anyone seriously supposing that since we are alone in our ability to speak a language (let's say) that our *function* is to talk? That we ought to talk *more*? If the move from what distinguishes humans to the human function is indeed illicit, then more needs to be done to convince us that the best life for us is the life of reason.

Perhaps of even greater concern to the modern thinker is Aristotle's conception of the natural world, in particular his view that natural kinds (animals, plants, even rocks) all have a purpose, or *telos*. On Aristotle's view, just as we can say that the purpose or function of hammers is to pound nails, we can say that the purpose of birds is to fly, the purpose of fish is to swim, and so on. But modern science (as we noted at §6.2) appears to have undercut this picture. We no longer conceive of the world as home to objects, each of which "strives" toward a perfected state, a state correlated with its essence. Sure, birds fly. But it's an entirely different kind of logical statement to say they *ought* to fly, that flying is their essence. At a deeper level, scientists are uncomfortable with the idea that in addition to all of the physical properties that constitute a particular organism (e.g., the atoms that comprise a snake), there is some non-physical property that somehow attaches itself to the snake: namely, its function, what it's *supposed* to do. But where exactly is this mysterious property? Inside its cells?

These criticisms did not, however, sink Aristotelians. For friends of function did not abandon their cause. Beginning in the 1970s, philosophers of biology attempted to resurrect (and make respectable) talk of functions. Driving the resurrection was Darwinian natural selection. The philosopher of biology Larry Wright (1973) proposed that we understand function-talk in terms of *selection*-talk. Take an easy case: the human heart. Modern biology provides a compelling case for the claim that the human heart pumps blood because it was selected for over evolutionary history. Perhaps, then, this is how we should understand the intuitively compelling idea that the human heart has a function: it was selected to pump blood and its selection explains its modern presence. Functions, then, can just be "read off" the record of evolutionary selection.

Some neo-Aristotelians have decided to run with this effort to legitimize function-talk. For example, the philosopher William Casebeer employs this modern conception of function as a way of (as he puts it) "bringing Aristotle up to date" (2003: 49). The trick is to swap out Aristotle's implausible conception of nature with a scientifically respectable one. As far as functions are concerned, Casebeer adopts an analysis introduced by the philosopher Peter Godfrey-Smith: "functions are dispositions to and powers which explain the recent maintenance of a trait in a selective context" (1994: 344). In other words, functions are those dispositions acted on by "recent" selective pressures. Casebeer believes that this "thoroughgoing naturalized conception of function" (2003: 53) is precisely what's needed to put Aristotle back on a firm footing. For with a scientifically respectable notion of function in hand, we can thus show that, as Casebeer puts it, "moral facts are functional facts" (2003: 53).[2] On this updated version of Aristotle, what we ought morally to do follows from the kinds of traits we ought to develop. And the kinds of traits we ought to develop follow from the kind of creatures we're meant to be. And (finally) the kind of creatures we're meant to be follows from our biologically given functions.

So what does all this mean in practice? The answer is less straightforward than one might hope. For teasing out our function(s) requires sustained empirical work. It's not merely (or hardly at all) a matter of just thinking really hard about our evolutionary past from the philosophical armchair. What's required is biological study. As a general matter, however, our functions will "nest" or "smoothly stack," according to Casebeer. Lower-level functions will, in general, subserve higher functions. For example, Casebeer stresses the social nature of our species, something we noted throughout part I. Thus, being a "good human" entails developing traits that subserve this higher-level function. There is, as Casebeer admits, a "rich complex" here, and sorting out this complex requires a degree of biological understanding that we do not, as yet, possess. At any rate, what Casebeer appears to have provided is a principled way of reconciling moral facts with an evolutionary account of moral development. It would be misleading to portray this account as a tracking account, whereby we evolved to "track" moral facts that somehow exist independently of us. On Casebeer's view, moral facts are no more mysterious than functional facts. And functional facts (at least as Casebeer understands them) are biologically respectable facts, facts that are indeed objective even if they are "not to be found in the environment *per se*, but rather within the organism" (2003: 48).

The philosopher Philip Kitcher offers a slightly different sketch of a naturalized virtue ethics. Since Kitcher only summarizes a position, a position he may or may not choose to develop further, I'm going to quote his idea in full:

The more immediate function of normative guidance (and the rules of proto-morality) was to reinforce the psychological capacities that made sociality possible for us in the first place. Those psychological capacities involved an ability to empathize with the needs and interests of *some* others and to *some* extent, and they were reinforced by directives to take greater account of other people's plans and projects, even where there is, at least initially, no empathetic response. We can say, then, that the primary function of morality is to extend and amplify those primitive altruistic dispositions through which we became social animals in the first place, and that this has the secondary effect of promoting social cohesion. On the account of functions I prefer, the function can be ascribed to the impact on our altruism, even though the process of selection (natural and cultural) may attend to differences in social harmony. We might say that the function of morality is the enhancement of social cohesion *via* the amplification of our psychological altruistic dispositions. (2005: 178)

As I understand Kitcher, evolution put in place some rudimentary capacities, capacities not entirely unlike the capacities Prinz suggested: namely to *feel*. In particular, the capacity to empathize with others, to feel their pain, to identify with their desires, etc. But these capacities are notoriously limited. Your friend's pain means more to you than a stranger's. Yet as we saw in part I, extending one's empathy to include those beyond your immediate circle yields real biological dividends. On Kitcher's view, that's morality's role: extending one's empathy to others. This implies that, as moral creatures, *our function* is to extend our empathic responses, to widen our altruistic tendencies. Virtue, then, is a matter of developing those traits that, as Kitcher puts it, amplify our biologically given disposition to altruism. Like Casebeer, Kitcher proposes a way of accepting the evolutionary account of our moral minds without giving up the idea that there are objectively better and worse ways of living. Just as you can be mistaken about the function of the human heart (e.g., to keep the beat), you can be mistaken about *your* function *as a human being*.

Attempts to naturalize Aristotle, to offer a scientifically grounded virtue ethics, are just beginning to circulate among moral philosophers. It is too early, therefore, to know how successful these offerings will be. We do know, however, what one of the major players in the debate, Richard Joyce, thinks about naturalizing virtue ethics. We'll consider his response at §12.5. Let's look first at one final option for the moral realist.

12.4 Option 4: Moral Constructivism

Perhaps Prinz was on to something. Recall that Prinz wanted to make room for moral facts but in a way that is perfectly compatible with (if not strongly dependent on) an evolutionary account of moral development. His solution was to adapt response-dependency views in a way that could accommodate the emotional basis of morality and moral realism. Moral facts are real, though mind-dependent. I believe that this is, in general, the way morality ought to be understood. Unlike Prinz, however, I believe that my account of morality yields the conclusion that moral facts are objective, not relative. Furthermore, my account is a straightforward *tracking account,* in the sense that our practical minds evolved in the way they did because they were tracking the moral facts. Had the moral facts been different, so would our moral minds.

My proposal has two parts. The first part involves a refinement of the story we told in part I about how we evolved to think morally. I argue that we developed a special sensitivity to how others would view our behavior (from a particular standpoint). The second part is a metaethical story, that is, a story about what moral judgments are and about what makes true moral judgments *true* (and, yes, I believe some moral judgments are indeed true). As I argue, these two stories together could be read to imply that the evolution of our particular moral sense was the result of the recognition of facts about *hypothetical agreement.* An early human, disposed to judge that others could reasonably object to what she was intent on doing and motivated by that judgment, enhanced reproductive fitness partly because such judgments were sometimes *true.* And this, by the way, constitutes a moral realism worthy of the name – or so I maintain.

First, we evolved a disposition to consider how others would likely react to our behavior. The adaptive pressures of social living would have put a premium on making judgments – often situated within emotions – to the effect that others could *reasonably disapprove* of some bit of conduct. An early human who cared deeply about how others who shared a particular social standpoint might respond to her action enjoyed the benefits of more cooperative exchanges than those early humans who did not. And this in turn conferred a reproductive advantage on that individual. Someone who did not consider and/or care about how others might respond to her behavior would not make for a trustworthy partner. After all, she would not restrain herself from performing acts that may harm or threaten others' interests.

But keeping track of how each of one's neighbors might respond to a range of behaviors would be difficult. And a miscalculation could be costly. For example, if you mistakenly think that Ogg doesn't mind being cheated (when it is actually his brother Agg who doesn't mind), you run a serious risk of being ostracized from the group. As I see it, an obvious – not to mention cheap – solution would be the adoption of a default standpoint: if your counterpart here were only seeking principles that all could agree to live by, would he have any reason to condemn your behavior? Bear in mind that the process leading up to this stage, like the processes leading up to mastery of syntax, say, would have been gradual. Over successive generations, the object of practical deliberation becomes increasingly abstract, to the point at which one is concerned with the evaluations of a *hypothetical observer*. Thus, by the time modern humans arrive on the scene, they have evolved moral minds that place special weight on how others – from a particular standpoint – would respond to proposed courses of action.

Of course it's one thing to speculate from the "armchair." How might contemporary research bear on this story? Several lines of empirical research provide indirect support for the view. First, psychologists have for some time now maintained that the mind is innately equipped with a "theory of mind" (TOM) module or system, whose function is to ascribe beliefs and desires to conspecifics as a means of explaining and predicting behavior (see Baron-Cohen 1995; Carruthers et al. 2005–6). While disputes remain about how to understand the TOM module (see Goldman 2006), a consensus has developed around the idea that our social understanding of the world is erected around a core set of assumptions about the mental states that move other people. But a TOM module is precisely the sort of cognitive precursor one would expect if one were independently drawn to the view that our moral sense is attuned to the evaluative attitudes of others. (And the fact that this ability develops quite early in children supports the adaptation hypothesis.) If the outputs of this module interface with one's first-person set of hypotheses about what sorts of experiences lead to what sorts of mental states, then through induction one can generate hypotheses about the sorts of evaluative attitudes others are likely to have under a range of circumstances.

Second, one of the more unexpected features of both many primate societies and extant hunter-gatherer tribes is a strong tendency toward *egalitarianism* (Binmore 1998; Boehm 1999; de Waal 1996). One explanation for this tendency is that "humans are singling out competitive or predatory behaviours that are likely to cause conflict, and, by suppressing them, they are, in effect, damping conflicts pre-emptively" (Boehm 1999: 85). Boehm thus supposes that "the first behaviour to be outlawed and controlled by a human group may well have been the expression of dominance" (1999: 97). It should be obvious then that an individual in such a climate would be careful to conform his behavior to standards his conspecifics could accept. After all, as we saw in chapter 4, people punish individuals who attempt to exploit or cheat other members of the group. Indeed, they will *pay* to do so. But these observations lend support to the prediction that individuals would be strongly inclined to govern themselves in ways that escape the condemnation of members of the group.

Third, in tandem with the previous studies, some biological anthropologists and game theorists argue that the earliest (recognizably) moral communities exemplify the social contract tradition of morality since, in the absence of a dominant ruler (or philosopher-king), decisions affecting the welfare of individuals in a group would have to be made collaboratively (see Binmore 1998; Skyrms 1996). Indeed, some experimental results show that when individuals across a wide cultural range are asked to choose principles of distributive justice, they almost always fix on the same principles that survive the constructivist approach sketched below (Frohlich and Oppenheimer 1993).

Finally, if, as I have argued, selection would have favored individuals who adopted a particular standpoint in evaluating the permissibility of a given action, a standpoint marked by hypothetical agreement, then one should expect to see evidence of this perspective embedded in cross-cultural norms. There is a presumption in favor of such evidence. From Buddhism ("Hurt not others in ways that you yourself would find harmful") to Judaism ("What is hateful to you, do not to your fellow man") to Islam ("No one of you is a believer until he desires for his brother that which he desires for himself"), core social norms appear to be constrained by considerations of fairness: one extends to oneself only those principles for social living that others could accept (see Hauser 2006: 357ff.). Apparently, even among divergent cultures, where a variety of norms obtain, there will remain a fixed deliberative point that commands our attention in practical matters.

So much for genealogy. The second part concerns the nature of morality itself. Recall Prinz's version of moral wrongness: an action is wrong just in case that action tends to produce feelings of disapproval in observers. This version of wrongness relies crucially on how things would be (or would have been) under normal conditions. Philosophers refer to this as a *counterfactual*. Counterfactuals, I believe, *do* play a crucial role in moral judgments. However, not exactly the role Prinz supposes. On my account, an action is wrong just in case others – who have an interest in general rules governing behavior – *would* tend to object to that action. This account extends the pioneering work of the philosopher T.M. Scanlon, who was himself following in the footsteps of the philosopher John Rawls. Scanlon argues that acts are wrong just in case they could be reasonably rejected by anyone seeking principles everyone could live with. Morality, therefore, is a construction or procedure. Right and wrong is whatever survives this hypothetical procedure.

Emotions, while they may regularly attend such judgments, need not. According to this "Scanlonian" picture, that someone *could reasonably object* to a particular behavior is enough to make that action wrong. *Moral constructivism* is the name some philosophers use to describe the view that facts about how others would respond to one's conduct constitute moral facts or truths themselves. On the constructivist account, moral facts are determined by, very roughly, the principles that would survive scrutiny from a particular standpoint. Evolutionary theory, then, does not undermine moral realism. I contend that evolutionary theory explains why moral realism is likely to be true.

There remain thorny questions here about realism and objectivity. Is the view I am proposing *realist*, in the sense that it identifies moral facts? Here I believe the answer is straightforward: yes. It's not difficult to suppose that, on some occasions at least, there *is* a fact of the matter as to what someone could reasonably object to, someone (that is) interested in finding rules everyone could live by. Moreover, moral facts are distinct in important ways from the attitudes people happen to have on a given occasion. What justifies a given moral principle *P* is *not* that *we think P* withstands scrutiny from the relevant procedure of construction, but that *P* withstands scrutiny from the relevant procedure, *whether or not anyone has bothered to consider the matter*. By virtue of depending on counterfactuals (i.e., what agents *would* agree to under certain conditions), at least some moral truths can be strongly mind-independent, obtaining even when evaluated against worlds in which there are no rational agents.

But what of objectivity? This is a more complicated question. On the one hand, the view does not support (what I'll call) *local relativism*, according to which moral facts are determined by what I or you happen to think or feel on this occasion. Indeed, moral facts are more independent still: even if *everyone* happened to think that a particular action was permissible, they could be wrong. They could be wrong because no one happened to consider whether that action could be rejected from the standpoint described above. This leads me to construe this view as a species of moral objectivity. We can actually discover which acts are wrong, and this discovery could demonstrate that we were all previously mistaken about its moral status. On the other hand, the view does not rule out (what might be called) *transcendental relativism*, according to which moral facts are relative to facts about human nature as we find it. Thus, if we can conceive of a world in which an act could not be reasonably rejected, although it *could* be reasonably rejected here in this world, then it would seem that the moral facts could change. It would be permissible there but impermissible here. It's hard to wrap one's mind around this possibility, but I don't see how to deny the possibility. Does this render the view relativistic? Well, as noted above, that might ultimately depend on the terms we use, not on the world itself. In the end, I suppose it's up the reader to make this decision.

12.5 Objections to the Realist Options

How promising are these options? Should the moral realist rest content that there *is* a place for moral facts in the world after all? The answer depends of course on how well these various options survive careful scrutiny. Richard Joyce has given what he considers close scrutiny to these options and is not persuaded. We have already discussed the virtues and vices of the first option – denying moral nativism. Joyce focuses his attention on the remaining options: response dependency, naturalized virtue ethics, and moral constructivism. In this final section, I'll present in brief Joyce's concerns about each.

Joyce lumps response dependency and moral constructivism into the same philosophical heap, on the grounds that they both see moral facts as determined by how certain observers would respond to certain acts. I myself noted the similarities between Prinz's view and my own, so this is not an entirely unwarranted move on Joyce's part. Joyce sees three problems facing (so-called) response-dependent views: the incompleteness problem, the practical relevance problem, and the content problem.

The incompleteness problem, according to Joyce, refers to the incomplete specification of the circumstances under which judges or observers make their responses. Joyce fixes his discussion on Prinz (though his objection presumably extends to my constructivist position). Joyce asks: "Moral wrongness (for [someone] X) is whatever would cause X disapprobation in circumstances of *full information*? of *impartial attention*? of *calm reflection*? or what?" (2008: 252). The reason this matters is because what would tend to cause disapprobation in X, if X is fully attending to the issue, is likely to be different than if X is somewhat distracted. And this matters because this means that whether or not some act is wrong will vary quite widely (not to mention arbitrarily). But even if we insist that wrongness depends on what would cause disapprobation in X *if X were fully attending to the matter*, there will still remain variation in what would cause disapprobation in X if X were raised in the wilds of Zambia or if X were a despondent American teen or if X were an elderly Jew in Tel Aviv. All this seems to introduce a degree of relativism far more extreme than initially supposed. According to Joyce, "the monster looming over Prinz's version of naturalism is relativism of the most radical and rampant rank" (2008: 252).

One might offer, on Prinz's behalf, the following solution. An act is wrong just in case it is disposed to cause X disapprobation assuming X has qualities *ABC* and is under circumstances *DEF*. That is, we stipulate in advance all the "correct" conditions. But this solution raises a new problem: *the problem of practical relevance*. In short, why should it matter *to X* that under these highly specified conditions *someone under the "correct" conditions* would feel disapprobation? Recall from §3.1 that one of the essential ingredients of moral judgments is their practical oomph: they *move us* (however slightly) to act in accordance with our judgments. Someone who claims that abortion is immoral but is not moved in the slightest to avoid having one (or to condemn those who have) raises obvious doubts about her claim. Now if moral wrongness amounted to an act's disposition to cause *someone* with qualities *ABC*, under conditions *DEF*, to feel disapprobation, this seems to short-circuit the practical oomph that moral judgments were supposed to have. After all, there doesn't seem to be anything particularly odd about my judging, on the one hand, that *someone* (under all the "right" conditions) might feel disapprobation toward some act and, on the other hand, that I'm not motivated at all to refrain from performing that act. Why? Because I feel no disapprobation toward that act!

Joyce summarizes his concern this way: "the kind of dispositional natural properties that [Prinz is offering] as the ontological constituents of the moral realm *don't come close* to satisfying the pretheoretical desiderata of what moral properties should look like" (2008: 253). In other words, if rightness and wrongness are supposed to look anything like the characterization offered at §3.1, then Prinz's view fails, for it offers a picture that does nothing to support that characterization.

Similar remarks are supposed to cover moral constructivism. Recall that moral constructivism construes wrong acts as acts that someone, *who was concerned about finding general rules to govern behavior*, could reasonably object to. But, Joyce asks, why should *I* care about what such a person could reasonably object to? Why should that fact give *me* a reason to resist performing that act? The practical relevance problem, in other words, is a problem for moral constructivism, too. A successful theory of morality should make it clear how the wrongness feature should be practically relevant to *me* – why it should move me. And, according to Joyce, moral constructivism does not make this clear.

In the same vein, moral constructivism confronts the incompleteness problem. Can we say with confidence that there *is* a determinate set of acts that *everyone* – even those concerned with general rules – could reasonably reject? Won't there be tremendous variation? (Joyce asks us to consider what "drunken Vikings," "medieval samurais," and "Soviet communists" might reasonably object to.) Joyce suspects that a similar kind of "radical and rampant" relativism to the one that plagued Prinz's view plagues moral constructivism.

But the problems (allegedly) don't stop there. The content problem is of a piece with the problems above. This problem concerns the question of whether the acts that response dependency and/or moral constructivism identify as wrong will line up with the acts that moral common sense identifies as wrong. Joyce foresees that both views will render acceptable some acts that are "intuitively immoral." "How do we know," Joyce wonders, "that even *being rational* (say) will exclude a preference for ethnic cleansing?" (2008: 257). Of course, one might attempt to avoid this absurd result by requiring that the agents deliberating over what could be reasonably rejected are *virtuous*, that is, have an intrinsic interest in rejecting immoral acts. Unfortunately, this move gets us nowhere. For wasn't immorality supposed to be understood in terms of what agents could reasonably reject? If so, then this won't remove the content problem. After all, what good does it do to add that the agents deliberating over what could be reasonably rejected have an intrinsic interest in deliberating over what could be reasonably rejected? On the other hand, if we characterized virtue (say) in terms of *fairness*, this might indeed get us somewhere. The cost of making this move, however, would be steep: moral constructivism is no longer doing any interesting philosophical work. It's a fifth wheel. If fairness (for example) is driving the decision-making *because fairness is objectively right*, then it's not the decision-making process that determines rightness – but fairness itself. Thus moral constructivism is not where all the moral action is.

As you no doubt suspect, defenders of response-dependency-style views are not rolling over dead. They are actively formulating responses. In the interest of keeping the focus, I will allow Joyce to get the last word here – not because (I believe) his objections are fatal, but because these metaethical debates are the subject of an entirely different book. At any rate, the suggested readings at the end of this chapter will provide the hungry reader with more meaty bits to chew on.

Let me close by discussing Joyce's reaction to naturalized virtue ethics. Recall that this moral realist option attempts to identify moral facts with functional facts, where functional facts are uncovered by modern biology. What it is to be a good human (or to live a flourishing human life) is to perform our human function(s) *well*. And what the human function(s) are is identified by the same method that identifies what the heart's function is and what the eye's function is and so on. Thus, just as we can say that the heart *should* pump blood at a given rate (and that a heart that fails to do so is a *bad* heart), we can say that someone *should* promote social harmony (say) or *should* be honest. And someone who doesn't is a *bad* person.

Joyce concedes that there is some sense in talking about what hearts and eyes *ought* to do. But, he argues, how "we get from 'Joe's heart ought to pump blood' to 'Joe ought to keep his promise' remains problematic" (2006: 170). What's problematic is the distinctive *normativity* (or reason-giving nature) of morality: the fact that moral claims have a special authority, that they are inescapable (again, see §3.1). Consider: it's one thing to say that the heart ought to pump blood. It's quite a different thing to say that the heart is *required* or *obligated* to pump blood – or that the heart *has a reason* to pump blood, in the sense of a practical demand. But this latter way of talking is precisely what characterizes *moral* oughts: you are required to keep your promises, you have a reason not to harm people unnecessarily. Apparently, biology doesn't seem able to provide the kind of normative force that the moral realm exhibits.

Think of things this way: What are we saying when we judge that a heart *ought* to pump blood? Isn't it something like: statistically speaking, most hearts tend to pump blood and so we predict that this one will, too? Now contrast this with judging that you ought to help someone who has helped you. Is this judgment *merely* (or at all) like saying: statistically speaking, most people tend to help those who have helped them, so we predict that you will, too? Surely there's more to the judgment than this. When I judge that you ought to help those who have helped you, I'm not pointing out what most people tend to do. I'm pointing out a *demand* on you, a demand that holds independently of what anyone else happens to do. Morality requires this. Moreover, if you refuse to help someone who has helped you, then you are (at least in principle) *deserving* of punishment. Why? Because you have transgressed a moral law. By contrast, it would be silly to suppose that a heart that fails to pump blood deserves punishment (if anything, it deserves a transplant!). So the biological ought seems too "wimpy" to account for the moral ought: "the normativity that may be squeezed from evolutionary biology comes nowhere near to accommodating this desideratum" (Joyce 2006: 174). The updated Aristotelian can either abandon the idea that morality has this normative force or promise to show that biology can supply it. The first choice looks drastic. The second choice is but an unfulfilled promise. At best, a naturalized virtue ethic is a work in progress.

12.6 Conclusion

The moral realist retains some interesting options. We have discussed four: rejecting moral nativism, response dependency, naturalized virtue ethics, and moral constructivism. The latter three options involve some fairly sophisticated metaethical moves. Response-dependency views like Prinz's identify moral facts with response-dependent facts, in particular facts about the emotional responses certain acts tend to produce in observers. For Prinz, morality is ultimately (only) *felt*. A related response-dependency view is moral constructivism, according to which moral facts are identified with facts about the rules people would freely accept (if they were seeking a set of rules to live by). Naturalized virtue ethics redirects the focus on *agents*, rather than acts. Here the aim is to develop and maintain traits of character, and which traits of character we ought to develop depends on careful Darwinian study of our function(s).

Given the resurgent interest in evolutionary ethics, no doubt more realist options – and more anti-realist responses – are forthcoming. Central to these coming debates is the empirical debate over the innateness of morality. This was our focus in part I. We asked: To what extent (if any) are our moral minds the result of evolution by natural selection? Because that issue has yet to be resolved, the metaethical story must be qualified in the following way. Claims about the nature of morality itself will need to be understood as conditionals: *if* natural selection is largely responsible for our moral minds, then the truth about morality is thus-and-so. If it's not, all bets are off. It's back to the drawing board.

At the same time, part of the debate will focus on *how real* moral facts must be in order to deserve the name moral realism. As we saw in chapter 11, Joyce and Street argue that we have no reason to believe that there is anything in the world that comes close to grounding moral facts. Real moral properties are an illusion. Contemporary realists, on the other hand, argue that there are indeed naturalistic properties that ground moral facts. This debate continues to rage in corners of moral philosophy quite apart from evolutionary considerations.

What we can all agree on, however, is this. If moral *realism* is to have a chance, then there needs to be a way of understanding, on the one hand, how natural selection played a critical role in shaping our moral minds and, on the other, how this can be reconciled with an account of moral facts that can sufficiently underwrite the distinctive character of moral judgment. Moral realists contend that such a view is available. Evolutionary anti-realists (like Joyce and Street) deny this.

For good or ill, the process of "biologicizing" ethics is under way. But this pursuit can take different shapes. It might take the shape of trying to understand how (if at all) our disposition to make moral judgments could have been the result of Darwinian pressures – the very same pressures that resulted in the tiger's stripes and the oak's leaves. We explored this pursuit in part I. On the other hand, it might take the shape of trying to understand how Darwinian principles can, directly or indirectly, reveal moral principles. Maybe what we ought to do, morally, follows directly from what our evolutionary past has disposed us to do (whatever that might be). This was our focus in part II. And finally, the pursuit of "biologicizing" ethics might take the shape of trying to understand the nature of moral properties *under the assumption* that we evolved to think morally. Evolutionary anti-realists claim that the evolutionary story *undermines* belief in an objectively *real* moral order. Realists counter this claim. We have waded through these debates in the last three chapters. Our understanding of these different pursuits will grow as our understanding of our evolutionary past grows. And it will grow as our understanding of morality itself grows.

Further Reading

Casebeer, W. (2003) *Natural Ethical Facts: Evolution, Connectionism, and Moral Cognition* (MIT).

James, S. (2008) The Caveman's Conscience: Evolution and Moral Realism. *Australasian Journal of Philosophy*, 87/2: 1–19.

James, S. and P. Carruthers (2008) Human Evolution and the Possibility of Moral Realism. *Philosophy and Phenomenological Research*, 77/1: 237–44.

Joyce, Richard (2006) *The Evolution of Morality* (MIT Press).

Joyce, Richard (2008) Replies. *Philosophy and Phenomenological Research*, 77/1: 245–67.

Kitcher, Philip (2005) Biology and Ethics. In D. Copp (ed.), *The Oxford Handbook of Ethics* (Oxford University Press).

Prinz, Jesse J. (2007) *The Emotional Construction of Morals* (Oxford University Press).

Prinz, Jesse J. (2008a) Acquired Moral Truths. *Philosophy and Phenomenological Research*, 77/1: 219–27.

Scanlon, T.M. (1998) *What We Owe to Each Other* (Harvard University Press).

Notes

Introduction

1 Unless of course you have had, say, significant damage to your ventro-medial prefrontal cortex, in which case you likely lack executive control over your behavior.
2 As those who are familiar with the conflagration following the release of E.O. Wilson's *Sociobiology* can attest.
3 Interested readers are encouraged to see Kitcher (1985) and Pinker (2002).

Chapter 1 Natural Selection and Human Nature

1 A powerful subsidiary force – *sexual selection* – operates according to the pressures associated with mating. There is, on the one hand, intrasexual competition whereby members of one sex compete for mating access to members of the opposite sex; this competition will tend to yield adaptations among intrasexual rivals (e.g. body mass among male primates). On the other hand, there is intersexual competition, whereby the preferences of one sex will tend to determine which qualities come to dominate among members of the opposite sex (e.g. the bright plumage of the male peacock).
2 During a critical period of early development, ducklings will come to associate the movements of a larger, independent object with their mother, and so follow that object wherever it leads. In most environments, such an organism *is* their mother, but in experimental settings ducklings can "imprint" on inanimate objects – or the legs of a scientist.
3 Just to be clear: there is no in-principle reason to think that, all things being equal, Mother Nature would not have selected for the oxygen-carrying substance had it appeared green to creatures like us.
4 I'm sweeping under the rug very large and very controversial questions. For example, what (if anything) is/was the purpose of moral sense? In later

chapters we'll do a thorough housecleaning job, addressing this question in its proper place.

5 A note of caution: while the enthusiasm for a specialized moral sense is highest among evolutionary psychologists, they are not the only researchers involved in the debate. Some researchers are pursuing the more general question of whether or not the mind contains any specialized faculties, independently of their evolutionary origin. The emphasis on evolutionary psychology in what follows is only meant to highlight one area of vigorous research. Important alternative models are suggested at the end of chapter 4.

6 Mixing our metaphors further, consider your house key. That key is useless in almost every other lock, but it's a cheap and very reliable key in the lock that counts: the one to your house.

7 For present purposes, I won't assume anything about the relationship between the mind and the brain; I will note, however, that it is a working assumption among psychologists that the mind is in some sense realized by the operations of the brain. But these are deep waters we need not enter.

8 Of course, how these rules are "encoded" in the brain is an entirely different matter, one that would take us across several different disciplines. My aim here is simply to offer a rough sketch of the evolutionary psychologist's program as a way of laying the foundation for our main discussion. For a more in-depth look at this field, see the Further Reading at the end of this chapter.

Chapter 2 The (Earliest) Roots of Right

1 One of the more striking cases came in 1996 when Binti Jua, a female western lowland gorilla at the Brookfield Zoo in Chicago, carefully cradled a 3-year-old boy who had fallen into the gorilla exhibit before delivering the boy to her trainers.

2 Sounds good on paper, but what do field tests show? More specifically, do the field tests show that alarm-calling in ground squirrels follows this inclusive fitness constraint? They do. In fact, not only are ground squirrels quite selective in their alarm-calling (almost only in the presence of kin), they're also selective in their assistance, rushing to help kin injured in conflict, but ignoring non-kin. See Sherman 2009.

3 According to a Spanish proverb, an ounce of blood is worth more than a pound of friendship,

4 Explaining *why* of course is notoriously difficult. For example, if someone demanded from you a justification for saving your brother first, what would you say beyond "He's my brother?" Most of us are inclined to think that that is justification enough. But surely something more can be said to defend the notion. What should we say?

5 A corresponding point can be made about selfishness: an organism is selfish on some occasion if and only if its motives on that occasion are self-interested. If it happens to help others on some occasion, we don't call it altruistic if its motives are self-interested.

Chapter 3 The Caveman's Conscience

1 Attempts to characterize what lies *beyond* our moral experience – i.e., the nature of the "moral world" itself – will be discussed in part II.

2 This does not mean that they have to do as they judge, or even that they have to judge correctly. Even Hitler would count as a moral creature in this minimal sense simply because (we'll assume) he could judge that some actions are forbidden. Being a moral creature has to do with what someone is *capable of* – not what he does.

3 If I seem overly cautious in my analysis of morality ("morality *appears* to be this and that," and so on), it's because serious debate continues in philosophy over whether or not these appearances are deceiving. Some philosophers, for example, are happy to admit that morality *appears* one way, but will insist that, in truth, it is another.

4 In study after study, males around the world consistently rank the attractiveness of females according to just those traits.

5 Strictly speaking, of course, the best guarantee that Ogg will avoid committing those types of actions (short of disabling him) would be to hard-wire Ogg in such a way that his behavior becomes inflexible. For reasons we'll get to shortly, this option faces real drawbacks.

6 In the next section we'll explore in more depth the connections between reputation, punishment, and morality.

7 See https://www.priestsforlife.org/magisterium/bishops/wuerl-2006-red-mass.htm.

8 Recent studies on the evolution of social behavior support this hypothesis, as we'll see in chapter 4.

Chapter 4 Just Deserts

1 In fact, the anthropologist Robin Dunbar has hypothesized that language evolved in humans precisely because it enabled us to *gossip*. The best way to learn about the behavior and reputation of others is to listen to the "dirt" that's going around. When the psychologist Jonathon Haidt and a student Holly Hom asked fifty-one subjects to keep a journal of longer conversations

they had with friends, they discovered that "gossip is overwhelmingly critical, and it is primarily about the moral and social violations of others" (2006: 54). "Gossip," concludes Haidt, "is a policeman and a teacher."

2 I take this to be especially important in coming to understand the nature of morality itself, as I argue in chapter 12.

3 Punishment appears to be costly in another way. Psychologists Kevin Carl-smith, Daniel Gilbert, and Timothy Wilson (2008) showed that revenge is not all that sweet. When subjects were exploited in a public goods game (by an undercover member of the experiment team who, after pleading with other members to invest heavily, defected), some subjects had the option to retaliate; other subjects did not. Those subjects who had the option to punish and did so "reported a significantly worse mood" after punishing than those subjects who did not have the option but expressed a wish to punish. Moreover, punishers ruminated far longer about the free-rider than those unable to punish. Evidently, contrary to folk wisdom, turning the other cheek can indeed be more satisfying.

4 As I write, the public is coming to grips with Bernard Madoff and the $50 billion investment fraud he committed. When asked by National Public Radio what Madoff's "biggest and hardest-to-forgive trans-gression" was, the rabbi Mark Borovitz said without hesitation: "The rape of trust. They call it 'affinity theft.' ... I get you to like me, I get you to trust me and then I not only steal your money, I steal your belief that people are good and decent and caring." So how will Madoff be punished if, according to Jewish tradition, there is no hell? "Mr. Madoff has to live with this himself ... There's nobody that he can turn to without seeing the harm that he's done. And being shunned, being ostracized ... *that's hell.*"

5 As quoted in the *Daily Telegraph*, August 8, 2008.

Chapter 5 The Science of Virtue and Vice

1 But this conservative explanation may not suffice to explain what Warneken and his colleagues saw (2009): chimpanzees were nearly as helpful as infants when someone was in need. And like the infants tested, the chimps were prompted to respond "even in the absence of encouragement or praise."

2 In some cases, patients exhibit other recognition impairments – for example, an inability to recognize common plants and animals or an inability to recognize places or facial expressions.

3 When we are exposed to images depicting individuals in severe distress (victims of car accidents, patients undergoing crude surgeries), our bodies react in characteristic ways: our heart-rate increases, our palms sweat, our

blood pressure rises. These are responses of the autonomic nervous system, a system that operates (mostly) independently of our will. Individuals identified as psychopathic do not show such reactions. They are indifferent to the distress of others.

4 The psychologist Joshua Greene reports that "the posterior cingulate gyrus, a region that exhibits increased activity during a variety of emotion-related tasks, was less active in the psychopathic group than in the control subjects" (2005: 343).

5 Just to be sure: in (1) "himself" *must* refer to *Bill*. In (2) "himself" could be just about anybody (as long as, I suppose, he's male). In (3), "him" could refer to just about anybody *but* Bill. *Bill* can't be the referent of "him" in (3). In (4) the correct imperative is "Is the boy who is happy missing?" And in (5) the correct imperative is "Was the duck sad that the chicken was missing?"

6 For example, while almost all human languages are either subject-verb-object (as is English: "He opened the box") or subject-object-verb (as is Japanese), virtually none is object-subject-verb. This should indeed be striking if, as non-nativists maintain, human language is not innately constrained.

7 Advertisers are forever crafting slogans that have just the right *something* to spread throughout the population of consumers. For (the thinking goes) the more people remember your slogan, the more they remember the product, and the more they remember the product, the more likely they are to purchase that product.

Chapter 6 Social Harmony: The Good, the Bad, and the Biologically Ugly

1 There are some constraints, of course. Variations in organismic form build off existing forms, so while one's offspring might, through some mutation, develop a thicker plumage, one's offspring won't develop a full plumage where none existed before.

Chapter 7 Hume's Law

1 This is really just the tip of a vast philosophical iceberg. At the risk of running us entirely off the tracks, I'm going to leave this discussion where it is, hoping that my reader has some sense of the distinction. For more on this, see the Further Reading at the end of the chapter.

2 Hume died eighty-three years *before* the publication of the *Origin*, so we cannot say, for obvious reasons, that Hume was a critic of Social Darwinism.

We could probably get away with saying that Hume *would have been* a critic of Social Darwinism.

Chapter 8 Moore's Naturalistic Fallacy

1 I am assuming that the question is not being asked jokingly or ironically – or in some other non-standard way made evident by the context. This is a question put forward sincerely.

Chapter 9 Rethinking Moore and Hume

1 The philosopher James Rachels (1990: 70–1) draws the distinction this way. It's one thing to offer a *definition* of a term (like "bachelor" or "water"); it's another thing to offer a *criterion* of a term.
2 One of the central tasks of normative epistemology is examining the nature of justification as it figures in claims to knowledge. Suffice it to say, much disagreement persists.

Chapter 11 Contemporary Evolutionary Anti-Realism

1 And many others besides Spencer. Joyce takes at aim at several recent attempts to vindicate a kind of moral realism in the context of evolution: Robert Richards (1986), Richmond Campbell (1996), Daniel Dennett (1995), and William Casebeer (2003).
2 This is not unlike the example I introduced in chapter 10 regarding the engine warning light on your dashboard. Since the light's appearance was not caused by an engine malfunction (but by some arbitrary short-circuit elsewhere), you are not justified in believing that there's an engine malfunction on the basis of the light alone.
3 To be fair, not all philosophers will gladly accept this. The view I am presupposing here is naive realism, according to which the world's properties are pretty much as we perceive them to be. The view receives unanimous(?) support from common sense. It receives mixed support from philosophers.
4 The philosopher Philip Kitcher presses the same point: "there's no issue here of perceiving moral truths . . . The criterion of success isn't accurate representation, but the improvement of social cohesion" (2005: 176).

Chapter 12 Options for the Evolutionary Realist

1 The philosopher Crispin Wright laments that "a philosopher who asserts that she is a realist about . . . ethics, has probably, for most philosophical audiences, accomplished little more than to clear her throat" (1992: 1).

2 Casebeer's proposal is unorthodox in more ways than one: virtue ethics is standardly thought to be a normative ethical position – not a metaethical position. That is, virtue ethics has traditionally aimed at giving us guidance on how to live, not at explaining the underlying metaphysical structure of moral talk and behavior.

References

Aristotle (1988/350 BCE) *The Nicomachean Ethics*, trans. D. Ross, ed. J.L. Ackrill and J.O. Urmson (Oxford University Press).

Barkow, Jerome, Leda Cosmides, and John Tooby (1995) *The Adapted Mind: Evolutionary Psychology and Generation of Culture* (Oxford University Press).

Baron-Cohen, S. (1995) *Mindblindness* (MIT Press).

Binmore, K.G. (1998) *Game Theory and the Social Contract, II: Just Playing* (MIT Press).

Black, Max (1964) The Gap Between "Is" and "Should." *The Philosophical Review*, 73/2: 165–81.

Blair, J. (2005) *The Psychopath: Emotion and the Brain* (Wiley-Blackwell).

Boehm, C. (1999) *Hierarchy in the Forest: The Evolution of Egalitarian Behavior* (Harvard University Press).

Boehm, C. (2000) Conflict and the Evolution of Social Control. *Journal of Consciousness Studies*, 7/1–2: 79–101.

Brockman, John (1995) *The Third Culture: Beyond the Scientific Revolution* (Touchstone).

Buller, David (2006) *Adapting Minds: Evolutionary Psychology and the Persistent Quest for Human Nature* (Bradford Books, MIT).

Burnstein, E., C. Crandall, and S. Kitayama (1994) Some Neo-Darwinian Decision Rules for Altruism: Weighing Cues for Inclusive Fitness as a Function of the Biological Importance of the Decision. *Journal of Personality and Social Psychology*, 67, 773–89.

Buss, David (2007) *Evolutionary Psychology and the New Science of the Mind* (Allyn & Bacon).

Campbell, R. (1996) Can Biology Make Ethics Objective? *Biology and Philosophy*, 11: 21–31.

Carlsmith, K.M., J. Darley, and P. Robinson (2002) Why Do We Punish? Deterrence and Just Deserts as Motives for Punishment. *Journal of Personality and Social Psychology*, 83: 284–99.

Carlsmith, K.W., T. Wilson, and D. Gilbert (2008) The Paradoxical Consequences of Revenge. *Journal of Personality and Social Psychology*, 95/6: 1316–24.

Carruthers, Peter, Stephen Laurence, and Stephen Stich (eds.) (2005–6) *The Innate Mind*, vols. 1 and 2 (Oxford University Press).

Casebeer, W. (2003) *Natural Ethical Facts: Evolution, Connectionism, and Moral Cognition* (MIT).

Chapais, Bernard, Liane Savard, and Carole Gauthier (2001) Kin Selection and the Distribution of Altruism in Relation to Degree of Kinship in Japanese Macaques. *Behavioral Ecology and Sociobiology*, 49/6: 493–502.

Chomsky, Noam and Carlos Peregrín Otero (2004) *Language and Politics* (AK Press).

Cima, Maaike, Franca Tonnaer, and Marc Hauser (2010) Psychopaths Know Right from Wrong But Don't Care. *Social, Cognitive, and Affective Neuroscience.* Advanced access: http://scan.oxfordjournals.org/content/early/2010/01/06/scan.nsp051.full.

Darwin, Charles (2003/1859) *On the Origin of Species* (Signet Classics).

Darwin, Charles (2009/1871) *The Descent of Man* (Dover Publications).

Darwin, Charles (2007) *The Life and Letters of Charles Darwin*, vol. 2 (Kessinger Publishing).

Dawkins, Richard (1982) *The Extended Phenotype* (Oxford University Press).

Dawkins, Richard (1986) *The Blind Watchmaker* (Norton).

Dawkins, Richard (1995) *The Selfish Gene* (Oxford University Press).

Dawkins, Richard (1999), Eating People Is Wrong. Interviewed by Mary Riddell, *New Statesman*, March 26. http://www.newstatesman.com/199903260013

De Waal, Frans (1989) *Peacemaking Among Primates* (Harvard University Press).

De Waal, Frans (1996) *Good Natured: The Origins of Right and Wrong in Humans and Other Animals* (Harvard University Press).

De Waal, Frans (2005) *Our Inner Ape* (Riverhead).

De Waal, Frans (2006) *Primates and Philosophers: How Morality Evolved* (Princeton University Press).

Deigh, Jonathon (1996) *The Sources of Moral Agency* (Cambridge University Press).

Dennett, Daniel C. (1995) *Darwin's Dangerous Idea: Evolution and the Meanings of Life* (Simon & Schuster).

Desmond, A. and J. Moore (1991) *Darwin: The Life of a Tormented Evolutionist* (Norton).

Dobzhansky, Theodosius (1964) Biology, Molecular and Organismic. *American Zoologist*, 4: 443–52.

Dreber, A., D. Rand, D. Fudenberg, and M. Nowak (2008) Winners Don't Punish. *Nature*, 452/7185: 348–51.

Dugatkin, Lee Alan (2006) *The Altruism Equation: Seven Scientists Search for the Origins of Goodness* (Princeton University Press).

Dunbar, Robin (1997) *Grooming, Gossip, and the Evolution of Language* (Harvard University Press).

Dunford, C. (1977) Behavioral Limitations of Round-Tailed Ground Squirrel Density. *Ecology*, 58: 1254–68.

Ehrlich, Paul R. (2002) *Human Natures: Genes, Cultures, and the Human Prospect* (Penguin).

Eisenberg, Nancy and Paul Henry Mussen (1989) *The Roots of Prosocial Behavior in Children*. Cambridge Studies in Social and Emotional Development (Cambridge University Press).

Emlem, S.T. and P.H. Wrege (1988) The Role of Kinship in Helping Decisions among White-Fronted Bee-Eaters. *Behavioral Ecology and Sociobiology*, 23/5: 305–15.

Essock-Vitale, S. and M.T. McGuire (1985) Women's Lives Viewed from an Evolutionary Perspective. II: Patterns of Helping. *Ethology & Sociobiology*, 6: 155–73.

Farmer, Colleen (1997) Did Lungs and the Intracardiac Shunt Evolve to Oxygenate the Heart in Vertebrates? *Paleobiology*, 23/3: 358–72.

Fehr, E. and Simon Gachter (2002) Altruistic Punishment in Humans. *Nature*, 415: 137–40.

Frank, Robert (1988) *Passions within Reason: The Strategic Role of the Emotions* (Norton).

Frohlich, N. and J.A. Oppenheimer (1993) *Choosing Justice: An Experimental Approach to Ethical Theory* (University of California Press).

Ghiselin, Michael T. (1974) *The Economy of Nature and the Evolution of Sex* (University of California Press).

Godfrey-Smith, P. (1994) A Modern History Theory of Functions. *Nous*, 28: 344–62.

Goldman, A. (2006) *Simulating Minds: The Philosophy, Psychology, and Neuroscience of Mindreading* (Oxford University Press).

Gould, Stephen J. (1992) *The Panda's Thumb* (Norton).

Gould, Stephen J. (1996) *The Mismeasure of Man* (Norton).

Greene, J. (2005) Cognitive Neuroscience and the Structure of the Moral Mind. In P. Carruthers et al. (eds.), *The Innate Mind: Structure and Contents*, vol. 1 (Oxford University Press).

Haidt, Jonathan (2006) *The Happiness Hypothesis: Finding Modern Truth in Ancient Wisdom* (Basic Books).

Hamilton, W.D. (1964) The Genetical Evolution of Social Behaviour, I and II. *Journal of Theoretical Biology*, 7: 1–16, 17–52.

Hamilton, W.D. (1998) *The Narrow Roads of Gene Land: The Collected Papers of W.D. Hamilton. Evolution of Social Behavior* (Oxford University Press).

Hauser, Marc (2006) *Moral Minds: How Nature Designed our Universal Sense of Right and Wrong* (Ecco).

Hitt, Jack (1999) This Is Your Brain on God. *Wired*, 7.1.

Howard, Jane (1978) *Families* (Simon & Schuster).

Hudson Institute (2007) *Index of Global Philanthropy* (Hudson Institute).

Hume, David (2009/1882) *A Treatise on Human Nature* (General Books LLC).

Huxley, Thomas (1863) *Evidence as to Man's Place in Nature* (Williams & Norgate).

Iredale, W., M. Vugt, and R. Dunbar (2008) Showing Off in Humans: Male Generosity as Mating Signal. *Evolutionary Psychology*, 6/3: 386–92.

Irons, William (2001) Religion as a Hard-to-Fake Sign of Commitment. In R. Nesse (ed.), *Evolution and the Capacity for Commitment* (Russell Sage Foundation).

James, S. (2008) The Caveman's Conscience: Evolution and Moral Realism. *Australasian Journal of Philosophy*, 87/2: 1–19.

James, S. and P. Carruthers (2008) Human Evolution and the Possibility of Moral Realism. *Philosophy and Phenomenological Research*, 77/1: 237–44.

Joyce, Richard (2006) *The Evolution of Morality* (MIT Press).

Joyce, Richard (2008) Replies. *Philosophy and Phenomenological Research*, 77/1: 245–67.

Kass, Leon (1997) The Wisdom of Repugnance: Why We Should Ban the Cloning of Human Beings. *The New Republic*, June 2.

Kitcher, Philip (1985) *Vaulting Ambition: Sociobiology and the Quest for Human Nature* (MIT Press).

Kitcher, Philip (2005) Biology and Ethics. In D. Copp (ed.), *The Oxford Handbook of Ethics* (Oxford University Press).

Levy, N. (2004) *What Makes Us Moral? Crossing the Boundaries of Biology* (Oneworld).

Locke, John (1996/1693) *Some Thoughts Concerning Education* (Hackett).

Lorenz, Konrad and Robert D. Martin (1997) *The Natural Science of the Human Species: An Introduction to Comparative Behavioral Research* (MIT Press).

Lumsden, C.J. and E.O. Wilson (1983) *Genes, Mind, and Culture: The Coevolutionary Process* (Harvard University Press).

Mackie, J.L. (1977) *Ethics: Inventing Right and Wrong* (Viking).

Mann, Horace (1855) *The Life and Works of Horace Mann* (Nabu Press).

Masserman, J.H., S. Wechkin, and W. Terris (1964) "Altruistic" Behavior in Rhesus Monkeys. *American Journal of Psychiatry*, 121: 584–5.

May, Rollo (1975) *The Courage to Create* (W.W. Norton).

Maynard Smith, J. (1974) *Models in Ecology* (Cambridge University Press).

Maynard Smith, J. (1982) *Evolution and the Theory of Games* (Cambridge University Press).

Mayr, Ernst (2002) *What Evolution Is* (Basic Books).

Mikhail, John (2009) The Poverty of the Moral Stimulus. In W. Sinnott-Armstrong (ed.), *Moral Psychology: The Evolution of Morality*, vol. 1 (MIT Press).

Miller, Greg (2002) Gene's Effect Seen in Brain's Fear Response. *Science*, 297/5580: 319.

Moore, G.E. (1903) *Principia Ethica* (Cambridge University Press).

Moore, Thomas (1868) *The Poetical Works of Thomas Moore* (D. Appleton).

Nichols, Shaun (2004) *Sentimental Rules: On the Natural Foundations of Moral Judgment* (Oxford University Press).

Nowak, M.A. (2008) Generosity: A Winner's Advice. *Nature*, 456: 579.

Nucci, L., E. Turiel, and G. Encarcion-Gawrych (1983) Children's Social Interactions and Social Concepts: Analyses of Morality and Convention in the Virgin Islands. *Journal of Cross-Cultural Psychology*, 14: 469–87.

Packer, C. (1977) Reciprocal Altruism in Papio Anubis. *Nature*, 265: 441–3.

Pinker, Steven. (1994) *The Language Instinct: How the Mind Creates Language* (Morris).

Pinker, Steven (1997) *How the Mind Works* (Norton).

Pinker, Steven (2002) *The Blank Slate: The Modern Denial of Human Nature* (Viking).

Pratchett, Terry (1999) *Hogfather* (Harper).

Prinz, Jesse J. (2007) *The Emotional Construction of Morals* (Oxford University Press).

Prinz, Jesse J. (2008a) Acquired Moral Truths. *Philosophy and Phenomenological Research*, 77/1: 219–27.

Prinz, Jesse J. (2008b) Is Morality Innate? In W. Sinnott-Armstrong (ed.), *Moral Psychology: The Evolution of Morality*, vol. 1 (MIT Press).

Quine, W.V. (1969) Natural Kinds. In *Ontological Relativity and Other Essays*. (Columbia University Press).

Rachels, James (1990) *Created from Animals: The Moral Implications of Darwinism* (Oxford University Press).

Richards, Robert (1986) A Defense of Evolutionary Ethics. *Biology and Philosophy*, 1: 265–92.

Rosaldo, M.Z. (1980) *Knowledge and Passion: Ilongot Notions of Self and Social Life* (Cambridge University Press).

Rottschaefer, William A. and David Martinsen (1995) Really Taking Darwin Seriously: An Alternative to Michael Ruse's Darwinian Metaethics. In P. Thomson (ed.), *Issues in Evolutionary Ethics* (SUNY Press).

Ruse, Michael (1986) *Taking Darwin Seriously: A Naturalistic Approach to Philosophy* (Oxford University Press).

Ruse, Michael (1995) Evolutionary Ethics: A Phoenix Arisen. In P. Thomson (ed.), *Issues in Evolutionary Ethics* (SUNY Press).

Ruse, Michael (1998) Evolution and Ethics: *The Sociobiological Approach*. In L. Pojman (ed.), *Ethical Theory: Classical and Contemporary Readings* (Wadsworth).

Ruse, Michael and E.O. Wilson (1986/1994) Darwinism as Applied Science. *Philosophy*, 61: 173–92; repr. in Sober (1994: 421–38).

Sadava, D., H.C. Heller, G.H. Orians, W.K. Purves, and D.M. Hillis (2008) *Life: The Science of Biology*, 8th edn. (Sinauer Associates and W.H. Freeman).

Sandel, M. (2004) The Case Against Perfection: What's Wrong with Designer Children, Bionic Athletes, and Genetic Engineering. *The Atlantic* (April); repr. in B. Steinbock, J. Arras, and A.J. London (2008) *Ethical Issues in Modern Medicine*, 7th edn. (McGraw Hill).

Scanlon, T.M. (1998) *What We Owe to Each Other* (Harvard University Press).

Schino G. (2007) Grooming and Agonistic Support: A Meta-analysis of Primate Reciprocal Altruism. *Behavioral Ecology*, 18: 115–20.

Searle, John R. (1964) How to Derive "Ought" from "Is". *Philosophical Review*, 73: 43–58.

Seyfarth, R.M. and Cheney, D.L. (1984) Grooming, Alliances, and Reciprocal Altruism in Vervet Monkeys. *Nature*, 308: 541–3.

Sherman, Paul (2009). Squirrels (with L. Wauters) and The Role of Kinship. In D.W. Macdonald (ed.), *The New Encyclopedia of Mammals* (pp. 150–61, 162–3) (Princeton University Press).

Singer, T. (2007). The Neuronal Basis of Empathy and Fairness. In G. Bock and J. Goode (eds.), *Empathy and Fairness* (pp. 20–30; discussion pp. 30–40, 89–96, 216–21) (John Wiley & Sons, Ltd).

Sinnott-Armstrong, Walter (ed.) (2008) *Moral Psychology: The Evolution of Morality*, vol. 1 (MIT Press).

Skyrms, Brian (1996) *Evolution of the Social Contract.* (Cambridge University Press).

Smith, Adam. (2010/1759) *The Theory of Moral Sentiments* (Penguin Classics).

Smith, M.S., B.L. Kish, and C.B. Crawford (1987) Inheritance of Wealth as Human Kin Investment. *Ethology and Sociobiology*, 8: 171–82.

Sober, Elliott (ed.) (1994) *Conceptual Issues in Evolutionary Biology*, 2nd edn. (MIT Press).

Sober, Elliott and David Sloan Wilson (1998) *Unto Others: The Evolution and Psychology of Unselfish Behavior* (Harvard University Press).

Sosis, Richard (2004) The Adaptive Value of Religious Ritual. *American Scientist*, 92: 166–72.

Spencer, Herbert (1851) *Social Statics* (John Chapman).

Spencer, Herbert (2004/1879) *The Principles of Ethics* (University Press of the Pacific).

Sripada, C. and S. Stich (2006) A Framework for the Psychology of Norms. In P. Carruthers, et al. (eds.), *The Innate Mind*, vol. 2 (Oxford University Press).

Sripada, C. (2008) Three Models of the Innate Structure that Shapes the Contents of Moral Norms. In W. Sinnott-Armstrong (ed.), *Moral Psychology: The Evolution of Morality*, vol. 1 (MIT Press).

Stich, S. (2008) Some Questions about *The Evolution of Morality. Philosophy and Phenomenological Research*, 77 (1): 228–36.

Stratton-Lake, Phillip (2003) *Ethical Intuitionism: Re-Evaluations* (Oxford University Press).

Street, S. (2006) A Darwinian Dilemma for Realist Theories of Value. *Philosophical Studies*, 127: 109–66.

Tancredi, Laurence (2005) *Hard-Wired Behavior: What Neuroscience Reveals about Morality* (Cambridge University Press).

Thomson, Paul (ed.) (1995) *Issues in Evolutionary Ethics* (SUNY Press).

Trivers, R.L. (1971) The Evolution of Reciprocal Altruism. *Quarterly Review of Biology*, 46: 35–57.

Trivers, R.L. (1985) *Social Evolution* (Benjamin/Cummings).

Trivers, R.L. (2002) *Natural Selection and Social Theory: Selected Papers of Robert L. Trivers*. Evolution and Cognition Series (Oxford University Press).

Turiel, Eliot (1983) *The Development of Social Knowledge: Morality and Convention* (Cambridge University Press).

Ulam, Stanislaw (1975) *Adventures of a Mathematician* (University of California Press).

Warneken, F. and M. Tomasello (2007) Helping and Cooperation at 14 Months of Age. *Infancy*, 11, 271–94.

Warneken, F. and M. Tomasello (2009) Varieties of Altruism in Children and Chimpanzees. *Trends in Cognitive Sciences*, 13/9: 397–402.

Warnock, Mary (1966) *Ethics Since 1900* (Oxford University Press).

Wechkin, S., J.H. Masserman, and W. Terris, Jr. (1964) Shock to a Conspecific as an Aversive Stimulus. *Psychonomic Science*, 1: 47–8.

Wilkinson, Gerald S. (1984) Reciprocal Food Sharing in the Vampire Bat. *Nature*, 308: 181–4.

Wilkinson, Gerald S. (1990) Food Sharing in Vampire Bats. *Scientific American*, February: 76–82.

Williams, G.C. (1966) *Adaptation and Natural Selection* (Princeton University Press).

Wilson, E.O. (1975) *Sociobiology: The New Synthesis* (Harvard University Press).

Wilson, E.O. (1978) *On Human Nature* (Harvard University Press).

Wimmer, H. and J. Perner (1983). Beliefs about Beliefs: Representation and Constraining Function of Wrong Beliefs in Young Children's Understanding of Deception. *Cognition*, 13: 41–68.

Wright, C. (1992) *Truth and Objectivity* (Harvard University Press).

Wright, Larry (1973) Functions. *Philosophical Review*, 82: 139–68.

Wright, Robert (1995) *The Moral Animal: Why We Are the Way We Are. The New Science of Evolutionary Psychology* (Vintage).

Young, L., F. Cushman, M. Hauser, and R. Saxe (2007) The Neural Basis of the Interaction between Theory of Mind and Moral Judgment. *PNAS*, 104/20: 8235–40.

Zahn-Waxler, Carolyn, E. Mark Cummings, and Ronald J. Iannotti (1991) *Altruism and Aggression: Social and Biological Origins*. Cambridge Studies in Social and Emotional Development (Cambridge University Press).

Index